Modern Politics and Go

Also by Alan R. Ball

British Political Parties (2nd edition)
Pressure Politics in Industrialised Societies (with Frances Millard)

Modern Politics and Government

Alan R. Ball
Principal Lecturer in Government
Portsmouth Polytechnic

FOURTH EDITION

MACMILLAN

First edition 1971
Reprinted 1973, 1974, 1975, 1976
Second edition 1977
Reprinted 1978, 1979, 1981, 1982
Third edition 1983
Reprinted 1985
Fourth edition 1988
Reprinted 1989, 1990

Published by
MACMILLAN EDUCATION LTD
Houndmills, Basingstoke, Hampshire RG21 2XS
and London
Companies and representatives
throughout the world

Typeset by Activity Ltd, Salisbury, Wilts

Printed in Hong Kong

British Library Cataloguing in Publication Data
Ball, Alan R.
Modern politics and government.—4th ed.
1. Political science
I. Title
320 JA71
ISBN 0–333–46412–5 (hardcover)
ISBN 0–333–46413–3 (paperback)

To Alison, Michael, Peter and Adam

Contents

PART THREE: STRUCTURE OF GOVERNMENT

PART FOUR: VALUES AND POLITICS

Preface to the First Edition

This book is intended as an introduction to the study of modern politics and political institutions. No exhaustive approach can be found within the pages of one book, especially in view of the wide-ranging nature of the subject, whose boundaries are still a matter of academic dispute. For some teachers of politics the problem of definition is solved by a concentration on the politics and political institutions of one country; for others the certainties of constitutional law become the only reliable guide to the complexities of what is termed the political process. The study of comparative government, with its advancing methodology, offers avenues of escape from a culture-bound prison, but it presupposes, from the nature of its approach, an awareness of the basic principles of the study of politics.

I have attempted to present a framework which will allow the student to understand the nature and the significance of political activity, the relevance of political institutions and the place of politics in the broader context of society. This approach hopes to raise more questions than it answers, yet intends to secure a firm foundation for students to follow more specialised courses in political science and, at the same time, to allow students who wish to specialise after the first year of degree studies in other social science disciplines to find a wider appreciation of the relevance of political studies to their own subject.

There are no attempts to see how particular countries are governed, or to examine in detail the political institutions of individual states. Instead, the contrasting political processes of various countries are used to illustrate the wider nature of the political process. The aim is to continually emphasise political interrelationships and therefore the field of reference is wide, yet, it is hoped, comprehensible to first-year undergraduates.

The book is divided into four parts. Part One examines the nature of political activity and some elementary problems of methodology, and attempts to relate these political institutions and societies by discussing such concepts as the political system, the political culture and political socialisation. Part Two concentrates on what are termed the 'inputs' of the political system, i.e. parties and pressure groups, and examines the impact of public opinion through elections and the mass media in the context of theories of representation. Part Three looks at the structure of government, not in a descriptive way, but in a search for the institutional connecting threads in political systems, and emphasises similarities, differences and the functions of government structures, which when studied in isolation may appear unique and incomparable. Part Four briefly examines the more difficult problems of evaluating political activity and political structures, and the pitfalls that accompany attempts to compare and measure the values of different systems. The place of political ideologies within the political system and their relationships to political change will also be examined.

This approach has the advantage of emphasising the interconnectedness of various aspects of political behaviour and of political institutions, and illustrates the basic unity of politics as an academic discipline. Also, by looking beyond the British political system it underlines the aspects common to all political activity, and there is then less danger of attributing certain political behaviour and institutions to isolated national genius or to an act of God. The difficulties that will be presented to the student by this wide field of reference are not underestimated, but the approach hopes to stir the imagination of the student by showing that the study of politics involves a wider and more fascinating field of investigation than perhaps was previously visualised.

I wish to thank my colleagues Mr Adrian Lee and Mrs Sylvia Horton for the help and advice they have given me with the subject matter and the structure of the book. The errors and lack of judgement are, however, my own responsibility.

Portsmouth *Alan R. Ball*
1970

Preface to the Second Edition

I have tried to minimise the changes in the second edition. There has been some revision of the supporting examples in view of recent political changes. I have also substantially altered Chapters 3, 5 and 13 to offer a less dogmatic approach and to elaborate the complexity of some of the problems of classification and conceptualisation. However, the structure of the book does remain basically unchanged.

I would like to thank my colleagues Sylvia Horton and Geoffrey Williams for the advice they have given – and, in particular, Frances Millard, without whose criticism this second edition would have been less necessary.

Portsmouth *Alan R. Ball*
September 1976

Preface to the Third Edition

In this third edition I have attempted to keep the basic framework intact while providing more recent examples and improving the notes and the bibliography. The increasing interest in corporatism has necessitated some changes to Chapter 6 and I have sought to ease student difficulties in understanding the problems of pluralism by introducing the concept much earlier, and it is now discussed more fully in Chapter 2. However, the major changes remain in the area of supporting examples and bibliography.

I would like to thank Terry Hanson of the Portsmouth Polytechnic Library for his help. My colleague, Sylvia Horton, was again invaluable with many constructive suggestions. My main thanks must be directed to Frances Millard for generous advice and for her suggestions for change. Without her encouragement the task of producing this edition would have been far more difficult.

Portsmouth
December 1982

Alan R. Ball

Preface to the Fourth Edition

In this fourth edition I have sought to keep the text up to date with developments in contemporary political events and to incorporate the more recent analyses that have appeared since the third edition was published. Thus the illustrations, references and bibliography have been extensively changed and improved. Also extensive changes have been made in those parts of the text such as political culture, elections and voting behaviour, where new approaches by political scientists have produced new insights and presented new areas for discussion and controversy within the discipline. I have also attempted to present a more simplified approach to those parts of the text dealing with political power and to offer students a guide to the complex arena of power distribution models.

I would like to thank my colleagues Sylvia Horton and Rob Atkinson for their help with various chapters and Terry Hanson of Portsmouth Polytechnic Library for his assistance in the search for the obscure and the difficult. Again my foremost gratitude must be directed to Frances Millard; she remains my main critic, but softens the criticism with helpful advice and guidance. However, I retain the onus of responsibility for all mistakes.

Alan R. Ball

Portsmouth
July 1987

PART ONE

The Nature of Politics

1 The Study of Politics

The problem of boundaries

There is a marked lack of agreement on what constitutes the best approach to the study of politics. The bewildering array of titles of degree courses in Britain at present illustrates some of the confusion: names such as Government, Politics, Political Institutions, Political Science are umbrellas protecting the various specialisms of Public Administration, Political Theory, Political Philosophy, Comparative Government and International Politics.[1] The Oxford English Dictionary defines politics as: 'The science and art of government; the science dealing with the form, organisation and administration of a state, or part of one, and with the regulation of its relations with other states'. The restriction of politics to that of concern mainly with public institutions and state activities is certainly disputed by most contemporary students of the subject, and the emphasis on the science of politics often leads to crude and confused analogies with the method of the natural sciences. Nevertheless, Professor W. J. M. Mackenzie has pointed to some advantages of the term political science:

> So far as I can judge, 'political science' is still the name which carries meaning to the general public ... The word science here indicates simply that there exists an academic tradition of the study of politics, a discipline communicated from teacher to pupil, by speech and writing, for some 2,500 years now. It does not mean that this discipline claims to be a 'natural science', or that it could be improved by copying the methods of physics and chemistry exactly.[2]

However, even with agreement on a title, or at least a recognition where the disagreements lie, there still remains the problem of the content and orientation of the subject. This difficulty has been underlined by the dominance of American political scientists, especially since 1945, and their emphasis on quantitative methods made possible by the vaster resources of American universities. There has also been a more extensive borrowing of methods and concepts from other social science disciplines, such as economics, sociology and psychology, with varying degrees of success. These new developments which have been superimposed on traditional approaches to the subject have led to confusion of terminology as well as method, and partly result from the political changes in the twentieth century, in which the certainties of liberal democracy have been assaulted by the rise of popularly supported totalitarian regimes. It is understandable that undergraduates fresh to the subject may feel rather uncertain as to what actually constitutes the study of politics. At the risk of promoting more confusion, it is proposed, therefore, to briefly survey the various approaches to the academic study of politics before examining, in Chapter 2, the nature of political activity itself.

Traditional approaches

Before 1900, the study of politics was largely dominated by philosophy, history and law. To use the label 'traditional' is neither a criticism nor a refutation of the obvious fact that they still play important roles in modern political studies although no longer monopolising the avenues of approach. The modern student of politics is still faced with the works of great philosophers such as Plato or Hegel that require textual analysis and new interpretations, but the search for universal values concerning political activity tends to be avoided. At present 'ought' questions are not fashionable, although not all critics of traditional political philosophy would travel as far as T. D. Weldon in his reduction to trivia and linguistic misunderstandings such ancient political concepts as freedom, justice, obedience, liberty and natural rights.[3]

It could not be thought that traditional political philosophy was concerned only with *a priori* deductions, that is, conclusions reached with little observation of political facts. Plato's search for his philosopher king, or Hobbes's 'leviathan', an all-powerful government that would end civil disorder, may be balanced by Aristotle's exhaustive collection of studies of the constitutions of Greek city-states, and Machiavelli's political advice resting on his observations and participation in the governments of Italian Renaissance states. But the seekers after the perfect state did base their answers on oversimplified assumptions on a wide variety of matters; thus Thomas Hobbes, with a generalised view of human nature, could speak of 'a generall inclination of all mankind, a perpetuall and restlesse desire of Power after power, that ceaseth only in Death'.[4]

The classical political theorists are still important even in regard to the nature of the questions they posed, and certainly ignorance concerning them would isolate any student of politics from much of the communications that pass between political scientists. Moreover, the descriptive work of these political philosophers, no matter how shaky their grand edifices, did supply the first explorations of the field of comparative government. Also, there is significant interplay between the political theories and the nature of the society and its politics in which the theory originates. We can learn a great deal of the English revolution of 1688, its origins, the character and political aims of the men who controlled and guided it, by reading the political philosophy of John Locke. The nature of the American constitutional settlement of 1788–9 becomes clearer after examining the propaganda of the Federalist Papers. No student of the government and politics of the Soviet Union could avoid reference to Lenin's reformulation of Marxist philosophy.

Given these particular approaches to political studies, it is easy to see why the historian has played such a significant part in the discipline. The historical–descriptive technique is to examine past events through what evidence is available and draw tentative conclusions as to some aspects of contemporary political activity. The sources will vary from memoirs and biographies of important statesmen to journalistic accounts of particular events. The historian becomes a synthesiser, using his own intellectual judgement and commonsense to fit the various parts of the jigsaw into a coherent pattern. It is clear that many of the political institutions and political practices of the present day are explicable in terms of these historical records, but past evidence does leave alarming gaps, and political history is often simply a record of great men and great events rather than a comprehensive account of total political activity. In British political studies, Sir Ivor Jennings, with his studies of parliament and cabinet government, favoured this approach, digging deep into nineteenth-century history to trace the growth of the office of prime minster or the rise of modern political parties. Robert McKenzie's pioneering work on British political parties lays great stress on their historical evolution. A similar orientation may be seen in the major work on the British cabinet by J. P. Mackintosh. An American scholar, Professor Samual Beer, devotes a major part of his analysis of British parties and theories of representation to historical development.

The study of constitutional law formed the third cornerstone of traditional political studies. There is now a closer relationship between the study of law and politics in the continental European tradition; in Anglo-Saxon countries the divorce has become more complete. Before 1900, a British student of politics would have devoted a major part of his energies to the study of legal institutions, and Dicey's *Law of the Constitution*, first published in 1885, loomed large on any politics reading list. Although arguments on such topics as the legal sovereignty of the British parliament, the rule of law and the separation of powers are not in their former context regarded as of first importance, the links between law and politics are not completely broken, the gap being bridged by bringing aspects of the judicial system firmly into the field of the political process.[5]

The strongest legacy that philosophy, history and law have bequeathed to the study of politics is in the field of descriptive and institutional approaches. Political scientists still, in spite of recent developments, concentrate chiefly on examining the major political institutions of the state such as the executive, legislature, the civil service, the judiciary and local government, and from these examinations valuable insights as to their organisation can be drawn, proposals for reform discussed, and general conclusions offered. However, despite the point that all description involves some conceptualisation, no wide-reaching theories are propounded from these studies. Bernard Crick's *Reform of Parliament* is representative of the British approach in this field, and Bailey and Samuel's *Congress at Work* offers an American example. They seek to explain how various political institutions work, and from that description come tentative proposals on how to remedy possible faults and inefficiencies.

There can, of course, be various different approaches within this descriptive–analytic field. If one were to study the contrasting examinations of the role of the president within the American system of government one could travel from the legal formalism of Edward Corwin's *The President – Office and Powers* to the invigorating emphasis on informal processes in Richard Neustadt's *Presidential Power*. Both, however, are concerned with the analysis of the president's role in American politics and seek to support their conclusions by citing case histories, personal observations and documentary evidence. They seek to show how that particular political institution works. It is interesting to note that some major contributions to this approach have been made not only by political scientists confined to their university desks, but by men actively engaged in public affairs. Walter Bagehot, for example, was a practising journalist when he wrote *The English Constitution* in 1867, but he produced a classic analysis of the working of the political process, an analysis that still has contemporary relevance.

Comparative studies

Comparative government and politics was to provide the link between the traditional approaches to political science and the more recent developments in the discipline. We have already noted that the comparative method is a very old one; its origins and development can be traced from Herodotus and Aristotle through Bodin and Montesquieu. Yet despite the longevity of comparative political studies, many problems remain. It is not simply the difficulty of collecting enough relevant facts about different political systems but the organisation of the information gathered. Comparative politics has been mainly concerned with the advance of European and North American states, but the enforced widening of horizons to countries referred to as 'developing' states, a pseudonym for 'poor', has led to a greater scrutiny of what units are to be compared. A comparison of formal institutions such as legislatures and executives may be attempted only in a broader context. One cannot extract a particular political institution from its organic context and compare it with institutions in other countries without taking into account the whole political system in which that institution is set. Robert Dahl attempted a comparison of political oppositions in various liberal democracies, and reached the conclusion that it is a concept that only has a particular meaning and relevance in the British system of government.[6] The attempted transfer of European political institutions to former colonial territories, especially on the African continent, has illustrated the difficulty in a practical way. Parliamentary procedures, competitive party systems, neutral civil servants and soldiers grow out of integrated relationships and cannot be individually exported and expected to function in a similar manner.

Of course, the comparative method does not necessarily mean that the comparison must be cross-national to be rewarding. The existence of fifty American states with some degree of independence of the federal government provides a fertile field for comparison. Even the apparent uniformity of English local government allows some scope for comparison.[7] Nor does the comparative method imply a disinterest in the political processes of one's own country; on the contrary it may be the most rewarding means of discovering information about the politics of one particular state. However, the recent advances in the methodology of the political sciences have resulted partly from the fact that the basic questions of the comparative approach such as 'Why do certain types of political institutions and political activity exist in certain states?' are still largely unanswered. To some extent it has been in response to these problems that political science has attempted to formulate general or partial theories and advance certain models in some way comparable to those used in the other social sciences.

New approaches

The publication of Graham Wallas's *Human Nature in Politics* and Arthur Bentley's *The Process of Government*, both in 1908, symbolised a change in political studies. There was to be a greater emphasis on the informal processes of politics and less on state political institutions in isolation. There was to be freer borrowing from other social science disciplines of sociology and psychology, and the new empirical orientation of political studies was ultimately to lead to an examination of such political concepts as power, authority and political élites. It should be remembered that these new approaches were neither uniformly accepted nor universally applied, and one should not ignore the nineteenth-century predecessors such as de Tocqueville or even Bagehot, who foreshadowed much of what is contained in this empirical aim of examining politics in action to discover what makes the machine tick.

Graham Wallas, an Englishman with practical political experience, was to emphasise a demand for a new realism in political studies. His central theme, borrowed from contemporary psychology, was that man was not a rational creature in that his political actions were not totally guided by reason and self-interest. Human nature was far too complex for simple explanations. Wallas was, therefore, attacking not only the deductive reasoning of the political philosophers, but also the *laissez-faire* approach of the classical economists that explanations could be found in man's eagerness to follow rationally his own economic self-interest. Wallas demanded facts and evidence, claiming that advances in the discipline should be attempted quantitatively not qualitatively. It is true that many of Wallas's methods and conclusions were to be extensively criticised and that political science's enthusiasm with psychology was not to bear the fruit that these early hopes had raised, but Wallas had carried the important message that to understand the political process one must examine how people actually behave in political situations, not merely speculate on how they should or would behave.

The other pioneer who symbolised new stirrings in political studies was Arthur Bentley. He too has been widely criticised,[8] but nevertheless his pragmatic realism and his demand for measurement and facts did succeed in weaning the discipline away from political philosophy and descriptive formalism. His aim was not to describe political activity but to provide new tools of investigation, and he believed that he had found these in the study of groups in politics: 'When groups are adequately stated, everything is stated.'[9] He was, therefore, prepared to ignore almost completely the formal political institutions. His behaviouralism owed much to sociology, and in this he was to point the way to the study of the roles of pressure groups, parties, elections and public opinion in the political process.

These new orientations have produced several dangers for political science. Firstly, politics has been seen as a subsidiary, a satellite of sociology, in that political activity and institutions reflect the nature of society and are determined and patterned to a large extent by divisions within society. Politics in this sense is to be seen as dependent on forces outside the political system, and as such ceases to have a major role as an independent social science. Thus the way people vote is seen to depend particularly on class, ethnic and religious divisions in society, and the activities of political parties and governments are regarded as less important. Giovanni Sartori has strongly argued for re-emphasis on the mutual contributions of politics and sociology, and recognition that political factors, governments and parties, independently affect political behaviour.[10] A second danger is that political sociology tends to emphasise only the 'inputs' of the political system, by which we mean emphasis on the role of political parties, pressure groups, voting behaviour, political communication and public opinion, to the detriment of other political factors such as governments, legislatures, administration and judiciaries. Linked to this is a third danger, which is that of examining only those aspects of the political system that are open to measurement or quantification. It has been part of the search for a pure science of politics in which the findings and conclusions would depend not on subjective judgements but on measurable factors. Quantitative methods would allow description and values in political studies to be banished, if not from the factory, at least from the research laboratories. The approach has been of immense advantage in some fields of political science, especially in those of voting behaviour and elections, in which mass behaviour could be more readily analysed by these tools.

Sample surveys used by opinion pollsters have shed much light on many aspects of political behaviour undiscoverable by other means, and used correctly in skilled hands have enriched the discipline. However, they are tools of analysis that can only be usefully employed in certain fields, and their findings have to be treated with care. It has been alleged that an American poll once found that a majority of Americans had views on a non-existent Metallic Metals Act.[11] The misleading conclusions of some opinion polls before the 1970 British general election may have led to a change of government in that year.[12] The problem is often that of a search for quantification as an end in itself, because there is something to be measured. Meticulous care is often taken to discover the class readership of newspapers and the political views of the editors before the more important question of whether newspapers actually influence political opinion is discussed. Size of the sample is a most important factor in deciding the utility of this approach, and variables not open to measurement have to be constantly borne in mind.[13]

The search for a science of politics and the fashioning of new tools of analysis and more sophisticated concepts was dominated after the First World War by Americans. Their lines of inquiry took them into the fields of psychology and the empiricism of quantitative methods. Political power became one of the key concepts of political scientists. The two giants of this approach were Charles Merriam[14] and Harold Lasswell,[15] who spoke of the 'science of power' and widened the discussion of such concepts as political élites. It is interesting to note that the development of the discipline from Merriam to his pupil Lasswell is also an indication of the relative failure of liberal democratic systems of government, especially in Europe, and the rise of totalitarian regimes of the fascist and communist varieties. Of course, a study of political power was not previously foreign to political science, and forerunners may be found in Machiavelli and Hobbes, just to mention two, but the new approach was far more rigorous and systematic, and was ultimately to blossom into the studies of communities and power in the 1950s with the arguments over methodology that they entailed.[16]

Systems analysis

David Easton published *The Political System* in 1953, claiming that he was attempting to construct a theory to embrace all the social sciences. He was emphasising the need to theorise about the whole political process, not simply about related aspects of it. Since then Easton has become one of the prominent supporters of the application of 'general systems' theories to political science,[17] and one of the few to come from within the discipline rather than from the other social sciences. Briefly, Easton focuses his attention on the system, that is, a pattern of related elements that are interdependent. He defines the political system as 'that system of interactions in any society through which binding or authoritative allocations are made'.[18] Authoritative allocations may be roughly translated as policy-making.[19] There are in this political system inputs from the various environments and these are converted into outputs, i.e. authoritative decisions. Feedback mechanisms put outputs back into the system as inputs, thus completing a complex, cyclical operation. Many demands will be made, or 'articulated', but some are lost in the conversion process and do not reach the output stage. If there are too many demands, or particular types of demand, stress arises, and the channels are then overloaded. There are various regulatory mechanisms to control demands and minimise overloading. Firstly, the structural mechanisms, 'the gatekeepers', e.g. pressure groups, political parties. Secondly, cultural mechanisms, the various norms which consider the appropriateness of the demands. Thirdly, communications channels, which can be increased. Fourthly, demands may be controlled in the conversion process itself by the legislators, executives and administrative bodies. Authoritative decisions that displease too many members of the system will lose support for the system.

The model is far more complex than described here, but the outline is sufficient to indicate the systemic approach. It is an attempt to provide a framework for organising and conceptualising information. The approach has been variously criticised for failing to adequately cater for concepts such as political power or for being unable to handle mass political behavioural aspects such as voting,[20] but it may be said to be one of the more ambitious attempts to construct a theoretical framework from within political science.

Another important offshoot from general systems theories is structural-functionalism.[21] It is a means of explaining what political structures perform what basic functions in the political system, and it is a tool of investigation. A political party is a structure within the political system that performs many functions, including those of communicating the wishes of the electorate to the government, informing the electorate on important political issues and allowing for wider participation by more people in the political system. The party helps to maintain the system because it performs these tasks, but other structures such as pressure groups or formal government institutions may also carry out these functions, and in other political systems may carry out these functions in the absence of political parties. A particular function may not be recognised or intended by the participants, and this is called a *latent* as opposed to a *manifest* function. The structural-functional approach has been more widely adopted in the field of comparative government because it provides standard categories for markedly different political systems.[22] The approach has been criticised partly because it is concerned with systems maintenance and as such tends, it is said, to justify the status quo.[23] Some of the criticisms can be met if the claims of the structural-functionalists are not exaggerated, and it is recognised that this approach, while rewarding, cannot provide a general theory for all aspects of political science.

Further developments

New approaches in the theories of political science have been borrowed from the technical advances of electronic communications and large-scale computers. Karl Deutsch is one of the foremost advocates of communication theory, and his approach is clearly set out in his book *The Nerves of Government, Models of Political Communication and Control*. 'This book', says Deutsch, 'concerns itself less with the bones or muscles of the body politic than with its nerves–its channels of communication and decision. This book suggests that it might be profitable to look upon government somewhat less as a problem of power and somewhat more as a problem of steering; and it tries to show that steering is decisively a matter of communication.[24] He then proceeds to talk of channels, loads, load capacity, flows. lag, etc. The chief point made is that communications set limits to any organisation, including political organisations, and therefore it is this process that should be intensely analysed. Games theory may be referred to at this point as another interesting development in political studies.[25]

In the search for new theoretical approaches, it may be said that the wheel has turned full circle, and the latest enthusiasm is for application of economic theory to politics. The title 'new political economy'[26] is given to this new approach to distinguish it from the political economy of the classical nineteenth-century liberal economists. The attempts to apply economic models to the study of politics are particularly associated with the names of Anthony Downs,[27] J. M. Buchanan and G. Tullock.[28] The essence of the approach is the view of the political process as a process of exchange; the vote, for example, is a type of money that can be exchanged for something else. Politics is a market place. The political economist sees the behaviour of individuals and organisations as rational and as the pursuit of self-interest. He is inclined to stress the co-operative elements in the political process as opposed to the conflict approach. Politics is concerned with the allocation of resources, the optimising of social welfare, and thus choices within the political process are concerned with government finance, budgets, types of taxes, and the effect of these choices on political structures. The application of economic models in competition with political sociology has resulted in an ironic state of affairs for the study of politics. In the words of W. J. M. Mackenzie: 'Hence a curious situation. Sociology and economics have both occupied the traditional territory of political science: but what is left to arbitrate their dispute–except political science.'[29]

Political science in the 1980s is left in a rather confused situation. Given the decline of enthusiasm for functionalism and systems analysis and the limits of behaviouralism, there have been no radical new departures. Certainly policy analysis gains more attention, and political scientists are directing more of their energy to what governments do and what are the consequences of government policies. This direction involves a return to organisational theory and a wider investigation of the constraints on policy-making and policy alternatives.[30] The 1970s also saw a revival of Marxist approaches to political science, although Marxist approaches themselves are characterised by a great deal of diversity.[31]

Political studies and practical politics

Aristotle once said that 'the end of politics is not knowledge but action', and certainly an overview of political studies must acknowledge the links between the academic approach and practical activity. There is, of course, a danger of being accused of political and social engineering in that the labours of the political scientist may be applied to normative ends. This is especially dangerous when university departments come to rely more and more on direct grants and particular private funds to conduct research, a danger more acute in the United States. But the history of political studies has illustrated the benefits received from practising politicians and the returns that political science has been able to repay. Machiavelli may not have secured the post in the Florentine government which he hoped would follow the dedication of *The Prince* to the Medici, but the realism of that treatise owes much to his former public service. The founding fathers of the American constitution are a foremost example of a mixture of political theory and practical realism; they wanted their system of government to embody certain political principles, but they also wanted it to work and endure. Herbert Morrison utilised his political and ministerial experience to provide valuable insights into the working of British governments. Lenin's *What Is to Be Done?*, a pamphlet of 1902, and Hitler's *Mein Kampf*, written in 1923, are superb examples of mixtures of political theory, political strategy and political propaganda.

American political scientists appear to be more willing to involve themselves in practical politics than their European counterparts. Zbigniew Brzezinski was an influential foreign policy adviser to President Carter in the late 1970s; Jeanne

Kirkpatrick taught political science in Washington before being chosen by President Reagan in 1980 to be American ambassador to the United Nations. Prominent British political scientists, such as Anthony King and Ivor Crewe, were actively engaged in advising the British Social Democratic Party, founded in 1981.

However, this level of involvement appears pallid when compared to that of the American political scientists of the Progressive era, the first two decades of the twentieth century, with their confidence in the future of liberal democracy, and their determination to set the world to rights. Woodrow Wilson not only wrote two important books on the nature of the American system of government, but was president between 1913 and 1920. Charles Merriam was a passionate and eloquent advocate of personal political involvement by political scientists amongst others, and was heavily involved himself in the politics of Chicago until 1920 as a political reformer, a passion reflected in his academic work.

It is argued that personal involvement in practical politics can only harm the work of the political scientist in that he will not achieve objective understanding of the nature of the political process unless he dispassionately stands aside. However, this raises the more important question of how neutral can the study of politics be? We will leave the discussion of that problem until we have looked at aspects of the political process.

The question of the political scientist's involvement in practical politics has become one of the central questions of the so-called 'post-behavioural revolution'. This movement is mainly a reaction to the post-1945 American behaviouralist school; as one political scientist has remarked: 'It is rumoured that the positivist–behavioural political science is moribund if not dead. It is said that we now live in the post-behavioural period of political science.'[32] The post-behavioural approach accepts the need to make political science relevant to real political problems; it is suspicious of the traditional defences of American pluralism, and emphasises that political scientists should perhaps seek some of their inspiration in traditional political philosophy.[33]

References

1. See B. Crick, 'The Tendency of Political Studies', *New Society*, 3 Nov.1966, for a brief survey of the position in Britain.
2. W. J. M. Mackenzie, *Politics and Social Science* (London, 1967) p. 17.
3. T. D. Weldon, *The Vocabulary of Politics* (London, 1953).
4. Thomas Hobbes, *Leviathan* (Everyman's Library ed., London, 1914) p. 49.
5. See Mackenzie, *Politics and Social Science*, pp. 283–7.
6. R. Dahl (ed.), *Political Oppositions in Western Democracies* (New Haven, Conn., 1966).
7. See J. G. Bulpitt, *Party Politics in English Local Government* (London, 1967).
8. See B. Crick, *The American Science of Politics* (London, 1959) pp. 118–30. For an excellent introduction to the problems of comparative government, see The Open University, *Comparative Government and Politics* (1974) D. 231, Block 4, Units 14,15 and 16. Also see P. G. Lewis, D. C. Potter and F. G. Castles, *The Practice of Comparative Politics*, 2nd ed. (London, 1978) particularly sections 3 and 4. See also L. Sigelman and G. H. Gadbois, 'Contemporary Comparative Politics', *Comparative Political Studies*, 16, 3 (October 1983) pp. 275–305.
9. A. Bentley, *The Process of Government* (Chicago, 1908) p. 208. See Also O. R. Young, *Systems of Political Science* (Englewood Cliffs, NJ, 1968) ch.6 for a discussion of the development of group theories after Bentley.
10. G. Sartori, 'From the Sociology of Politics to Political Sociology', in *Politics and the Social Sciences*, ed. S. M. Lipset (Oxford, 1969).
11. D. Butler, *The Study of Political Behaviour* (London, 1958) p. 70.
12. See D. Butler and M. Pinto-Duschinsky, *The British General Election of 1970* (London, 1971) p. 177.
13. See Butler, *The Study of Political Behaviour*. ch. 4 for a discussion on the uses and abuses of quantitative methods in political studies.
14. Charles Merriam, *New Aspects of Politics* (Chicago, 1925) and *Political Power* (New York, 1934).
15. Harold Lasswell, *Politics: Who Gets What, When, How?* (1936, reprinted Glencoe, Ill., 1951), and with A. Kaplan, *Power and Society: A Framework for Political Enquiry* (London , 1952). See Crick, *The American Science of Politics* chs 8 and 10 for a discussion of the work of both Merriam and Lasswell.
16. See Mackenzie, *Politics and Social Science* pp. 227–43.
17. For a brief discussion of general systems theory, see Young, *Systems of Political Science*, ch. 2.
18. David Easton, *A Framework for Political Analysis* (Englewood Cliffs, N.J., 1965) p. 50. Also D. Easton, 'Systems Analysis in Political Science Today', *Political Science Review*, 19, 1 (1980) pp. 1–25.
19. See *The Political System* (New York, 1953) for Easton's famous definition of politics as 'the study of the authoritative allocation of values in a society'.
20. See Young, *Systems of Political Science*, pp. 37–48, and Mackenzie, *Politics and Social Science*, pp.102–10, for a brief appreciation of Easton's work.
21. See R. E. Jones, *The Functional Analysis of Politics* (London, 1967) for an introduction to the approach. See also A. Madian, 'The anatomy of a failure', *Government and Opposition*, IV 2 (1969).

22. See particularly G. A. Almond and G. Bingham Powell, Jr, *Comparative Politics, System, Process and Policy*, 2nd ed. (Boston, Mass., 1978) and G. A. Almond and J. Coleman (eds.), *The Politics of Developing Areas* (Princeton, NJ, 1960).
23. See Young, *Systems of Political Science*, p. 36.
24. K. Deutsch, *The Nerves of Government* (New York, 1966) p. xxvii.
25. See Mackenzie, *Politics and Social Science*, pp. 119–37 for an outline of aspects of games theory.
26. See W. C. Mitchell, 'The Shape of Political Theory to Come: From Political Sociology to Political Economy', in *Politics and the Social Sciences*, ed. Lipset, ch 5.
27. A. Downs, *An Economic Theory of Democracy* (New York, 1957).
28. J.M. Buchanan and G. Tullock, *The Calculus of Consent* (Ann Arbor, Mich., 1962).
29. Mackenzie *Politics and Social Science*, p. 152.
30. See S. S. Nagel and M. Neff, *Policy Analysis in Social Science Research* (London, 1979); C. Pollitt (ed.), *Public Policy in Theory and Practice* (London, 1979); T. R. Dye, *Policy Analysis: What Makes Governments Do, Why They Do It and What Difference It Makes* (Alabama, 1976); T. R. Dye (ed.), *The Determinants of Public Policy* (Farnborough, 1980); S. S. Nagel (ed.), *Improving Policy Analysis* (London, 1980).
31. For Marxist approaches to political science see R. Miliband, *The State in Capitalist Society* (London, 1973), R. Blackburn (ed.), *Ideology in Social Science* (London, 1972); N. Poulantzas, *Political Power and Social Classes* (London, 1973).
32. Ellis Sandoz, 'The Philosophical Science of Politics. Beyond Behaviouralism', in *The Post-Behavioural Era. Perspectives on Political Science*, ed. G. J. Graham and G. W. Carey (New York, 1972).
33. See H. S. Kariel, *Saving Appearances: The Re-establishment of Political Science* (Massachusetts, 1972).

2

Politics, Power and Authority

The nature of politics

A British housewife, asked whether people should take an interest in politics replied: 'Well, not too much. Sufficient interest. You don't want to waste too much time on it. There are many other things of more interest ... You have got to have a certain amount of interest ... I think everybody should be interested without being rabid. Everybody must be, because it affects your life.'[1] This hesitant recognition of the importance of political activity has found numerous echoes amongst political leaders. Thus Quintin Hogg, defining the attitude of British Conservatives towards politics, he said: 'For Conservatives do not believe that political struggle is the most important thing in life ... The man who puts politics first is not fit to be called a civilised being, let alone a Christian.'[2]

However, this approach to political activity does tend to raise some problems. Firstly, it is often assumed that politics is only concerned with the public sector, with parliaments, elections, cabinets, and has little relevance to other spheres of human activity. Secondly, there is the danger of confusing politics solely with party politics, that it is somehow concerned with having a political opinion, or that it at least implies a distaste with the intrigues and tricks of party politicians seeking power. Political activity is, on the contrary, a far more universal phenomenon. It involves disagreements and the reconciliation of those disagreements, and therefore can occur at any level. Two children in a nursery with one toy which they both want at the same time present a political situation. There is conflict and there is the need to resolve that conflict. The two children could resort to violence, with the stronger claiming the toy, or the mother could appear and use her stronger position to arbitrate between the quarrelling children. The possibilities are numerous, but the essence of the political situation remains: that of conflict and the resolution of that conflict. A Hapsburg emperor, Charles I, once said of his relations with the French King: 'Francis I and I are in complete agreement. We both want Milan.' The attempts to resolve this particular 'agreement' alternated between military clashes and summit conferences. It does raise the interesting point of whether physical force is the end of politics, or the continuation by other means.

The failure to recognise these basic elements of politics gives rise to various confusions and misconceptions even if we concentrate our attention on the arena of public affairs. British civil servants are said to be politically impartial, but this does not mean that they do not make political decisions, i.e. decisions that resolve conflict. Nor does it mean that they will not sometimes apply their own standards and values in reaching a decision. Political neutrality, in the context, merely implies that they will not openly support or favour one or other of the main political parties. Judges are in a similar position. Their political neutrality, in one sense, is a vital aspect of the confidence people show in their competence, but this does not mean that conflict-resolving decisions are not made by judges within the discretion allowed to them by the written laws.

The constant demands for an all-party government in some countries or the desire to turn government functions over to individuals who have displayed competence in other fields, such as business men, is again evidence of these misconceptions about political activity. Competing parties or factions are evidence of disagreements, not causes of those disagreements, and coalitions and all-party governments are attempts to cure an illness, if political conflict could be regarded as unnatural, by treating the symptoms not the cause. George Washington, the first American president, at the end of his second term of office criticised what he called 'the baneful effects of the spirit of party', but the factionalism of the young conservative United States stemmed partly from disagreement on how wide the powers of the national federal government should be over the individual states. The parties were expressing this disagreement. The new political institutions and growing political parties were successful means of reconciling those differences while preserving the unity of the country. The disagreement was the cause of party growth. When the parties and other political institutions failed to continue to reconcile that particular disagreement in the middle of the nineteenth century, the result was civil war.

Single-party states do not signify an end to disagreement between political leaders. Khrushchev was overthrown by his Communist Party colleagues in 1964 because, amongst other things, they disagreed with his foreign policy and his economic policy.[3] British political parties buried some of their disagreements between 1940 and 1945 because of the demands of total war, but conflicts still continued even at parliamentary level, on such issues as personal liberties, social welfare and the nature of the governments to be supported in former enemy-occupied territories.[4]

Perhaps the need to resist foreign invasion represents what must be nearest to the general or national interest, that is, wide agreement on particular ends and means for the good of all, as opposed to sectional interests.[5] The belief that a general interest exists is held by those who hold that the promotion of certain interests and opinions is for the good of all, not recognising the sectional nature of those interests. It may result from a deliberate attempt to confuse people as to the selfish aims of a particular group by disguising those claims. Usually, this concept of the general interest is a criticism of the political process, and a failure to understand that political activity is concerned with conflict and conciliation. Thus the Duke of Norfolk, criticising the party electioneering before the 1970 British general election, said: 'This is not a time for politicians to get at one another's throats. It must be clear that in the interests of the nation they must come together with reasoned consideration and sane appreciation of all problems ... We must not be divided and embattled, but think of the nation and what we can do together to help the nation.[6] This seemed to be a plea not merely to take politics out of general elections, but really to substitute one form of political activity for another, simply to change the arena of the political conflict.

Sources of political conflict

Political activity may result from the scarcity of resources. An expensive space research programme may only be possible at the cost of ignoring social problems such as housing, education and the relief of poverty. An increased road-building programme may necessitate increased taxation. Political activity results from the necessity of choosing and coming to a decision about alternative policies when only one is economically possible. Differences between individuals and groups provide reasons for disagreements. Whites may dislike black people and seek means of maintaining white political and economic superiority which then provides additional reasons for dislike. The poor may be jealous of the rich and form groups and political parties to work for a more equal distribution of wealth. Men may wish to perpetuate the inferior position of women in society, and struggle may ensue for the political emancipation of women. This is not to say that all differences are a source of potential conflict at public level; the differences between tall men and short men do not give rise to political conflict. Some differences are more important than others, and there will be variations between different countries. However, economic differences appear to provide a universal source of political disagreement.

The diversity which gives rise to conflict need not have an objective base such as economic or racial differences. Opinions not directly linked to objective differences may form the source of political activity. Teetotallers may wish to impose complete abstinence on drinkers. Religious diversity may replace race and social class as the chief basis for political conflict. Personality may be a factor in the disagreement, such as Hitler's desire to impose his will on others, irrespective of his views on German nationalism, Jews or class differences. The degree of diversity in a society may vary, but diversity of some form is the norm of every society. It is a permanent feature, and therefore political activity is not an abnormal aspect of human behaviour. It is the process of accommodating the conflict that stems from that diversity.[7]

Means of reconciling political conflict

At public levels there are various means of reconciling political conflict. An election decides which of the competing parties or individuals may translate their programme into public policy. A debate in the legislature or in a legislative committee allows opponents to express their views and provides an opportunity to try to defeat unwelcome legislation. A revolt in a political party or a cabinet crisis may force the resignation of a particular leader and reversal of his policies. A constitutional court may have the authority to declare certain government actions or legislative enactments unconstitutional. Pressure groups, such as business organisations or trade unions, may effect a change in government policy, or seek to balance and defeat the counter-claims of opposing groups by aiming for closer relations with political leaders. These political institutions and political processes provide a framework within which political conflict may be channelled and reconciled and decisions reached. However, there must be agreement that these are the most acceptable means of accommodating disagreements. If some groups are barred from participating, or feel that a particular political institutional framework is a means of frustrating their political demands, they may seek means of effecting change by acting outside the recognised political channels, illegally or unconstitutionally, and attempt to provoke violence, or seize power by a *coup d'état*. A comparison of national and international politics provides an interesting contrast in this respect. There is more stability in national politics because of a greater willingness to work through the existing institutions, and to recognise the legitimacy of existing political processes. Relations between states are more anarchic, and the efforts to reconcile conflicts by institutional means such as the United Nations Organisation are less successful. This difference, of course, partly stems from reasons of historical development, and from the inability to impose sanctions, short of war, at international level.

It is important not to overemphasise the formal and institutionalised aspects of the political process, such as elections, cabinet meetings, parliamentary debates. The reconcilation of conflict may be achieved at various levels, which are accepted but not formalised. *Ad hoc* arrangements may equally be a necessary part of the political process. Professor T. H. Williams has provided an interesting and informative example of the settlement of political conflict in Louisiana in the 1920s. Governor Parker had promised in his election campaign that he would impose a tax on private companies such as Standard Oil which were exploiting the natural resources of the state. He asked the companies, informally, to agree to small tax, but they refused. Parker then threatened a smaller tax which would be pushed through the state legislature whether the companies agreed or not. The combined opposition of the companies collapsed, and in return for their agreement Parker not only promised not to raise the level of the tax in the future, but even allowed representatives of the larger companies to draft the proposed legislation imposing the tax. Unfortunately for Parker, the state legislature was not committed to the governor's 'gentleman's agreement' with the companies, and wanted a higher tax imposed. Whereupon Parker called the legislative leaders and company representatives to a meeting which actually took place on the steps of the governor's home, and various concessions and compromises were proposed and accepted. The tax was limited; it was not to be increased for a set period, and part of the proceeds of the tax were directed to help the constituencies the legislators represented. As Professor Williams observes: 'Every party to the controversy got something, and everyone seemed satisfied.'[8]

Political activity is simply a means of reconciling differences. In itself it is neither good nor bad. Particular politicians or political methods of achieving certain goals may be disliked, but politics itself is neutral. However, this should not lead to the acceptance of the liberal view of political activity, which holds that governments are neutral and merely hold the ring between competing interests in society. Governments are composed of different opposed interests, and may be dominated by one particular interest. Certainly governments generate interests of their own, even if it is simply that of preserving the status quo.

If political activity is based on diversity, and is the attempt to reconcile conflicts flowing from that diversity, through, at public level, a political framework of accepted political institutions and processes, political activity is then universally applicable to all types of governments. No political regime has succeeded in suppressing differences, none has established a uniformity of behaviour, nor have any ended disagreement. Therefore politics cannot be confused with liberal freedoms such as the rights of individuals in society, or denied to socialist or fascist states. Politics is an activity, not a moral prescription; it is a universal activity. The propaganda myths that propose the end of conflict with the realisation of certain social and economic changes should not be accepted as the actual realisation of those aims.[9]

Political power

So far in the discussion we have avoided any direct reference to the concept of political power. It is a key concept in the study of politics: for if politics is the resolution of conflict, the distribution of power within a political community determines how the conflict is to be resolved and whether the resolution is to be effectively observed by all parties. However, there are numerous terminological difficulties, for political scientists disagree on the definitions of such terms as 'power', 'authority' and 'influence'.[10]

Political power may be broadly defined as the capacity to affect another's behaviour by some form of sanction. Sanctions may take the form of coercion or inducement: power may be backed by the carrot or the stick and it may be exercised in a positive or negative fashion. Thus political leaders may acquire compliance with their wishes by promising wealth or honours to their supporters; or they may threaten to deny such rewards to their opponents. Most exercises in political power include both elements. The negative penalties for opposing the holder of power may be extreme, such as imprisonment or death. These penalties are usually in the hands of those who control the institutions of the state, and those who control the state usually wield the greatest political power. However, it is the fear of these coercive sanctions which promotes obedience, not the coercion itself. Indeed, too frequent use of these penalties may be an indication of the weakening of political power.

Political power must also be seen as a relationship: the holder of political power has the capacity to make another behave in a manner that he, she or it was unwilling to do before the threat or application of sanctions. Thus Robinson Crusoe had no power until the arrival of Man Friday on the island. The actors in a power relationship may be individuals, groups, or institutions. If political power implies a relationship, it is important to discover who or what has power in relation to whom or what. The claim that a Secretary of Education in the central government is more powerful than the chairman of a local authority education committee is a different type of statement from that which concludes that the British Prime Minister is more powerful than the American President. The first statement is clearly concerned with decision-making in the field of education. The second could refer either to the ability of the Prime Minister and the President to change the behaviour of a third party, say the Prime Minister of Canada, or to their respective power relationships with their own cabinets, assemblies, or civil servants.

It is also important to compare like with like. The claim that modern British cabinets do not control the decision-making processes of modern government as effectively as nineteenth-century cabinets, where all major decisions were considered, ignores the limited scope of cabinet decision-making a hundred years ago. Then government responsibility was confined chiefly to matters of foreign policy, defence and internal order, not to economic regulation or the wide field of social welfare.

There are further problems in deciding who or what has power. The individual, group or institution may be initially unwilling to act in the manner desired by the wielder of power, and obviously there can be no agreement between the actors in the relationship. Thus if a prime minister asks for the resignation of a member of the cabinet and the resignation takes place with little or no political damage to the prime minister, we can say that in relation to the resigning member of the cabinet, the prime minister has political power. However, if the cabinet member resigned for other reasons and it was a coincidence that his resignation occurred at the same time as the prime minister's request, we have no evidence either way about the power of the prime minister in this relationship. Similarly, if a trade union threatens industrial action in order to compel a government to agree to changes in the law regarding the legal position of trade unions, and the government successfully resists the union's demands, we cannot claim the union is powerful if, as a result of the consequent industrial action there is economic dislocation. The union is not powerful as a result of consequences it did not primarily intend.

Political power cannot be measured satisfactorily. Any attempt to measure the amount of political power that individuals or groups hold must be a very careful exercise. The relevant questions involved in this exercise include the following: how many times has A effected a change in the behaviour of B in the manner intended? Did B's behaviour change dramatically, or was B almost at the position that A desired? Was the change in B's behaviour relatively permanent or did B quickly return to the position previously occupied before A's exercise of power? Was A trying to change only the behaviour of B at the time or were there attempts to change the behaviour of C, D and E? What were the political costs to the actors involved? If A induced a change in B's behaviour at enormous political costs to A and few costs to B, then A's power is less than if the reverse was the case. As Pyrrhus, the ancient king of Epirus, remarked: 'One more such victory over the Romans and we are utterly undone'.

Measurement of political power is not the only difficulty facing the political scientist. There is also the problem of non-decisions. An actor may be powerful enough to keep certain issues off the political agenda. A political élite may have sufficient political power to keep out of the political debate any issue which would provide a threat to its own power and the élite may attempt to restrict political conflict to 'safe' issues.[11] It is difficult to analyse decisions which seek to prevent the making of decisions.

There is also the complex issue of potential power. Those with power may act in such a way to avoid creating political opposition; they anticipate the possible or potential power of groups, individuals or institutions that as yet have not emerged as opponents of the power-holders. Yet although the power relationship is not overt, it is difficult to claim that a power relationship does not exist.[12]

Political authority and influence

Obedience secured solely by the threat of sanctions is unstable. Political power is usually accompanied by authority. Political authority is the recognition of the right to rule irrespective of the sanctions the ruler may possess. Thus a ruler may be obeyed because of the belief that he was chosen by divine authority, and obedience to the ruler is obedience to God's laws. Supporters of the theory of the Divine Right of Kings could seek verification in the New Testament: 'Let every soul be subject unto the higher powers. For there is no power but of God: the powers that be are ordained of God. Whosoever therefore resisteth the power, resisteth the ordinance of God ...'[13] Shakespeare's distorted view of King Richard III was that of a man who monopolised the coercive powers of the state, but whose right to rule was disputed, and the challenge to his authority, because he had usurped political power, was the reason for his ultimate downfall. Thomas Hobbes's prescription of strong government to end the civil wars was a concentration on the coercive powers of governments, but Rousseau was nearer the truth underlying political stability when he observed: 'The strongest is never strong enough to be always master, unless he transforms strength into right, and obedience into duty.'[14]

The German sociologist Max Weber suggested a threefold classification of the sources of political authority in the modern state. Firstly, traditional authority, the right to rule resulting from the continuous exercise of political power. Hereditary ruling families fit into this classification. Secondly, charismatic authority, which results from exceptional personal characteristics of the political leader, e.g. Hitler. Thirdly, legal-bureaucratic or legal-rational, in which authority emanates from the political office the individual holds, not from the individual who holds the office. The American president is obeyed because he is the American president, not because of the particular individual holding that office. Here the emphasis is on the acceptance of constitutional rules. Weber recognised that none of these categories existed in pure form. The British system would provide an example of a mixture of traditional and legal-bureaucratic sources of authority. American presidents often combine charismatic authority with legal-bureaucratic.[15]

We have noted that political power may be divorced from political authority in that the right to exercise political power may not be recognised. Some political leaders may possess political authority but be unable or reluctant to translate it into political power. General de Gaulle's authority was recognised in German-occupied France, but the coercive powers of the German and pro-German French governments prevented the conversion of that authority into political power. Political authority is buttressed and perpetuated by the use of symbols such as the use of the national flag or a coronation ceremony, but an important basis of political authority can be found in the pattern of political ideas.

Political influence, like power and authority, implies the ability to change the behaviour of other actors. However, here the cause of the behavioural change is not the application of sanctions or the acceptance of the authority of those seeking a change in the behaviour of others. The change in behaviour is the result of rational persuasion or of mutual recognition of the advantages of co-operation. Influence differs from power in the sense that with the former the behavioural change is not reluctant. Naturally, it is often difficult to ascertain clearly the degree of unwillingness on the part of those whose behaviour is changed.

Distribution of power

Political power is not distributed evenly in any political system. The rich possess more political resources than the poor in that they can finance election campaigns, bribe supporters and opponents, and purchase other political advantages such as a good education. The rich may be individuals or they may be corporate bodies. Some individuals have more political skills than others in that like Hitler or Lloyd George, they may be able to influence audiences by their oratory or political intelligence. Prestige gained in non-political activities such as the army and the church may be translated into political power. Even those in possession of certain political skills and resources may be reluctant to turn them into political assets. However, all theories concerned with the distribution of political power agree on one main point: political power in all political systems is unequally distributed. Nevertheless, there are key differences between the various models of how political power is distributed.

Pluralism

An influential approach to the distribution of political power in modern political systems is that adopted by the pluralists. The pluralists hold that political power in liberal democracies is widely distributed, that there is continual competition between groups and that new groups constantly emerge. Decisions are seen as the outcome of bargaining between influential groups, and although political power is not equally distributed, no one group has a monopoly. The membership of the groups overlaps and the leadership interacts to produce an overall consensus on the aims of the political system and the methods for maintaining political stability; there is élite consensus. The resolution of conflict tends to be non-violent, taking the form of bargaining and procedural devices such as elections.

Modern pluralism is partly the result of the behavioural revolution in political science that emerged in America after the Second World War. However, there are many varieties of pluralism. Some early pluralists adopted what came to be known as the 'balance of power' theory, implying a dynamic equilibrium between competing groups.[16] Dahl, the most influential of the American pluralists, however, has never held such views and he is far more explicit on the relationship between political and economic inequality: some are more equal than others.[17] Another area of disagreement among pluralists is concerned with the degree of neutrality of the modern state; whether the state is a passive mediator between competing interests or whether the state has interests of its own.[18]

The pluralist model of the distribution of power has also been applied to socialist systems of the USSR, Eastern Europe and China. As industrial society develops, so there emerges a multiplicity of interests and functional specialisation. This does not imply that these societies are liberal democratic or that spontaneous autonomous organisations emerge, but that the dominant political party must share political power and accommodate different demands.[19] None of these approaches imply that Soviet 'pluralism' is akin to that of liberal democracies and it usually bears titles such as 'bureaucratic' or 'institutional' pluralism.

The pluralist approach to the distribution of political power, particularly in liberal democracies, has been widely criticised. It ignores non-decisions, it ignores social class as a basis for élite rule: 'The flaw in the pluralist heaven is that the heavenly chorus sings with a strong upper-class accent'.[20] Pluralists, it is alleged, have tended to isolate important decisions, but this methodological approach tends to create a criterion of 'importance' which underpins the pluralist conclusions. Critics argue that the alleged balance of groups, countervailing power, does not exist. Pluralists unfairly distinguish between legitimate rule and illegitimate protest, and term 'extremist' those of whom they disapprove. Above all, pluralists are criticised for faults in their methodology that their approach intended to avoid: namely the adoption of an approach that favours their own political preferences.[21]

Elitism

Elitist models of the distribution of political power share many of the characteristics of pluralist approaches. However, all élite theorists accept one key element which separates them from the pluralists and brings them close to Marxist views: all societies are divided into two groups, the rulers and the ruled. The smaller group, the political élite, controls the majority. Mosca, an early twentieth-century originator of modern élite theories, said: 'In all societies ... two classes of people appear – a class that rules and a class that is ruled. The first class, always the less numerous, performs all the political functions, monopolises power and enjoys the advantages that power brings, whereas the second, the more numerous class, is directed and controlled by the first in a manner that is more or less legal.'[22] The wishes of the smaller group generally prevail over the wishes of the majority,[23] and the élite is cohesive and united on most important issues. This closed nature of the political élite and its common social background is common to all political systems.[24]

There are several important differences between the élite theorists; élite models do not agree on the sources of power of the élite, whether it is economic, social, the possession of certain psychological characteristics such as the will to power, and/or the ability of the élite to organise. The major division among élite theories is whether the power of the élite stems from the occupation of certain political offices, such as party or military leadership, or whether élite power stems primarily from economic and social bases.[25] However, whatever these differences, élitists differ from the pluralists on the crucial point of the concentration of power; they differ essentially from the Marxists over the sources of that élite power.

Elite models, like those of the pluralists, are criticised for a flawed methodological approach; a concentration on those assumed to have political power will result in the conclusion that they do indeed have political power. Pluralists will not accept that power is cumulative; as Robert Dahl has observed: 'Neither logically nor empirically does it follow that a group with a high degree of influence over one scope will necessarily have a high degree of influence over another scope within the same system.'[26] Also, élitists have been criticised for inadequately dealing with the problem of political change in society and importantly, the problem of identifying the élite itself.

Marxism

As with pluralism and élitism, there are numerous, varied Marxist models of the distribution of political power. However, the essential basis of all Marxist approaches is that the economic order of society determines how political power is distributed; political power is concentrated in the hands of a ruling class as a consequence of the concentration of economic power in the hands of the few. The state is a coercive mechanism designed to keep the ruling class in power. Marxism recognises divisions within the ruling class and as a result of these divisions, the state has a degree of autonomy and regulates political and economic conflicts. Moreover, to maintain the stability of the ruling class domination, the state will attempt to mitigate the worst consequences of the division of political power, and to appease those who may seek to disturb the status quo.

Marxism in all its varieties offers a rich and complex explanation of the distribution of power. Unlike élitism it offers a more persuasive explanation of change in political societies. However, there are serious divergences between Marxists themselves and many trenchant criticisms of the Marxist approaches.[27] The concentration on the importance of social class, the conflicts over the nature of the state, a monocausal approach to the nature of political change and the inability to test certain Marxist assumptions empirically are some of the criticisms levelled at this explanation of the distribution of political power. Yet it is important to remember that all these conflicting approaches to power have strong normative overtones; these theories are not merely concerned with what is but with what should be. Given the ideological framework of the investigators, no approach to the study of political power is value free; political enquiry is not a neutral occupation.

Corporatism

Corporatist approaches are the most recent of the investigation of where power lies. Modern corporatism emerged in the 1970s to analyse power distribution in the contemporary liberal democratic state. Corporatism stresses the incorporation of certain groups in society into the decision-making process, The state benefits from the co-operation and expertise of groups such as industrialists and trade unions in the implementation of political decisions, while the groups gain from a share in political power and the recognition of their monopoly as representatives of certain societal sectors.[28] As a result of this incorporation of key groups, large areas of the decision-making process are depoliticised, that is the formal bodies such as cabinets and assemblies only appear to make the decision reached by other means. Corporatism implies that the state is not, as the Marxist claims, a repressive means or coercion but a means of engineering consent.

There are many different emphases among corporatists, and none claim that it is a complete theory of the distribution of power nor that it can be applied to all political systems. Its empirical foundations are disputed,[29] and there are serious divergences on the role of the state. To some corporatism is merely 'a variety of pluralism.'[30]

Power distribution in modern societies

Thus the student of politics is faced with competing and complex models seeking to explain how political power is distributed. They all agree that power is not distributed equally but disagree on whether is concentrated in the hands of an élite or ruling class, or whether it is more widely distributed between competing élites. The debate is of crucial importance since the whole approach of the political scientist will be coloured, unconsciously or not, by the ideological assumptions implicit in the competing models. Politics is concerned with conflict and the resolution of that conflict, but how the resolution takes place and the consequences of that resolution will be coloured by the investigator's 'bias'. The different institutions of the state, executives, bureaucracies, assemblies and judiciaries, plus parties, pressure groups and the procedural devices such as elections, are analysed within each political investigator's ideological preferences. Political study cannot be completely value free.[31]

References

1. G. A. Almond and S. Verba, *The Civic Culture* (Princeton, N J, 1963) p. 93.
2. Quintin Hogg, *The Case for Conservatism*, 2nd ed. (London, 1959) pp. 12–13.
3. See R. J. Osborn, *The Evolution of Soviet Politics* (Illinois: Dorsey Press, 1974) pp. 182–90.
4. For an interesting account of the opposition to the policies of the National government during the Second World War, see A. Calder, *The People's War* (London, 1969).

5. See J. D. B. Miller, *The Nature of Politics* (London, 1965) ch. 4.
6. *The Times*, 3 June 1970.
7. See Miller, *The Nature of Politics*, chs 1 and 2 for a fuller discussion of diversity and political conflict.
8. T. H. Williams, *Huey Long* (London, 1970) p. 144.
9. See B. Crick, *In Defence of Politics*, 3rd ed. (London, 1982) for the argument that 'Politics is the way in which free societies are governed' (p. 5).
10. See A. Cox, P. Furlong and E. Page, *Power in Capitalist Society* (Brighton, 1985) pp. 14–44 for a view of these differences.
11. See P. Bachrach and M. S. Baratz, 'Two Faces of Power', *American Political Science Review* 56 (1962) pp. 947–52. Also see a case study in the area of non-decisions, M. A. Crenson, *The Un-Politics of Air Pollution* (Baltimore, 1971).
12. See D. Truman, *The Governmental Process* (New York, 1951).
13. Romans: 1 and 2.
14. *The Social Contract* (Everyman's Library ed., 1913) p. 6.
15. See Max Weber, *The Theory of Social and Economic Organisations*, Trans. A. M. Henderson and T. Parsons (Glencoe, Ill., 1947).
16. See J. K Galbraith, *American Capitalism* (London, 1952).
17. See R. A. Dahl, *Dilemmas of Pluralist Democracy* (London, 1982).
18. See Earl Latham, *The Group Basis of Politics* (Ithaca, 1952) p. 390. He depicted the state as a body which 'referees the group struggle'.
19. See, for example, J. Hough, 'The Soviet System: Petrification or Pluralism', *Problems of Communism*, March-April 1972, pp. 25–42. D. Hammer, *U.S.S.R.: The Politics of Oligarchy*, 2nd ed. (Boulder, Col., 1987).
20. E. E. Schattschneider, *The Semi-Sovereign People* (Homewood, Illinois, 1960) p. 35.
21. For criticisms of the pluralist approaches see W. Connolly (ed.), *The Bias of Pluralism* (New York, 1969); R. Miliband, *The State in Capitalist Society*, (London, 1973); P. Dunleavy and B. O'Leary, *Theories of the State. The Politics of Liberal Democracy* (London, 1987) pp. 59–70.
22. Gaetano Mosca, *The Ruling Class* (New York, 1939) p. 50. For a general view of élite theories see G. Parry, *Political Elites* (London, 1969).
23. See R. Michels, *Political Parties* (Glencoe, Illnois, 1958 reprint) p. 418 for his famous depiction of élite rule in his 'Iron Law of Oligarchy'.
24. For examples of the application of élite models to the United States, see C. Wright Mills, *The Power Elite* (London, 1956); G. W. Domhoff, *Who Rules America* (Englewood Cliffs, N J, 1967).
    For the Soviet Union see R. Conquest, 'The Soviet Order' in R. Wesson (ed.) *The Soviet Union: Looking to the 1980s* (Stanford, 1980).
25. For examples of the 'positional élite' argument see Mills, *The Power Elite* and E. Nordlinger, *The Autonomy of the Democratic State* (London, 1981).
26. R. Dahl, 'Critique of the Ruling Elite Model', in F. G. Castles *et al* (eds.), *Decisions, Organisations and Society* (London, 1971).
27. There is not the space to identify the wide literature, but see Karl Marx and Friedrich Engels, *The Communist Manifesto* (London ed., 1967); B. Jessop, *The Capitalist State* (London, 1982); R. Miliband, *Marxism and Politics* (London, 1977).

28. For corporatist theories see P. Schmitter and G. Lehmbruch (eds.), *Trends Towards Corporatist Intermediation* (London, 1979); T. Smith, *The Politics of the Corporate Economy* (Oxford, 1979); K. Middlemas, *Politics in Industrial Society* (London, 1979); O. Newman, *The Challenge of Corporatism* (London, 1981).
29. See M. Heisler, 'Corporate Pluralism Revisited. Where is the Theory?', *Scandinavian Political Studies*, 2 (new series), 3, 1979, pp. 285ff.
30. G. Almond, 'Corporatism, Pluralism and Professional Memory', *World Politics*, 35, 2 (January 1983) p. 251.
31. For example, standard texts on British politics differ accordingly to the model adopted by the authors, thus R. M. Punnett, *British Politics and Government*, 4th ed. (London, 1980) uses the pluralist perspective, whereas J. Dearlove and P. Saunders, *Introduction to British Politics* (Cambridge, 1984) employ a Marxist model.

3

Classification of Governments

Aims of classification

Attempts to produce a classification of political institutions can be dated back to the beginnings of the study of political science. Aristotle made one of the earliest attempts to classify government structures. He distinguished between states ruled by one person, by the few and the many – monarchy, aristocracy and mixed government. His intention was not only to describe but to evaluate and thus he extended his classification scheme to their 'perverted' forms, which he labelled tyranny, oligarchy and democracy. He realised, however, that these types did not exist in their pure forms, thus noting that classification in political science is a search for 'ideal' types.[1]

Jean Bodin, writing his *Six Books on the Commonwealth* in the sixteenth century, pushed Aristotle's classification further. Although he was still primarily concerned with the question, 'Which type of constitution is best', his immense arsenal of facts on contemporary constitutions and his insistence that the type of government depended on economic and geographical factors as well as political factors allowed him to make significant advances in the study of politics. There was still the emphasis on legal sovereignty that was to be the hallmark of political science until the twentieth century.[2]

Montesquieu, a French philospher of the eighteenth century, produced one of the most famous schemes of classifying governments: 'There are three species of government: republican, monarchical and despotic.'[3] Montesquieu's classification differed from Aristotle's in that aristocracy and democracy were part of his republican type of government, but his categorisation was firmly in the classical mould since the type of government depended on the number of people holding power. Republican government divides power between the many or the few, 'the more an aristocracy borders on democracy the nearer it approaches perfection: and in proportion as it draws towards monarchy, the more it is imperfect'.[4] Monarchy is a system of government in which power, although in the hands of a single person, is regulated by fundamental laws and by the power of other groups in the society. Despotism is the worst form of government since power is in the hands of one man. There is in Montesquieu the important recognition of the relationship between the type of government and the type of society. Education, morals, patriotism and the level of economic equality all help to determine the type of government, and a most important variable is the extent of the state's territory: 'A large empire supposes a depotic authority in the person who governs',[5] a monarchical state possesses moderate territory, but 'It is natural for a republic to have only a small territory otherwise it cannot long subsist.'[6]

These brief glimpses at former attempts to produce schemes of classification help to illustrate some of the difficulties in their construction. Classification is essentially an attempt to isolate the most important characteristics of the political system from the less important. Classification presupposes a comparative approach,[7] and classification in political science is no different in terms of aims from those of natural science; it is to simplify, to ensure the grouping of like with like, to allow for significant comparison and thereby extend our understanding.

It is important to remember, however, that all classification in the social sciences is somewhat arbitrary; the classification scheme depends on what aspect of the political system one wishes to isolate and emphasise; therefore there can be no one scheme of classification that is suitable for all purposes. It is important to ask the question: 'What is the purpose of a particular scheme of classification?' Although one's conclusions can only be tentative, the mark of good categorisation is simplicity.

Several examples will illustrate the importance of the question being asked. We noted Weber's classification of different types of political authority in Chapter 2, but like other typologies it has its limitations; it only provides answers to the question that it asks and it is concerned solely with the sources of political authority. Robert Dahl has emphasised this point: 'Even as a scientific classification, however, Weber's typology seems deficient, since it makes no place for a number of distinctions that most students of politics would regard as interesting and significant.'[8] If one were concerned to emphasise civil liberties, one might distinguish liberal democracies from non-liberal democracies and discuss the emphasis that certain civil freedoms appear to receive in political systems of the former type. However, if one wanted to examine the degree of executive independence of the legislature, it would be rewarding at some stage to compare presidential systems of the type found in the United States and the parliamentary systems prevalent in most of Western Europe. If we asked questions concerning the degree of public participation in the decision-making process, we would find a distinction between presidential and parliamentary systems most unrewarding; even a distinction between democratic regimes and non-democratic regimes would produce difficulties. There is a distinction between participatory systems which may include the Soviet Union and the United States and non-participatory systems such as Saudi Arabia. However, to emphasise the role of ideology in the political system, some political scientists, as we shall see later in the chapter, find it important to distinguish between the United States and the Soviet Union.

The classification scheme may point to interrelations between different variables. The connection between the type of political system and the socio-economic structure is an important one in this respect. The French writer, Alexis de Tocqueville, emphasised this relationship when examining the basis of American democracy in the early nineteenth century: 'Among the lucky circumstances that favoured the establishment and assured the maintenance of a democratic republic in the United States, the most important was the choice of the land itself in which the Americans live. Their fathers gave them a love of equality and liberty, but it was God who, by handing a limitless continent over to them gave them the means of long remaining equal and free. General prosperity favours stability in all governments, but particularly in a democratic one.'[9]

This relationship between socio-economic development and the type of political system has been echoed by S. M. Lipset. He has argued that a liberal democratic system is only possible where relative social and economic equality produces political stability, and where economic and industrial development has produced a high level of material prosperity.[10] Basically, there is a relationship, in his view, between the capitalist mode of production and liberal democracy, and there is the presumption that liberal democracy is not consistent with a peasant, non-industrial base. Non-liberal democracies may therefore be a product of economic underdevelopment.

Barrington Moore developed this link between the type of political system and other socio-economic factors.[11] He isolated three types of political system, the democratic or parliamentary, such as Britain, France and the United States; the fascist, such as pre-1945 Germany and Japan; the communist regimes, such as the Soviet Union and China. He allowed for types of political system that do not follow this threefold pattern of development, giving India as the main example of this hybrid type. Moore argued that the interaction of lords, peasants, the middle class and government bureaucracies will tend to produce in certain circumstances a particular type of political system.

Thus it can be seen that the number of typologies is very wide and the choice will depend on the type of variables that are being considered, but more importantly on the nature of the question being asked. Before any particular scheme is adopted the aim of the classification must be clear, but even with this qualification in mind there are still innumerable problems of methodology that must be identified before moving to any examination of particular schemes of classification.

Problems of classification

Thus an aim of all schemes of classification is simplicity, although the choice may be arbitrary depending on the nature of the question being asked. Yet even given these qualifications to the utilisation of particular typologies, there are certain fundamental problems that are common to all schemes of classification. There is the problem of defining the concepts being used. Thus civil liberties may mean something different in the United States than they mean in the Soviet Union; therefore the claim that the Soviet government ignores fundamental civil rights will be meaningless unless there is some form of agreement on what the respective regimes mean by 'civil liberties'. Moreover, the problem of quantification complicates the already difficult question of conceptualisation. Weber's concept of 'charisma' provides an illustrative example here; how does one measure charisma? If one claims that the source of a leader's authority is charismatic rather than legal-bureaucratic, how much charisma is necessary before this claim is made and how is it measured? Hitler was certainly obeyed because he had outstanding powers of leadership, but he was also appointed chancellor in a legal manner by the German president; how are we accurately to estimate the different contributions to his authority over the German people?

The problem over labels is another difficulty in the classification of political systems. Political institutions with the same label may perform similar functions in different political systems.[12] The British monarchy has similar political functions and political influence to those of the West German president. The French president of the Fifth Republic has more political power than either; the president of the United States combines, in some respect, the political features of the British prime minister and the British monarchy. We will see in Chapter 5 that the labels of multi- or two-party systems may be most confusing in terms of how the party system actually works. Thus it is very important and often very difficult in the construction of typologies to make sure that like is being compared to like.

Another difficulty concerns value judgements. Classification is sometimes used to praise or condemn a particular regime. Regimes are labelled 'democratic' or 'autocratic' not simply to describe, categorise and analyse the political institutions, but to indicate preferences. To a certain extent all political scientists are culture-bound; they use the political institutions and the political processes with which they are familiar as a yardstick with which to measure others. They seem to state preferences almost unconsciously; they see types of governments they dislike as resting on force or fraud. Political descriptions then become full of words of abuse. Bernard Crick has pointed out the difficulties of using the word 'democratic', given the desire on the part of practising politicians and political scientists to consecrate different regimes with this holy description:

> Democracy is perhaps the most promiscuous word in the world of public affairs. She is everybody's mistress and yet somehow retains her magic even when her lover sees that her favours are being, in his light, illicitly shared by many another. Indeed, even amid our pain at being denied her exclusive fidelity, we are proud of her adaptability to all sorts of circumstances, to all sorts of company. How often has one heard: 'Well, at least the Communists claim to be democratic'? Bur the real trouble is, of course, that they do not pretend to be democratic. They are democratic in the sound historical sense of a majority actively willing to be ruled in some other way.[13]

The dangers are, in some cases, unavoidable, but awareness that value judgements may interfere with a more objective analysis is of great importance in the process of classification.

A further difficulty in the development of typologies is the failure to recognise that regimes change; any system of classification must allow for the processes of change, avoiding excessive rigidity. Both the Spanish and Portuguese political systems underwent various changes in the 1970s and they are now substantially different from the Franco and Salazar dictatorships. It was already difficult to classify these regimes before the deaths of their respective enduring dictators. They were commonly described as 'fascist' to allow comparison with the regimes of Hitler and Mussolini, but this was too simplistic. The respective changes in the 1970s, and especially the relative rapidity of those political changes, certainly warn against the dangers of too rigid a scheme of classification.

Systems of classification

Many of the problems of classification can be appreciated by examining particular examples of classifying political systems and political institutions. We have seen in Chapter 1 that the political system includes all types of political activity within a society, not only the formal political institutions. We also saw that a political system implies the interdependence of the various parts of the system and that changes in one aspect of the system will affect other parts. There are many different ways in which political systems have been classified,[14] but for the purpose of underlining the difficulties associated with typologies as well as indicating some of the advantages, the following broad typology would be sufficiently representative:

1. Liberal democratic systems.
2. Socialist democracies.
3. Authoritarian autocracies.

The liberal democratic system could be characterised as follows:

1. There is more than one political party competing for political power.
2. The competition for power is open, not secretive, and is based on established and accepted forms of procedure.
3. Entry and recruitment to positions of political power are relatively open.
4. There are periodic elections based on universal franchise.
5. Pressure groups are able to operate to influence government decisions. Associations such as trade unions and other voluntary organisations are not subject to close government control.
6. Civil liberties, such as freedom of speech, religion, freedom from arbitrary arrest, are recognised and protected within the political system. This assumes that there is a substantial amount of independence and freedom from government control of the mass media, i.e. radio, television, newspapers.

7. There is some form of separation of powers, i.e. a representative assembly has some form of control over the executive, and the judiciary is independent of both executive and legislature.

This broad description of the possible attributes of liberal democracy bristles with dangers. The difference of degree becomes very important and the measurement of this degree difficult, as we saw earlier with civil liberties. A major problem is the relative importance of the different variables. For example, South Africa has a competitive party system, but it is doubtful whether civil liberties are more rigorously protected in South Africa than in Tanzania, where there is only one political party. Competition between political parties in South Africa is confined to white political parties and the majority of the population are excluded from the institutionalised political arena. The degree to which the judiciary is independent of executive control or the mass media free of government censorship are very important questions. Critics of the government of Indira Gandhi after the declaration of the state of emergency in 1975 argued that the government's control of the press and imprisonment without trial of political opponents no longer entitled India to be categorised as a liberal democracy. But here we meet the problems of change and the fact that few political systems are static. The British government possessed the most far-reaching powers during the Second World War, including powers of imprisonment without trial, to ban newspapers, to direct labour, to seize property by new procedures; there was, moreover, a postponement of elections and an electoral truce between the political parties. Did all this imply that Britain ceased to be a liberal democracy? Of course, the nature of the emergency, the agreement of all the main political parties and the apparent consent of the British people to these draconian powers were very important considerations, yet the example does underline some of the difficulties in classification.

There is no doubt that the problems are formidable. Jean Blondel has observed: 'Liberal democracy is ... difficult to define, as the major components of the combined index (free elections, existence of an opposition, etc.) seem to defy rigorous operationalisation.'[15] However, in spite of all the problems, the concept of liberal democracy is flexible enough to be able to group together various systems by emphasising certain essential characteristics and usefully to contrast these systems with other broad categories of political system. The political systems of Britain, France, Sweden, the United States, West Germany, etc. can be grouped together under the label 'liberal democratic', thereby stressing certain important characteristics these political systems possess in contrast to other political systems.

The second category, that of socialist democracy, presents far more operational problems than that of liberal democracy. This category is often given the alternative title of 'totalitarianism' and Friedrich and Brzezinski produced their famous characterisation of totalitarian regimes as those political systems with an official ideology, a single mass party, the government use of terror, communications and the use of force monopolised by the government and where there is central direction of the economy.[16]

The difficulties with the use of 'totalitarian' abound and the critics are many.[17] The description would seem to fit the regimes of Stalin and Hitler rather than any contemporary political system and the category appears to lay stress on socialist ideology and the use of terror. There are now large differences, especially economic, that underly the bases of these systems, for example the peasant economy of Vietnam and the industrialised structure of East Germany. Therefore the use of socialist democracy instead of totalitarian would have fewer normative overtones and these regimes could be characterised as having the following:

1. An official socialist ideology.
2. Political domination by one political party.
3. Fewer distinctions between the public and private spheres of activity than in liberal democracies, with private associations subject to a larger degree of state supervision.
4. The absence of the liberal democratic concept of the separation of powers with subsequently less judicial independence.

This form of characterisation, despite the difficulties, would be more useful than the totalitarian label, and the use of the term 'socialist' would offer a clearer contrast with liberal democracy. It is the label that these systems use themselves and therefore less open to the accusation of political bias. In this category one could place the political system of the USSR and the East European systems of Poland, Hungary, Yugoslavia and Bulgaria, etc. and the less economically developed systems of Vietnam and Cuba. China would provide another good illustration of these characteristics.

The third category, autocracy, probably gives rise to more difficulties of conceptualisation than either liberal democracy or socialist democracy. It becomes a heterogeneous collection of all the political systems that cannot be fitted into the other two categories. Furthermore, the political systems that can be classified as autocratic are often unstable and likely to change more rapidly than others and therefore the examples are often soon dated. Descriptions such as modernising regimes or third world states are useful in certain exercises, but tend to emphasise only certain aspects of the political system. The level of socio-economic development, the nature of the party system, and the role of the military are all important variables; but the classification cannot rest on these alone. Certainly, characteristics such as limitations on open political competition, the role of ideology, the overt deployment of coercion, weakly supported civil liberties, lack of judicial independence and the role of traditional or military élites are important and perhaps would allow a way forward. Thus oligarchic or authoritarian regimes as opposed to liberal democratic or socialist regimes may be classified as follows:

1. Conservative regimes:
   (a) Traditional monarchies, with traditional ruling groups and little political institutional infrastructure, e.g. Saudi Arabia, Morocco and Nepal.
   (b) Conservative dictatorships where the personality of the leader is important and there are few institutional forms of legitimacy, e.g. Paraguay and Malawi.
   (c) Theocracies, revolutionary regimes that attempt to mobilise mass support. The few examples can be drawn from the Islamic states such as Iran.

2. Façade liberal democracies where there are competitive elections but restrictions on the opposition and limited civil liberties. Examples in this category could include South Africa and Mexico.
3. Military regimes:
   (a) Direct military rule. The military has usually seized power in a *coup*, there are no elections, there is a poor level of economic development, and often a marked degree of political instability. Examples are to be found in contemporary Nigeria, Bangladesh and Ghana.
   (b) Civilian–military regimes. These portray far more political stability than those regimes with direct military rule but the power relationship between the civilian and military within the government is difficult to assess and subject to constant change. Chile, Brazil, Egypt and Syria would fit into this category.
   (c) Radical military regimes. This provides a most controversial category since there is considerable overlap between this and categories (a) and (b) above and even with the socialist systems. Tentatively, one could put Angola, Mozambique, Ethiopia and Algeria into this category.[18]

Certainly, it would not be difficult to quarrel with any of these categories and with the examples chosen to illustrate them. The exercise illustrates the advantages of attempting a form of classification and also underlines the pitfalls. All systems of classification should be tentative and flexible and possess a clear idea of the purpose of the classification exercise.

Classification of political structures

Attempts to classify particular elements of the political system are fraught with the same difficulties outlined above. We shall see this more clearly when we examine different types of party system in Chapter 5. However, if we recognise such limitations, the comparison of different structures or processes assists us in understanding the working of various aspects of the system, especially in terms of the relationship of the separate parts to the whole. The division between a federal and a unitary system or that between parliamentary and presidential systems can serve to illustrate the advantages of such an approach.

Federal and unitary division cuts across the threefold typology outlined for political systems. A federal form of government is one in which political power is divided between the central federal government and the constituent states or provinces that form part of the federal union. The federal structure can lead to significant differences in the way in which the political process works. We shall see in later chapters that federalism affects the working of the party system, the operation of pressure groups, the relationships between assemblies and executives, the status of the judiciary and the organisation of the bureaucracy. Therefore, for certain patterns of interrelationships, the division between the federal systems of the United States, Canada, Australia and West Germany on the one hand and the unitary systems of Great Britain, Sweden and France on the other is an advantage in the examinations of individual systems and the comparison of these systems.[19] The usefulness of the division even extends to the examination of the politics of the Soviet Union. It is sometimes argued that in spite of having a federal constitution, the decision-making process in the Soviet Union bears a closer resemblance to that of unitary systems because political power is highly centralised. It is certainly true that Soviet federalism differs enormously in practice from that of the United States (but comparison of different types of federalism is useful in itself); but it is simply not true that federalism in the Soviet Union does not have profound effects on the operation of the political system.[20]

Another useful division is that between presidential systems and parliamentary systems. A comparison of the two throws up certain important distinctions between the two, emphasises the essential characteristics of each, and, moreover, further underlines the limitations of any form of classification.

The major characteristics of the parliamentary type of government could be listed as follows:

1. There is a nominal head of state whose functions are chiefly formal and ceremonial and whose political influence is limited. This head of state may be a president, as in West Germany, India and Italy, or a monarch, as in Japan, Sweden and the United Kingdom.
2. The political executive (prime minister, chancellor, etc.), together with the cabinet, is part of the legislature, selected by the legislature, and can be removed by the legislature if the legislature withdraws its support.
3. The legislature is elected for varying periods by the electorate, the election date being chosen by the formal head of state on the advice of the prime minister or chancellor.

There are significant differences within parliamentary types of government. The legislature may consist of one chamber or two; there are variations in the methods of selecting the second chamber; there are variations in the power of the executive to dissolve the assembly and call an election; there may be a supreme court to interpret the constitution, or the position may be that of Britain, where the legislature is legally supreme. The number and type of political parties will have important consequences for the operation of these systems.

The chief characteristics of the presidential type of government are as follows:

1. The president is both nominal and political head of state.
2. The president is not elected by the legislature, but is directly elected by the total electorate. (There is an electoral college in the United States, but it is of little political significance).
3. The president is not part of the legislature, and he cannot be removed from office by the legislature except through the legal process of impeachment.[21]
4. The president cannot dissolve the legislature and call a general election. Usually the president and the legislature are elected for mixed terms.

The outstanding example of the presidential type of government is that of the United States. Most other examples are imitations of the American system, found chiefly in Central and South America.

The division between presidential and parliamentary regimes can be most useful. There are numerous examples of political scientists using a comparison of, say, the United States and Britain, in terms of this division in order to emphasise significant aspects of both systems.[22] But there are serious limitations to this approach. We have already hinted at one difficulty: the small size of the sample of presidential systems. Also, all our examples come from liberal democratic systems. The Soviet Union has been left out of this division because socialist systems in general do not recognise the separation of powers; the party system may be of far greater significance for the working of the political system than the formal distinctions between presidential and parliamentary systems.

France of the Fifth Republic is a good example of the limitations of this approach. France adopted a new constitution in 1958 after the accession of de Gaulle to power. Formerly under the Fourth Republic (1946–58) French political institutions could be firmly classed as 'parliamentary'. The constitution of the Fifth Republic strengthened the political power of the president and he ceased to be merely the ceremonial head of state. Basically, the new constitution demoted the National Assembly, as the president is not dependent on its support but is elected for a fixed term by the whole electorate. French political institutions are no longer parliamentary, but the political structure cannot be clearly classified as a presidential type of system on the American model. S. M. Lipset has spoken of 'the American' elements introduced into French politics by de Gaulle,[23] and another commentator has described the Fifth Republic as 'a fundamentally ambiguous regime, as it appears to constitute the logical outcome of the crisis which destroyed the traditional model and an attempt to evolve a new system'.[24]

These examples of France and the Soviet Union serve to highlight some of the empirical difficulties we encountered in attempts to compare political systems or their constituent elements. Few political systems fit neatly into one pigeon-hole. Categories are elaborated in terms of general, abstract characteristics, while each political system is in some respect a unique combination of particular features. Thus the more general a category, the more difficult is the problem of empirical fit. This factor has led many political scientists to succumb to the temptation to proliferate their categories by adding further divisions and sub-divisions.[25] To carry this process to its logical conclusion would be to obviate the purpose of classification, for it would result in a separate category for each political system.

It seems more useful, then, to accept the utility of various types of classification, recognising their fluid nature and accepting that for some purposes it will be useful to treat certain countries as having crucial similarities, while for others the systems concerned will appear diametrically opposed to one another.

References

1. *The Politics of Aristotle*, trans. with an introduction by Ernest Barker (Oxford, 1946) particularly bk IV.
2. See J. W. Allen, *A History of Political Thought in the Sixteenth Century* (London, 1957) ch. 8.
3. Baron de Montesquieu, *The Spirit of the Laws*, trans. T. Nugent (London, 1966) bk II, ch. I, p. 8.
4. Ibid, bk II, ch. III, p. 15.
5. Ibid, bk VIII, ch. XIX, p. 122.
6. Ibid, bk VIII, ch. XVI, p. 120.
7. See chapter 1.
8. R. A. Dahl, *Modern Political Analysis*, 4th ed. (Englewood Cliffs, NJ, 1964) p. 30.
9. Alexis de Tocqueville, *Democracy in America* (London, 1968) I, 345.
10. See especially S. M. Lipset, *The First New Nation* (London, 1963).
11. Barrington Moore, *Social Origins of Dictatorship and Democracy* (London, 1967).
12. See G. A. Almond and G. B. Powell, *Comparative Politics, System, Process and Policy*, 2nd ed. (Boston, Mass., 1978).
13. B. Crick, *In Defence of Politics* (London, 1964) p. 56.
14. There are many examples of different typologies: see Maurice Duverger's distinction between pluralist systems and monolithic systems, *The Idea of Politics* (London, 1966) pp. 92–5; See also S. E. Finer, *Comparative Government* (London, 1970), and B. Crick, *Basic Forms of Government: A Sketch and a Model* (London, 1973).
15. J. Blondel (ed.), *Comparative Government* (London, 1969) p. xxxviii.
16. C. Friedrich and Z. Brzezinski, *Totalitarian Dictatorship and Autocracy*, 2nd ed. (Massachusetts, 1965) p. 22.
17. For wide ranging discussion of the usefulness of the concept of 'totalitarianism', see, *inter alia*, C. J. Friedrich, B. R. Barber, and M. Curtis, *Totalitarianism in Perspective: Three Views* (London, 1969); L. Schapiro, *Totalitarianism* (London, 1972); R. Burrowes, 'Totalitarianism: the Revised Standard Edition', *World*

Politics, vol. 21, no 2 (Jan. 1969) pp. 272–89; R. Cornell (ed.), *The Soviet Political System* (Englewood Cliffs, NJ, 1970).

18. For a discussion of the problem of classifying radical military regimes see J. Markakis and M. Waller (eds.), 'Military Marxist Regimes in Africa', *The Journal of Communist Studies,* Vol. 1, Nos 3 and 4, Sept/Dec., 1985.
19. For a discussion of aspects of federalism, see K. C. Wheare, *Federal Government*, 4th ed. (Oxford, 1963), and W. H. Riker, *Federalism: Origin, Operation, Significance* (Massachusetts, 1964); also, Ivo Duchacek, *Comparative Federalism* (New York, 1970).
20. For an examination of Soviet federalism, see E. Goldhagen (ed.), *Ethnic Minorities in the Soviet Union* (Praeger, N Y, 1968).
21. For the impeachment process in the United States, see R. Berger, *Impeachment. The Constitutional Problems* (New York, 1974).
22. See the essays by R. Neustadt in *The British Prime Minister*, ed. A. King (London, 1969).
23. *Archives Européennes de Sociologie*, I, 1(1960).
24. P. Avril, *Politics in France* (London, 1969) p.18.
25. See particularly the categories used by S. E. Finer, *Comparative Government* (London, 1970).

4

Political Culture

The nature of the political culture

A political culture is composed of the attitudes, beliefs, emotions and values of society that relate to the political system and to political issues.[1] These attitudes may not be consciously held, but may be implicit in an individual or group relationship with the political system. Nor are they necessarily amenable to rigid definition, but, nevertheless, an awareness of the basis of the political culture will allow a more detailed picture of the political system to emerge. This would be difficult if reference were made only to the political institutions and the policy issues of the political process. In Britain there is increasing dissatisfaction with the way the country is governed and weaker attachment to the institutions and processes of government. Consequently, there is now much more discussion of reforming political institutions and more support for political innovations such as membership of the EEC, changes in the electoral system, and for a strengthening of civil liberties.[2] However, there is still a fundamental consensus on the major aspects of the political system and lack of support for revolutionary changes, so that we can say that a degree of consensus exists. Where this consensus is weak, there is greater likelihood of the political system being challenged by public disorder or even revolution. The consensus may exist on the goals of the political system as well as the means of reaching those goals.[3]

That is not to claim that even in politically stable societies the political culture is homogeneous; where differences between one group and others are marked, there is said to exist a political sub-culture. This is not a distinct set of attitudes, beliefs and values, but a set of attitudes some of which are in common with other sub-cultures. Thus many Spanish Basques feel that loyalty to their group is more important than loyalty to Spain as a whole, and because of the strength of these attitudes there is a strong separatist movement in the Basque provinces. The blacks in the United States constitute a political sub-culture. The growth of the Scottish National Party, especially in terms of electoral support, has illustrated the strength of separatist feelings within the United Kingdom. Most political cultures are in fact heterogeneous.

Political cultures differ according to the degree of participation in the political process by the citizens of the political system. In some systems, individuals take a more active role in the political process, possess a great deal of political information, and expect to influence decisions made by governments. In the United States, despite an increasing political cynicism and mistrust of political leaders, political participation generally remains high, although electoral turn-out is low.[4] Similarly in the political culture of the Soviet Union citizens are expected and encouraged to participate in the political life of the country, to be conscious of the activities of the Soviet government, and are encouraged to join groups which participate in politics. Yet at the same time, the ruling élite expects obedience from the governed and conformity to the directives of the organs of government.[5]

The West German political culture presents interesting contrasts. West Germans profess to be very interested in politics, possess impressive political knowledge, but while electoral turn-out is high, other types of political activity are fewer, and West Germans are less likely than Americans to believe that they have the ability to influence the government.[6]

Foundations of the political culture

A political culture, whether diverse or homogeneous, is a product of many interrelated factors. Political continuity is important in Britain, and the older values have been allowed to merge with modern attitudes, undisturbed by violent internal strife or domination by a foreign power. An interesting example was the acceptance of the first Labour government by the leaders of the other political parties in 1924. Baldwin, leader of the Conservative Party, welcomed the change as an opportunity to impress the problems of responsibility on the relatively new party to allow the acceptance of the existing political norms. The Labour leaders themselves were anxious to prove the moderation of their programme and their ability as members of the government party. Thus there was no challenge to the political system.[7]

France offers a sharp contrast in historical development. The revolution of 1789 violently overthrew the existing political structures, and the political conflicts and antagonisms of the nineteenth and twentieth centuries may be said to be largely determined by the attitudes, values and beliefs formed by that revolutionary upheaval.[8] Violent historical changes may result in a conservative consensus. The American War of Independence, although accompanied by certain social changes, was primarily an attempt to break the political links with Britain. It established agreement on certain liberal democratic procedures which were affirmed by the American constitution. Thus, although there was no complete rejection of the past, the Revolution did establish a stable political system based on new egalitarian and competitive values which were not fundamentally changed by the later industrialisation and mass immigration.[9]

The impact of European colonial domination on many new states in Africa and Asia is an important factor explaining some aspects of the political culture of these states. The extent of this colonial influence is disputed,[10] but one may recognise the different effects of, for example, British and French control, or even, in Nigeria's case, a more flexible policy of the colonial power to different areas of the same colony. The northern area of Nigeria was subject to indirect rule and the coastal areas were controlled more directly by British administrators, a policy which was to re-emphasise the different political cultures of the north and south, and was to have profound consequences on the post-independence politics of the country.

India provides an illustrative example of colonial domination extended over a long period of time, and the gradual introduction of the Westminister model of government. There was indirect rule in the case of the princely states, but the British system of conciliar local government was established in other areas.[11]

Besides historical development, geography is another important factor in fashioning a political culture. Britain's island insularity protected the country from foreign invasion. The limitless frontier of America of the developing United States is said to have forged the political values of independent egalitarianism in spite of ethnic differences, but the United States also possessed an abundance of natural resources and was protected from hostile neighbours, and therefore it is essential to emphasise the interrelations between the various factors.[12]

The impact of ethnic differences on a particular political culture varies. Ethnic differences have only recently begun to affect attitudes in Great Britain. Yet the United States, with a more polyglot population, has succeeded in assimilating the vast numbers of immigrants, at least the voluntary ones, so that different groups think of themselves primarily as Americans, owing allegiance to the government of the United States. However, European immigration into Canada and South Africa has not removed entirely the consciousness of being members of different ethnic groups, and the party systems reflect this consciousness. The dominant Nationalist Party in South Africa represents the Afrikaaners, descendants of the Dutch immigrants, while the English tended to dominate the former United Party. The newly strengthened Progressive Federal Party, despite having Afrikaaners among its leaders, still reflects white ethnic divisions, attracting most of its membership from English-speaking white South Africans. It is significant that in the South African and Canadian examples, unlike America, the different ethnic groups have retained their own languages, and reinforced their separate identities by retaining the link between ethnic group and religion. Religion, in fact, not language was used by the Irish to emphasise their separateness from the British in the long struggle for independence before 1922.[13]

The instability in the political system caused by ethnic groups' loyalties being directed to themselves and not to the national government is increased if allegiances are also directed to another state. European history is littered with such historical accidents, and the inclusion of Serbians in the Hapsburg Empire, and of the Germans in the Czechoslovakian state were important factors in the events leading up to the 1914 and 1939 European wars. The arbitrary boundaries of former European colonies in Africa were drawn with little reference to the divisions of tribal groups.[14]

The socio-economic structure is another determinant of the political culture. A predominantly urban, industrialised society is a more complex society, putting a premium on rapid communications. Educational standards are higher, groups proliferate, and participation in the decision-making process is, of necessity, wider. Rural societies are not geared to change and innovation, and states with a predominantly peasant population tend to be more conservative. We observed in Chapter 3 that there is not always a direct link between the level of socio-economic development and participatory liberal democracies, but nonetheless there are repercussions on certain political attitudes and values. Loyalty to the national, as opposed to the regional, group is more a characteristic of an industrialised society, but the examples of such states as Belgium warn us that this is not a rigid correlation. Moreover, a simple division between urban-industrialised states and agrarian ones may be too crude a categorisation. American farming, even when it employed the majority of the working population, was always a more capitalist and commercial activity than farming is, or was, in predominantly peasant societies, and therefore the values were those more associated with modern industrialised states. Modern New Zealand and Denmark are illustrations of farming economies with this commercial foundation. In societies in which peasants form the major part of the population, there tends to be linked with conservative attitudes a resentment of government activity and an ignorance of its scope. There is an emphasis on what the central administration does, but little awareness of how these policies can be changed and influenced.

An industrialised society will have a complex class structure, but the distinctness of class as a sub-group will vary. In the United States it is claimed that the working class have been *embourgeoisified* and lack the consciousness of European working classes. But even in Britain, where social class is more closely parallel to voting for the different political parties, consciousness of class membership does not mean that the working class see their values and interests as being in conflict with those of other social classes.[15] One observer has pointed to the dominance of middle-class values and attitudes in British society.[16] A greater conflict between class sub-cultures may be seen in certain European liberal democracies, such as France and Italy, where hostile attitudes to the values of the dominant political élites can be illustrated by the electoral support for the communist parties and fascist parties.

Aspects of the political culture

There are two important components of a political culture: attitudes to the political institutions of the state, and the degree to which citizens feel they can influence and participate in the decision-making process. However, there are problems of measuring both how much pride people have in the political system and their perceptions of political efficacy.[17] A distrust of the holders of political offices may not affect positive feelings about the political institutions themselves. Americans express great support for the American political structure as a whole, admire the Constitution and will not support any anti-system parties. Yet Americans are also critical of particular political institutions, have become more electorally volatile and independent in terms of party support, and are disillusioned with politicians. Generally, they support the system as a whole, but distrust the office-holders.

Italians on the other hand, show far less support for the total political system, are more inclined to vote for anti-system parties, but have expressed an increasing pride in the economic system.[18] One could therefore presume that political stability in Italy rests more on the satisfactory performance of the economic system than on the structure of representative parliamentary democracy. In Britain, surveys consistently show that there is often admiration for political leaders and a desire for strong government even if particular political leaders are not greatly liked. Margaret Thatcher has been regarded as a strong, decisive leader and this image was strengthened by the Falklands conflict of 1982. Yet, she was also regarded an as opinionated and unsympathetic individual whose policies were politically divisive. She led the Conservative Party to three successive general election victories.[19]

Change can also pose problems for an evaluation of political cultures. Almond and Verba's pioneering work of 1963 comparing political cultures in several political systems was extensively re-evaluated in 1980. Besides the methodological problems invloved in cross-national comparisons, the contributors to the new study found evidence of important changes in the political cultures of the countries investigated.[20]

In stable liberal democracies, the boundaries of the political system are fairly firmly drawn. There is a belief in the limitation of government activity. Thus the freedom of the individual is emphasised, and at the same time there is an expectation of benefits for the individual ensuing from government activity. This again stems from the basis of trust in political leadership, and a belief that the unwritten rules of the political game will be respected by all the participants.

The degree of stability in the political system is linked to the level of socio-economic development. We have noted the effects of relative economic prosperity on Italian attitudes, and the level of education will affect the sense of competence on the part of the citizens. In Britain, the relative economic decline and the accompanying rise in educational levels have reduced the importance of deference in the political system, deference being the belief that socially superior individuals are best suited to political decision-making. Deference in Britain is now largely confined to the older generation.[21]

In West Germany, the 'economic miracle' of the post-war years may have assisted the emergence of more positive attitudes to political institutions in the 1980s than were found in the 1950s, and there developed a greater willingness to participate politically, especially among the young. Of course, there are other variables involved such as the longevity of the Republic itself. Yet there is a link between political consensus and political stability and a comparison between the contemporary West German system and the Weimar Republic is indicative of a link. The economic development of Spain and Portugal in the 1960s and 1970s assisted in the weakening of the legitimacy of the former dictatorial regimes and more positive attitudes to the development of representative democratic institutions.

Poland provides an interesting non-liberal democratic illustration of the legitimacy of the regime and its economic performance. Since 1975 economic difficulties have led to a decline in the regime's legitimacy and Solidarity represented an attempt to replace the old, discredited trade unions. However, it must be remembered that Poland is different in many respects from its Eastern neighbours, since the Catholic Church wins the most trust and the ruling Communist Party the least of all Polish national institutions according to surveys of Polish opinion.[22]

Symbols and the political culture

Political attitudes and values in a society are symbolised by such things as the flag and the national anthem. The monarchy may be a symbol of national pride in the political system. These symbols express the idealised elements of the political institutions and are not necessarily related to the level of political knowledge and competence of the people whose emotions are channelled through such symbols. Bagehot, writing in the middle of the nineteenth century, recognised the importance of such symbols, arguing that '... we have whole classes unable to comprehend the idea of a constitution – unable to feel the least attachment to impersonal laws. Most do indeed vaguely know that there are some institutions besides the Queen, and some rules by which she governs. But a vast number like their minds to dwell more upon her than upon anything else, and therefore she is inestimable.'[23] Although the relationship between political symbols and stability is difficult to analyse, there are still problems of initiating a rational public debate about the place of the monarchy in the British system, as its role does not seem open to utilitarian analysis, and the treatment given to critics is a measurement of the strength of the emotional attachment.[24]

The American president gains a similar emotional adherence in spite of the more overt political role he performs. President Kennedy was more popular after his death than before, perhaps because he was no longer a politician, and the publicity and importance given to President Johnson's oath-taking ceremony on television after Kennedy's death illustrated the symbolism of the act more than the legal requirements of the succession.[25] Desecrating the national flag is regarded as a punishable offence in America,[26] and certainly it could not be used in the commercial way one finds in Great Britain.

All political systems place great emphasis on the use of symbols. They give reality to abstractions and embody some aspects of the dominant political values, such as the hammer and sickle emphasising the unity of workers and peasants. The uniforms and the flags of the Nazi mass rallies presented an image of strength, unity and authority. Lenin's memory is used as a symbol of the continuity and ideological purity of the present Soviet leadership.

Religious symbols may take the place of secular symbols in some political cultures. Profound significance is attached to coronation ceremonies in the national church, national holidays are chosen from the church calendar, and particular saints are used to symbolise national unity.

Myths play an important role in the political culture. They may be very important as a foundation of national identity. Myths about certain historical periods are used to evoke a sense of national greatness. The 'Elizabethan age' is important in the British context, the image of small ships defying the overwhelming might of Spain, basing their victories on superior courage and seamanship. A former prime minister, Harold Wilson, constantly evoked the 'spirit of Dunkirk' in his political speeches. Myths emphasise certain half-truths and therefore are distortions, although politically important distortions. They were especially important in totalitarian systems; thus the Bolsheviks are portrayed as playing the major role in the 1917 revolution, and the parts played by other groups are largely ignored. Hitler emphasised the 'stab in the back'; the German armies were not defeated by the western allies in the 1914–18 war, but were betrayed by traitors at home.

It is interesting to note that the more artificially created state of West Germany has been unable to evoke a sense of national unity or national pride by the use of the various symbols of flag and national anthem. West Germans are less patriotic since 1945 and in spite of official efforts, the new flag does not inspire the reverence paid to former national symbols.[27]

The symbols need not be directly relevant to the existing political system, and may be regarded with incredulous amazement by outsiders. Thus the Protestants of Northern Ireland symbolise the religious unity of their allegiance to the British crown by yearly celebrations of the victories of William III in the late seventeenth century, and the anniversary of his defeat of the Catholics at the Battle of the Boyne is treated as a sectarian holiday.

The emotional intensity that embraces these symbols is a means of identifying the political values and attitudes in the political system, but these symbols are also used by governments to ensure their own legitimacy and foster national unity. This is particularly important in new nations or in states that have experienced a profound political upheaval. Efforts are made to eliminate memories of previous regimes by new anthems, flags, rewriting history, in some cases inventing it, establishing new national heroes or resurrecting forgotten ones, changing street names and even those of towns, and a constant ritual bombardment of the population to provoke manifestations of national unity. This sense of unity can often be intensified by whipping up feeling against foreign symbols such as foreign embassies.

Development of a political culture

A political culture is not static but will respond to new ideas generated from within the political system or imported or imposed from outside. Japan furnishes an interesting example of a state subject to these internal and external pressures, resulting in bewildering and rapid changes within the last hundred years. In 1868 the Meiji Restoration ended a long period of centralised feudalism; it also coincided with the intrusion of the western industrialising societies after long international seclusion. Japan then embarked on a period of rapid industrialisation that was to make the country the equal of the western nations in economic and military strength, and also adopted some of the forms of European autocratic government, especially those of the German Empire. The total military defeat in 1945, the occupation until 1952, and the imposition of the liberal democratic constitution by the Americans in 1946, all have superimposed great changes on an already changing society. The result has been the coexistence of traditional norms and modernising western characteristics, which, while not completely conducive to political stability, has, nevertheless, produced a viable political system. As one observer has pointed out: 'Modern Japan has inherited a remarkably integrated ethos which, despite rapid changes, has always provided a source of stability.[28]

Industrialisation is an important factor in changing values and attitudes. Rapid influxes of immigrants, war, and especially defeat in a major war, revolution, all may provoke changes in political values and beliefs, with subsequent strains on the political system. The relationship of change and continuity is illustrated by the course of twentieth-century American foreign policy. The end of isolationism, or rather the increased intervention in world affairs since 1900 made possible by American industrial and economic developments, was made more acceptable to the American public by projecting American values onto a world stage. Thus American foreign policy was designed to encourage liberal democracies and national self-determination. These were factors in American political development which, it was believed, had led to American prosperity and power. This sense of mission to extend American values to less fortunate nations was readily amenable to an anti-communist crusade, especially after 1945, a crusade to which American liberals more eagerly subscribed than the conservative isolationists.[29]

The stability of a political system is underlined by the relative success or failure of the assimilation of new attitudes into the existing value structure, and we must now examine the means of effectively transmitting the political culture from generation to generation.

Political socialisation

Political socialisation is the establishment and development of attitudes to and beliefs about the political system. The process may encourage loyalty to the nation, the fostering of particular values, and it may increase either support for or alienation from the system. It is particularly important in the degree of participation in political life that is expected of groups and individuals. Political socialisation is not a process confined to the impressionable years of childhood, but one that continues throughout adult life.

Before examining the agencies of the socialisation process, some words of qualification are needed. Firstly, work in this field is relatively new, and various conclusions are disputed. It is easier to examine the deliberate attempts of governments to influence the socialisation process than to come to some firm views about the effects of those attempts, especially as it is easier, for example, to conduct a survey of mass opinions in Great Britain than in the Soviet Union. Secondly, the values and attitudes developed by political socialising agencies are often mistakenly confused with voting intentions and party allegiances, partly, one suspects, because it is easier to measure the latter. While there may be considerable overlap between voting and party partisanship and broader political values and attitudes, they are not the same. Thirdly, one needs to distinguish clearly between intentional efforts to influence the establishment of political values and socialisation processes over which the government has no influence. With the former, manifest, as opposed to latent, political socialisation, we are usually referring to political indoctrination. Non-political experiences, such as participation in school societies and sporting clubs, may be as important in later adult political life as a weekly civics course on the structures of the country's political institutions. Finally, one needs to be aware when examining the agencies of the political socialisation process of the interrelationships between them, and this in turn can lead to general conclusions as to whether they can complement each other or whether there is conflict between them. In stable political systems there are fewer antagonisms between such socialising institutions as the family, school and the various voluntary groups in society.

Agencies of socialisation

The principal determinants of the development and establishment of various attitudes and values about the political system may be listed as (1) the family; (2) the schools and other institutions of education; (3) voluntary groups, work and informal relationships; (4) the mass media;[30] (5) government and party agencies. We have noted the necessity of remembering the overlap between them; they cannot be examined in complete isolation. Moreover, all are affected, in varying degrees, by other factors, such as social and geographical mobility. For example, people moving upwards on the social class ladder tend to acquire new values and attitudes, whereas those whose social class is lower than their parents' are more likely to retain former political attitudes. Geographical mobility has several consequences, such as the reluctance to discuss political questions or participate in political activities after moving into a new district.

The influence of the family in the process of political socialisation seems obvious. The family is the child's first window on the world outside; it is the child's first contact with authority; it is here that the first differences in the role expectations between the sexes are implanted, and surveys have shown the strong link between the voting behaviour of parents and their children.[31] Of course there are other agencies exerting influences on the child from an early age, and it may be that the family is divided in its political attitudes, and the political values of the child may be formed in opposition to one of the parents. Also, the longer the period of formal education and the higher the intelligence of the child, the smaller will be the extent of parental influence.

Yet a great deal will depend on the relationship with other socialising agencies. In Britain and the United States the family tends to encourage many of the values that will find support in later life, whereas it is claimed that in the Soviet Union the constant propaganda efforts of the government and the emphasis on political education in the schools are evidence of the regime's relative failure to eradicate the deviant influences of the family. In West Germany the position is complicated by the profound political changes in recent times, and by the difficulties parents have in explaining the support for the Hitler regime and at the same time giving support to the liberal democratic government's efforts to inculcate new values in generations that did not experience the Nazi government. However, there is evidence in West Germany as elsewhere that the role of the family is becoming less important.[32] Political attitudes are not formed in terms of opposition to parents, however much they may differ, but parents are only one agency, and not always as influential as one would suspect, at least in terms of political values if not in terms of party allegiance.

The educational system has important effects on the process of socialisation, the more so if it is extended to cover higher and university education. The values imparted by schools and universities may not be the result of direct political indoctrination, but are none the less important. A decentralised educational system may prevent direct government interference and may encourage and support sub-cultures. In France there is a high degree of centralisation, but the states' control of schools in the United States allows the existence of regional loyalties, witness attitudes to racial segregation in the southern states, attitudes in which family attitudes are reinforced by the schools. American education, however, does tend to support the major values apparent in the political system; it encourages the notion of equal and democratic participation, and there are strong links with the parents which temper authoritarian tendencies on the part of the schools. The structure of British education is more likely to encourage inequality and deference, especially with the existence of a strong private sector of education for middle-class children, with its emphasis on character-building and other individual and social virtues.[33] The arguments over comprehensive schools in the state sector of British education are more concerned with social inequalities than academic or administrative arguments. The implicit inculcation of political attitudes in any educational system can be in the role that religious education plays and in the different expectations of boys and girls.

Yet manifest socialisation is important in many political systems. The educational programme of Soviet schoolchildren includes an overt element of 'moral education' with stress on discipline, Soviet patriotism and proletarian internationalism and dedication to the goals of the community, the state and the Communist Party.[34] Civics courses have been a necessary part of American education to allow for the assimilation of vast numbers of immigrants from diverse backgrounds. The teaching of history is an important part of any education course; accounts of past national heroes, coupled with a timely neglect of other aspects of history, are an effective means of encouraging patriotism and a general pride in the achievements of the state. It is noticeable that for understandable reasons recent history is a neglected aspect in many West German schools. American blacks have become more vocal in their criticisms of the neglect of Black contributions to American history as outlined in American schools and textbooks, and have successfully demanded the inclusion of 'black studies' programmes in many colleges.

The effect of education on political values can be partly illustrated by the upsurge of student radicalism in the late 1960s, especially in more industrialised countries, even though it may represent only a minority. The students' role in the French crisis of May 1968, and the American student opposition to the Vietnam war are illustrative examples. However, the impact of university on political values is complex, and it may be that a university environment merely heightens political awareness without affecting basic political attitudes.[35]

The other agencies of political socialisation are regarded as less direct (or measureable) and are closely interrelated to the influence of family and school. Political parties are more diffuse because of their need to win wider support. Direct government intervention may be a sign of failure to receive the support of either the family or school. The West German government gives financial support to voluntary youth groups and organisations and the political parties to encourage political education. Youth movements do play an important part in the process of national integration in developing countries, e.g. the youth wing of UNIP in Zambia. Nearly all Soviet schoolchildren are members of the Party-controlled Octobrists and Pioneers, as are the majority of university students members of the Komsomol, the youth wing of the CPSU. The mass media, whether directly controlled by the government or not, tend to reinforce existing political values, and this aspect also highlights a negative weapon of the government, that of political censorship. Perhaps the most important socialising agency in this voluntary category is the church. Its effect on political attitudes is less apparent when it reinforces other socialising agencies, but the role of Roman Catholicism in many European countries, liberal democratic and socialist, offers illustrations of its conflict with both state and education, and is possibly a vital factor in the political behaviour of women in some countries. It is worth noting the socialisation role of compulsory military service in some states.

Socialisation and the political system

We have seen that manifest socialisation may be the result of several socialising agencies, and that interrelationships are important. One cannot simply seek links between, for example, an authoritarian family structure and the establishment of values that expect a subject role in the political system. There are too many variables, such as generational differences, the greater adult socialising influences on political leaders, and the question of individual personality, which is more defiant of analysis. Yet the values established need neither be coherent nor consciously held to contribute to the stabilisation of the political system. Some processes of socialisation are more homogeneous, and the various agencies will complement each other rather than conflict; yet this does not preclude change, nor does it stifle variety. Political socialisation is a continuous process, and as such is not completely static. The test for a stable political system is whether the socialising agencies are sufficiently flexible and interdependent to allow change without violent disruption.

References

1. See D. Kavanagh, *Political Culture* (London, 1972) pp. 9–19.
2. See D. Kavanagh, 'Political Culture in Great Britain: The Decline of the Civic Culture', in *The Civic Culture Revisited*, G. A. Almond and S. Verba (eds) (Boston, 1980) pp.140–3.

3. For a discussion of the term 'consensus', see P. H. Partridge, *Consent and Consensus*, (London 1971) pp. 71–95.
4. See A. I. Abramowitz, 'The United States: Political Culture under Stress', in *The Civic Culture Revisited*, pp. 177–211.
5. See F. C. Barghoorn, *Politics in the U.S.S.R.*, 2nd ed. (Boston, Mass., 1972) ch. 2. One excellent study emphasises the persistence of the predominantly centralised, collectivist political culture which the Bolsheviks inherited in 1917: see S. White, *Political Culture and Soviet Politics* (London, 1979).
6. See L. J. Edinger, *West German Politics* (New York, 1986) pp. 95-100.
7. See R. Miliband, *Parliamentary Socialism*, 2nd ed. (London, 1973) pp. 99-100.
8. See D. Thompson, *Democracy in France*, 2nd ed. (Oxford, 1952) ch. 1. for a brief outline of the impact of the revolutionary tradition.
9. See F. Thistlethwaite, *The Great Experiment*, 3rd ed. (Cambridge, 1967) for a broader view of the development of the American political culture.
10. I. Wallerstein, *Social Change: The Colonial Situation* (New York, 1966) lays stress on the relatively short period of colonial rule, and the importance of the pre-colonial history of these states.
11. The old *panchayat* system of village self-government in some areas assisted the import of English local government systems into India. This should be contrasted with what could be described as the invention of the office of village chief in early British rule in Kenya, to act as a civil servant and replace the local ruling group. See D. M. Lyon, 'The Development of African Local Government in Kenya, 1900–1962' (unpublished PhD thesis, University of Nottingham, 1967).
12. See S. M. Lipset, *The First New Nation* (London, 1963). Hugh Seton-Watson, remarking on the effect of these interrelationships, has observed: 'one reason for the prevalence of autocracy in Russian history is military. Russia has no natural boundaries except the Arctic ice and the mountain ranges of Caucasus and Central Asia. It was subject for centuries to invasion from both west and east. Imagine the United States without either the Atlantic or the Pacific, and with several first-rate military powers instead of the Indians, and there would be some form of parallel. ... In America the open frontier meant opportunity, and so freedom: in Russia it meant insecurity, and so subjection' (*The Russian Empire 1801–1917* (Oxford, 1967) pp. 12–13).
13. See E. Norman, *A History of Modern Ireland* (London, 1972) pp. 237–41, for an account of Irish cultural nationalism in the early twentieth century, especially the attempts of the Gaelic League to revive the Irish language.
14. For a discussion on national identity of new states, see F.R. von Mehden, *The Politics of Developing Nations*, 2nd ed. (Englewood Cliffs, NJ, 1969) ch. 3.
15. See D. Butler and D. Stokes, *Political Change in Britain*, 2nd ed. (London, 1974) pp. 67–94.
16. F. Parkin, 'Working Class Conservatives: A Theory of Political Deviance', *British Journal of Sociology*, XVIII (1967) pp. 278–90.
17. See A. C. MacIntyre, 'Is a science of comparative politics possible?', in *The Practice of Comparative Politics*, ed. P. G. Lewis *et al.* (London, 1978) pp. 266–84, for a discussion of the problems of comparing political cultures.
18. For an overview of the Italian political culture, see G. Sani, 'The Political Culture of Italy: Continuity and Change', in *The Civic Culture Revisited*, pp. 273–324.
19. See D. Kavanagh, *Thatcherism and British Politics. The End of Consensus?* (Oxford, 1987) pp. 270–4.

20. See G. A. Almond and S. Verba, *The Civic Culture* (Princeton, NJ, 1963) and *The Civic Culture Revisited.*
21. See R. Rose, *Politics in England*, 4th ed. (London, 1985) pp. 141–2.
22. See D. S. Mason, *Public Opinion and Political Change in Poland, 1980–1982* (Cambridge, 1985). For a wider approach to East European political cultures, see A. Brown (ed.) *Political Culture and Communist Studies* (London, 1984).
23. W. Bagehot, *The English Constitution* (Fontana Library ed., London, 1963) p. 85.
24. See R. Rose and D. Kavanagh, 'The Monarchy in Contemporary Political Culture', *Comparative Politics*, 8, 4, (1976) pp. 548–76.
25. For a detailed emphasis on that particular oath-taking ceremony and its significance, see W. Manchester, *The Death of a President* (London, 1967).
26. During the Second World War the United States Embassy protested to the British government over a company's plans to market ladies' underwear emblazoned with the Stars and Stripes for sale to GIs.
27. Edinger, *West German Politics*, p. 101.
28. A. W. Burks, *The Government of Japan*, 2nd ed. (London, 1966) p. 267.
29. For an attack on the role of 'liberals' in American foreign policy, see N. Chomsky, *American Power and the New Mandarins* (London, 1966) ch. 1.
30. The influence of the mass media will be examined in Chapter 7.
31. For a discussion of the family and the socialisation process, see B. Stacey, *Political Socialisation in Western Society* (London, 1978) pp. 1–18.
32. See Edinger, *West German Politics*, p. 108. Also see H. W. Ehrmann, *Politics in France*, 4th ed. (Boston, 1983) pp.66–71.
33. See Rose, *Politics in England*, pp. 170–77.
34. D. Lane, *Politics and Society in the U.S.S.R.* (London, 1978) p. 491.
35. See Stacey, *Political Stabilisation in Western Society*, pp. 92–9, for a discussion of American student opposition to the Vietnam war.

PART TWO

Parties, Pressure Groups and Representation

5

Political Parties

Definition

Political parties may be principally defined by their common aim. They seek political power either singly or in co-operation with other political parties. As Joseph Schumpeter has observed: 'The first and foremost aim of each political party is to prevail over the others in order to get into power or to stay in it.'[1] It is this goal of attaining political power that distinguishes political parties from other groups in the political system, although the distinction is rather blurred at times, especially in regard to pressure groups. This flexible definition presupposes organisation, and to distinguish political parties from legislative cliques there must be the assumption that the organisation has local bases of support. Otherwise one would have to include within the definition of parties the pre-nineteenth-century West European parliamentary organisations that differed markedly in structure and in functions from modern political parties.[2]

Given this definition we can avoid evaluative approaches to the study of parties, whether parties are 'conspiracies' against the rest of the nation, whether they are inimicable to the 'national good', etc. Political parties exist in differing forms in various political systems, and while not essential to the political process, it is difficult to imagine the political consequences of their absence in the vast majority of states. Also the definition avoids the necessity of examining the ideological and programmatic aspects of political parties. We can ignore Edmund Burke's famous definition of party 'as a body of men united for promoting by their joint endeavours the national interest upon some particular principle in which they are all united',[3] It is important for the functioning of the political system whether a party is ideologically united or simply exists as an electoral machine, but it does not determine the right to monopolise the title of political party. Again it is important whether particular parties compete against each other for political power, but this does not mean that we can only meaningfully discuss political parties in liberal democracies and deny their existence in certain socialist systems.

The capture of political power, or indeed its retention, can be achieved within existing political structures or by overthrowing them. Working within the political system, parties can present candidates and leaders to the electorate and seek to mobilise the support of the electorate by propaganda, organised activities and by emphasising ideological differences with other parties in competitive party systems. The overthrow of the existing system can be achieved by *coup d'état*, civil war, guerrilla activities against the existing government, or by capturing power by legitimate electoral means and then changing the political structures. Thus Hitler attempted to obtain power in Bavaria in the early 1920s by a coup; it failed and he later reverted to constitutional electoral means of capturing power. In this he was successful, the Nationalist Socialist Party became the largest single party in the Reichstag in 1931 and 1932, and after being installed as chancellor by President Hindenburg in 1933, Hitler promptly abolished all electoral competition to the National Socialist Party. A similar suppression of competitive party activity followed the Communist Party's assumption of power in Czechoslovakia in 1948.

Methods of seeking power are better explained and discussed in the context of the analysis of type of party and type of party system, but a reference was necessary at this stage to distinguish the conscious efforts to seek and retain political power from the performance by the political parties of important fuctions within the political system which do not constitute the main aims of the parties, but which are significant by-products.[4]

Functions of political parties

One of the most important functions of political parties is that of uniting, simplifying and stabilising the political process. Political parties tend to provide the highest common denominator. They do not divide, in spite of the claims of advocates of non-party or coalition-national governments, they unite. Parties bring together sectional interests, overcome geographical distances, and provide coherence to sometimes divisive government structures. The American Democratic Party has long provided a bridge to bring together, albeit uneasily, southern conservatives and nothern liberals. It was a sectional split in the Democrats that encouraged the outbreak of the American Civil War a century ago. The French UDF gives a parliamentary coherence to a loose group of locally based notables whose only elements in common have consisted of an anti-Catholic and anti-Marxist platform. The German Christian Democratic Party (CDU) has likewise bridged the gulf between Protestants and Catholics in West Germany. All political parties in federal systems emphasise the uniting of different government structures, the extreme example being the one-party system of the Soviet Union which almost completely undermines the federal constitutional division of decision-making. Even in such politically homogeneous systems as Great Britain's, the structural bridging function of political parties may be seen in the unity of cabinet and House of Commons.

This bridging function of political parties is an important factor in political stability. There are many other variables, but nevertheless political parties in their search for political power do form order out of chaos. They seek to widen the interests they represent and harmonise these interests with each other. This 'aggregation' of interests is carried out by other groups in the political system as well as political parties, but in the main the function is performed by the parties. The representation of interests is a safety valve; it brings diverse interests into the political process, and appears, at least, to be attempting to satisfy their demands. We have already noted this harmonising aspect of the American Democratic Party. The British

Conservative Party, one of the most successful parties in competitive party systems, has, in spite of the nature of its internal organisation and distribution of power, won the support of diverse economic, social and geographical sections in British politics. All parties seek to widen their support, whether they are parties fighting competitive elections or single parties dominating the political process, and in doing so they not only reflect divisions in society, but tend to mitigate them.

Political parties provide a link between government and people. They seek to educate, instruct and activate the electorate. They use the mass media and local organisations to maintain contracts with the relatively politically inactive and lead them to the awareness and acceptance of various policies. They seek to mobilise the population. These activities may be restricted to election periods, with various methods of increasing the party's votes, but they may extend far beyond electoral propaganda, and the party may seek to mobilise support by channelling supporters' non-political activities. Thus there may be trade unions, cultural and leisure organisations controlled by the party. The French Communist Party provides an excellent example of this 'occupational and social implantation'.[5]

The mobilisation of support by activating the population may be carried further by mass rallies, uniforms, flags and other displays of unity, to emphasise the identification between the individual and the political party. This aspect of political mobilisation is usually associated with parties in totalitarian systems, and the German Nazi Party provides some spectacular illustrations:

> There were posters, always in red, the revolutionary colour, chosen to provoke the Left; the swastika and the flag, with its black swastika in a white circle on a red background, a design to which Hitler devoted the utmost care; the salute, the uniform and the hierarchy of ranks. Mass meetings and demonstrations were another device which Hitler borrowed from the Austrian Social Democrats. The essential purpose of such meetings was to create a sense of power, of belonging to a movement whose success was irresistible.[6]

While increasing the scope of political activity and widening popular participation, political parties perform the important function of recruiting political leaders. This is very important in socialist regimes where the party provides the only avenue to political power, but it is as significant in competitive party systems in which the main source of political recruitment is through the political parties. In political systems where political parties are absent or very weak, the political élites are recruited from traditional élites, such as hereditary ruling families, or through religious or military organisations. The recruitment of political élites without the more popular base of party leaders has significant effects on the stability of the regime.[7]

Parties present issues; they set value goals for the society. All political parties have philosophical bases, no matter how blurred and no matter how divorced from the actual political behaviour of the party these foundations may be. The more coherent this philosophical base is, the more inclined we are to talk of ideological parties. The ideology may be important for the party workers to justify their commitment to the party, but it also serves to distinguish the party from others and allows the party to attempt to organise public opinion in a given ideological direction. The ideology of the party may be a challenge to the prevailing ideologies, as when socialist parties appeared in western Europe at the end of the nineteenth century to oppose the existing conservative and liberal consensus among the political élites. The ideology may, on the other hand, be an expression of agreement between the parties on existing political structures and political goals.

The different levels of ideological commitment could be illustrated by distinguishing between American political parties, European social democratic parties and parties in socialist states. American political parties are emphatically pragmatic; Robert Dahl speaks of 'ideological similarity and issue conflict'.[8] This does not mean that American parties are not ideological, but that they agree fundamentally on the goals of American society: there is no challenge to existing orthodoxies, and those few parties, socialist or radical right-wing, that have challenged the consensus have failed even at state level. It is of little importance in this context that the consensus is maintained through agreement between the political élites and the apathy of the majority,[9] but merely that it exists. The Irish parties, Fianna Fail and Fine Gael, are the nearest European equivalents of the American parties in respect to ideological differences.[10]

This degree of pragmatism is less emphasised in West European communist and social democratic parties, for although they wish, theoretically, to challenge the existing social and economic system, they do not aim to overthrow the prevailing political structures, and they are content to work through them, attempting to realise their goals gradually. Party members who do not subscribe to the ideological goals of the party may be disciplined, and more passion is often spent on doctrinal feuding than on the mechanics of winning elections. Of course there are wide differences between social democratic parties that have dominated government for long periods, as in Sweden, and communist parties that have formed opposition groups for long periods, as in Italy, for example. It is easier to remain ideologically pure without the responsibility for pragmatic adjustments of government. Yet the ideological base of these parties is sufficiently flexible to allow accommodation to parliamentary forms of government, and the parties tend to be dominated by their legislative wings.

Single parties in socialist or fascist systems set more rigid ideological goals for society. The German Nazi Party emphasised racial purity; communist parties proclaim the dictatorship of the working class, and economic and social equality. The aims of the party become the total aims for the society, and the party goals take the form of a secular religion.

It is difficult to imagine modern political systems without political parties; certainly liberal democratic institutions imply political parties, and the reliance on parties is greatest in socialist regimes. This is not to overlook the distorting features of political parties. They may polarise opinion in ways dangerous to the stability of the political system. The French Fourth Republic was near to collapse as early as 1951, with the pending successes in the general election of that year of two parties, the Communist and the Gaullists, hostile to the existing constitution.[11] The German Weimar Republic collapsed as a result of the polarisation of the electorate between the Nazi and Communist Parties. The Portuguese military rulers feared that the election results of the 1976 general election would polarise opinion between the left and the conservative parties. The military had in fact banned the more conservative parties in previous elections that followed the 1974 coup.[12]

The legislative isolation of large parties could mean the effective disenfranchisement of their supporters. Moreover, the various functions of the political parties may clash within the political system; thus Fred Greenstein has observed that the supporters of the decentralised, consensual party system in the United States have emphasised the success and consequent stability of that system, whereas its critics argue that it has been achieved at the expense of democratic control of government, and at the expense of efficient and effective government.[13]

Party structure

The structures of political parties relate very closely to the functions and the methods political parties employ to realise their aim of capturing or retaining political power. Thus parties which wish to widen their electoral support and operate at a parliamentary level will need a different structure from a party forced underground by restrictive legislation, or from a party conducting guerrilla operations from a rural base against urban-centred political élites. Parties which demand wider democratic participation, such as the extension of the franchise, may have, in theory, a more democratic structure than parties which seek to perpetuate the power of existing political élites.

An important analysis of party structure has been offered by the French political scientist Maurice Duverger. Duverger put forward a fourfold classification of party structure.[14] These were (1) the caucus; (2) the branch; (3) the cell; (4) the militia. The caucus or committee is characterised by its small membership and its resistance to seeking wider mass membership; it emphasises quality in its membership. It concentrates mainly on electoral activities, remaining dormant between elections. Its members consist either of local notables elected for their individual qualities and local influence ('direct caucus'), or of delegates of local organisations which have combined to form the party ('indirect caucus'). Duverger cites the French Radical Party and the British Labour Party before 1918 as two examples of this type of party, and he argues that the caucus-type party declines with the extension of the franchise.

The branch party is the product of the extension of the franchise in Western Europe. Unlike the caucus, the branch party is a mass party seeking to enrol the maximum membership. It usually has a centralised party structure, the basic units being distributed geographically according to the consituency arrangements. Moreover, its political activities are permanent, not merely confined to election periods. The branch structure was invented by the European socialist parties after the extension of the franchise to the working class, and has been imitated by Catholic and conservative parties with varying degrees of success. The German Social Democratic Party (SPD) provides a good example of this type of organisational structure. Delegates are elected via the branches and the regions to the biennial party congress, which in theory is the highest policy-making body in the party. The congress elects the party executive, which controls the party organisation outside the German parliament. (Although a new competing organisation, the party presidium, was established in 1958, which is more tightly controlled by the SPD parliamentary group.) The real centre of power in the party is, in fact, in the hands of the parliamentary group, which consists of all SPD members of the Bundestag, the West German lower chamber. The organisation of the SPD is similar, in many ways, to that of the British Labour Party, especially in regard to the distribution of power inside the party.[15]

Duverger's third type of structure, the cell, is an invention of the revolutionary socialist parties. Its organisational structure is based on the place of work, not, as with the branch parties, on geographical areas, although some area cells do exist and in some parties are quite important. The cell is smaller than the branch and is geared to continual political activity. The cell structure was essentially conspiratorial; it was designed to ensure that the whole party structure was not imperilled by the infiltration or destruction of one cell as there was no contact between individual units at the same level. The secretive activities of the cell were more widely political and more demanding on the individual than in branch parties. Cell-structured parties tended to regard the winning of elections as of secondary importance. Elements of the former cell structure still remain in European parties, but there is hostility among French Communist Party members to this form of structure. The French Communist Party, like other Western European Communist parties, has long attached far more importance to winning parliamentary elections, and the structure of the party now resembles more closely parties with a branch form of structure.

Duverger's fourth form of party structure is the militia type of organisation in which the structure takes on the hierarchical character of an army. Like the communist party cell structure, the militia form of organisation is adopted by revolutionary parties, and the two principal European examples have been Hitler's Storm Troopers and Mussolini's fascist militia. But Duverger does point out that 'no political party has ever been exclusively formed on the basis of the militia'.[16] In fact he goes further, arguing that his basic types are more likely to be found in mixed rather than pure form.

The critics of Duverger's classification scheme are many.[17] Jean Blondel wishes to describe 'caucus' and 'mass' parties as parties of 'indirect rule' and parties of 'direct rule', stressing not membership but the nature of the links between leaders and followers: 'It follows that the real distinguishing factor between mass party and party of committee is not directly related to questions of membership; the type of allegiance is the crucial problem.'[18]

In any examination of party structure, the following factors should be considered:

1. The role of the leadership and the method of selecting it.
2. The degree of organisational centralisation.
3. The power of the leadership in relation to the rank and file; the extent of disciplinary powers; participation in decision-making and policy initiation.
4. The control of the party bureaucracy.
5. The relationship of the parliamentary wing to the rest of the party.
6. Basis and extent of membership.

Determinants of party structure

We have already seen that the ideological framework of the party is an important factor in how the party relates to the rest of the political system, and therefore will have an important bearing on the structure of the political party. If the party sees its goals as antagonistic to the existing political structures, its organisation will reflect not only the party's hostility to the prevailing norms, but also a readiness to defend itself against any repressive measures that this hostility has produced among the dominant political élites. The organisational structure of the party also responds to the existing political institutions and structures of government. A federal structure of government is more likely to produce decentralised parties; presidential elections will have different effects on the nature of the party leadership than the less individual parliamentary elections. It must be remembered, of course, that parties are not passive in this context, but, as we have seen, in their turn affect the functioning of these different structures of government.

Socio-economic factors are also important in the determination of party structures. The level of economic development will influence the nature of the party competition and whether that competition endures and so affects the structure of the parties. There will be a different response to urban and rural societies, and to those in which class conflict is a significant aspect of the political process. Nationalism and religious divisions may be more important than class in forming the basis of some political parties.[19] Of course, the attitudes and values prevalent in society, the political culture, may be of vital significance in determining the types of political parties that emerge in any society. Parties with what are regarded as undemocratic structures may find difficulties in electoral competition in stable liberal democratic systems. The violence endemic in the autocratic structure of the British Union of Fascists in the 1930s was thought to be an important factor in the movement's alienation of much public support, and partly accounts for the ease with which coercive legislation, in the form of the 1936 Public Order Act, was passed.[20]

Historical factors are of the utmost significance in the determination of party structures. Parties are creations of modern political processes, and their emergence presupposes a necessary degree of urbanisation and development of mass communications. Parties arise when historical changes occur, and these are not subject to scientific laws. Therefore the development of parties is more haphazard and uneven than general classifications make apparent. Certainly particular changes are necessary, such as the need for the dominant political élites to seek wider political support, and for a significant change in political attitudes. In western Europe the extension of the franchise forced the existing conservative and liberal parliamentary groups to form national organisations to appeal to a wider electorate in order to capture or maintain power. Thus the 1867 Reform Act in Britain, which extended the right to vote to some of the working classes, was immediately followed by the formation of the National Union, a vote-catching organisation of the Conservative Party in parliament. The slight extension of the electorate in 1832 had led to the setting up of local registration societies which were limited in their scope.[21]

In this context it is important to know whether the parties were extensions of groups already existing at the legislative level, or whether the parties were created outside the legislature with the aim of gaining a foothold inside.[22] Externally created parties involve challenges to the existing dominant élites, they tend to be more centralised and are less deferential to the existing political institutions, although the British Labour Party is a powerful exception to the last point.

Naturally, not all political parties originated in relation to the legislative structure. The Russian Bolsheviks had no alternative to secret, conspiratorial organisation and activities given the hostility of the Tsarist regime. Colonial liberation movements are not given the option of constituting a parliamentary opposition to the existing government, and originate either as urban underground parties or as rural guerrilla organisations. They can be said to grow out of crisis situations in which the legitimacy of the established political élites is no longer recognised, and new groups seek to replace them.

All these factors, ideology, structure of government, level of socio-economic development, political culture and historical 'accidents', are interrelated. Thus, for example, American parties are primarily electoral machines, decentralised, laying little emphasis on ideological differences, exercising little disciplinary control over their members, and recruiting many of their presidential and congressional representatives from outside the party structure. For explanations for the development of parties with these characteristics, one needs to look at the federal system of government, the separation of powers, the presidential form of government, the liberal consensus, immigration and industrialisation, ethnic differences and the extension of the franchise in the early nineteenth century before the rise of an urban working class of significance. West European communist parties have a predominantly working-class membership, place great emphasis on ideological purity, are highly centralised with power largely in the hands of the leadership, and exercise a strong degree of control over their parliamentary representatives. For explanations for some of these characteristics, one would note the predominantly parliamentary, unitary political structures of western European states, the extension of the franchise long after the appearance of an urban working class, the political dominance of traditional conservative and liberal élites, and the success of the Bolshevik revolution in Russia and the consequent attempt to establish a Moscow-dominated conformity on western communist parties. Naturally, the relationship of party structures to these various factors is one of great complexity, and far more analytical detail is needed for any explanation to be entirely satisfactory.

Party systems

The structures of political parties and the factors that assist in determining those structures are only one set of factors which guide us in determining how political parties function in the political system. Parties operate within party systems, and the type of system will have profound effects on party behaviour. There are various classifications of party systems but it is difficult to classify party systems according to one single criterion. The most useful factors to take into account are: (1) the number of parties; (2) the relative strength of the parties; (3) the ideological differences between the parties; (4) the structure of the parties. Using all these criteria with varying degrees of emphasis, we could arrive at the following classification:

1. *One-party systems*. The Soviet Union offers the example of a system where only one party is allowed to compete and that party dominates the nomination and election processes within the system. Tanzania and Kenya provide examples of party systems where only one party is allowed to compete but there is a greater degree of competition within the party; this even leads to the defeat of prominent politicians at the polls.[23]
2. *Dominant party systems*. In India the Congress Party has dominated federal politics since 1947 and won 403 of 544 seats at the general election in 1985. Other parties compete but only rarely collectively match the strength of the Congress Party. Likewise the Mexican dominant party, *Partido Revolucionario Institucional* (PRI) has never lost an election since 1917, but allows its insignificant rival, the *Partido Accion Nacional* (PAN) to compete in elections at every level, and it is believed to give financial encouragement for this form of party competition, presumably for as long as the challenge is ineffective. The East German Communist Party (SED) allows other parties to compete, even middle-class parties, but they are rigidly controlled by the Communist party through a national-front organisation which selects the party lists for all the parties; it is this which prevents the East German example from being comparable with India and Mexico. Moreover, the East German Communist Party's control over all the agencies of government and the role of its detailed ideology in the political system make the East German party system comparable with that of the Soviet Union.
3. *Distinct two-party systems*. New Zealand offers the best example of a system which consists of only two parties in the legislative assembly. The two parties, the Labour Party and the conservative National Party achieve overall

majorities in the legislature, govern alone and rotate in office. Although there are more than two parties in the Australian federal assembly, the system operates basically in a similar fashion to that of New Zealand. Power alternates between the conservative Liberal Party, supported at federal level by smaller parties, and the Labour Party.[24] The United Kingdom remains a two-party system at the parliamentary level despite the existence of eleven distinct groups in the House of Commons after the 1987 election. Despite the distribution of the votes at general elections, the Conservative and Labour Parties win the majority of seats, have consistently governed alone since 1945 and since then have generally rotated in terms of government power. Only twice since 1945 have either of these parties failed to win an overall majority of seats in the House of Commons.[25]

4. *Indistinct two-party systems*. The Irish Republic and the United States provide useful examples of this type of party system. Although in terms of numbers they are similar to the New Zealand party system, the parties in the Irish Republic and in the United States lack centralised hierarchical structures and lack mass membership. Ideologically, the differences between the two major parties in each system are not clear cut. The political divisions between Fianna Fail and Fine Gael originated in a political quarrel over the status of the British monarchy in 1922, and the Republican and Democratic Parties of the United States often have more internal differences than inter-party differences. It is certainly difficult to place any of these four parties within a clear left-right spectrum. However, to underline the difficulties of any system of classification, whilst there are only two parties represented in the American Congress or which capture control of the American presidency, the Irish party system sometimes resembles the West German system. Thus before the 1987 February election the second largest party, Fine Gael, could only form a majority government with the support of the much smaller Labour Party.

5. *Two-and-one-half party systems*. These are party systems in which there are two dominant parties but the larger parties rarely command an overall majority and need the support of other parties to form a government. The small West German Free Democratic Party has held the balance between the two larger Christian Democratic and Social Democratic Parties since 1969. It has formed governments with first the Social Democrats until 1982 and since then with the Christian Democrats. The picture has been slightly complicated by the emergence of the Greens, a party which won 42 seats in the January 1987 election, but this party lacks the central bargaining position of the FDP. Austria provides another instance of this type of party configuration. Until the autumn of 1986, the Socialist Party governed Austria with the support of the much smaller Liberal Party (the Freedom Party). However, the Freedom Party moved significantly to the right and after the November 1986 election, a grand coalition was formed between the two largest parties, the Socialists and the People's Party (Conservatives) leaving the Liberals with the smaller Greens to provide the opposition. Between 1966 and 1969, the two largest West German parties formed a similar coalition.
6. *Stable multi-party systems*. In this type of system the relative strength of the parties makes multi-party coalitions a necessity on many occasions but the ideological differences between the parties are sufficiently muted to allow coalitions to be formed. Usually, coalitions are easy to form and have a long tenure. In Sweden the Social Democrats have often governed alone, but the party has not found it difficult to form coalitions in the past with the Centre or Liberal parties. Between 1976 and 1982, the three right-of-centre parties, the Moderates (the Conservatives), Liberals and Centre generally found few difficulties in forming a stable coalition in spite of the arguments over nuclear power in 1978. The Netherlands provides another example of a system with nine parliamentary parties after May 1986 but with a stable coalition of Christian Democrats and two Liberal Parties.

7. *Unstable multi-party systems.* Italy provides the best European example of this type of system. Although there are thirteen parties represented in the Italian parliament after the 1987 election, the basic problem of coalition building stems from the presence of Communists, constituting the second largest party to the Christian Democrats, and their exclusion from government power since 1947. Governments are unstable, lasting on average for only six months, and the Italian party system bears a strong resemblance to that of the French Fourth Republic between 1947 and 1958; in that example both the Communists and Gaullists were unwelcome to the other parties as coalition partners. The Belgian system may be placed in this category, a system complicated by the division of the Christian Democratic, Socialist and Liberal parties into Flemish and Walloon sections.

There is no one universal system of classification of party systems, and the foregoing classification is less complex than most. However, it does illustrate both the problems of classification and the diversity of party systems. Above all it stresses the need to take into account all aspects of the system. The Netherlands and France have the same number of groups represented in the assembly, but the relative strength and ideological differences in the French party system makes it perform more like a dual party system rather than a multi-party system. The two-party systems of New Zealand and the United States are distinguishable by structural and ideological considerations. The West German FDP has determined the fate of each West German government since 1969 with only a quarter of the seats of each of the two larger parties, yet the Italian Communist Party with over a quarter of the total seats is permanently excluded from power. Moreover, all party systems are susceptible to change.

Change and party systems

The factors determining and causing changes in a particular party system are complex and difficult to isolate. There may be no perceptible changes in the party system in spite of profound changes in other parts of the political system and deep changes in the social and economic systems. Secondly, change may be gradual, taking place over a period of time. Thirdly, changes in the party system may be dramatic and sudden.

The party system of the United States has not significantly altered during the period of rapid growth and industrialisation of the country, and the political parties still reflect early nineteenth-century characteristics.[37] Few party systems demonstrate this degree of stability. Most party systems are fluid and subject to greater change, and the degree of change is the factor which makes classification difficult. The British party system in the twentieth century provides a good example of this second type of change. Early in the twentieth century, the British Liberal Party was replaced as the second largest party in the British Parliament by the Labour Party,[28] and for a period the party system changed from a system with two major parties, the Conservatives and the Liberals, with minor parties such as Labour and the Irish Nationalists (before 1918), to a three-party system with Conservative, Labour and Liberal roughly equal.[29] The Liberals took a long time to die and cease to present a serious electoral challenge, and even as late as May 1928 *The Economist* could state: 'The three-party system has come to stay and we have got to learn to work it.' The two-party system, the Conservative and Labour Parties alternating as majority governments with a small Liberal Party never having more than thirteen seats, dominated British politics from 1945 to 1974. The result of the two elections in 1974 revived fears that the two-party system was no longer a feature of British politics, and even the results of subsequent elections have not removed doubts about its future.[30]

Sudden and dramatic changes in party systems are more likely to be the consequence of political revolutions, war or foreign occupation. The emergence of single-party systems in the Soviet Union after the October Revolution of 1917, or in some of the Eastern European states after 1945, provides examples of sudden change. These changes were not the result of the relatively slow political, economic and social changes that can be seen in the British example; they were the result of a forcible seizure of political power by a revolutionary group or invading army.

Thus party systems are not static and they do change, and the causes of change are many and complex. However, there is one factor which is claimed to have important causal relationships with party systems: the electoral system.

Electoral systems and political parties

The electoral system is only one factor in the evolution of a party system, but the effects of different electoral systems can be found in the structure, ideology, the pattern of party interaction and in the number of parties that compete in the political system.[31] An electoral system consists of more than the methods of counting the votes cast by the voters. A full description of an electoral system would include such factors as the extent of the franchise, i.e. who is entitled to vote. It would include the rules relating to candidates and parties and those regulating the administration of elections, especially the provisions against corruption. The method of casting the vote, i.e. 'is the ballot secret?' is part of an electoral system. Although the secret ballot may be almost universal, some aspects of electoral systems remain a characteristic of certain political systems, e.g. states such as Australia enforce compulsory voting; and primary elections are a feature of the electoral system of the United States. The size and shape of the constituency is an important aspect of electoral systems; the Netherlands and Israel have one constituency for the whole country, for example. However, the aspects of electoral systems that gain the most attention are the methods of casting the vote, the ways in which these votes are counted and the translation of votes into seats.

We can distinguish between the following main types of electoral systems:

1. *Single-member constituency and single vote.* This is usually referred to as 'first-past-the-post', and provides the electoral system for countries such as Britain, Canada, New Zealand and the United States.
2. *Single member and second ballot.* If one candidate does not receive an absolute majority of the ballot, a second one is held with the weaker candidates either choosing or being

required to retire. This system is used in France with the complication of provisions for alliances of the parties at the second ballot.[32]

3. *Single member with preferential vote.* This system allows the elector to place the candidates in order of preference, the votes of the weaker candidates being distributed to the stronger ones according to second, third, etc. preferences. Australia uses this system allowing for an alternative preference vote.
4. *Proportional representation.* There are many variations of PR in use throughout the world but the essence of all the different types is that seats are allocated in proportion to the votes cast in multi-member constituencies. The two principal types of PR are:
   (a) *The list system.* The elector votes for a list of candidates presented by a political party and each party wins the number of seats in that constituency according to the votes for that party list. In Belgium, Sweden, Denmark and Italy the voter is allowed to vary the order of the candidates in the party lists. The list system is the most popular European electoral system.[33]
   (b) *Single transferable vote.* This system is used in Eire, Tasmania, Northern Ireland, and Malta. It was used for the English university seats before 1948, and was recommended for Britain by the Speaker's conference of 1917. The voters in multi-member constituencies may mark all the candidates in order of preference. When the votes are counted, an electoral quota is established, that is the minimum number of votes needed by a candidate to win one of the seats; the surplus votes are redistributed to the other candidates according to the voters' order of preference. When all the surplus votes are redistributed in this way, the weakest candidates are then eliminated and their votes are redistributed according to the voters' second, third, etc. preferences. The quota is established according to the formula:

$$\frac{\text{Total votes}}{\text{Number of seats} + 1} + 1 = \text{Quota}$$

Thus in a four-member constituency with 100 000 votes cast, the quota would be 20 001.

It is inevitable that the electoral system does affect the relative strength and number of parties in the legislature. Dr Cheddi Jagan's People's Progressive Party was ousted from power in 1964 in what was then British Guiana by the British government changing the electoral system to one of proportional representation.[34] This is not to say that proportional representation 'causes' an increase in the number of parties, but that it tends to prevent a reduction. It has been estimated that if the British general election of June 1983 had been conducted with proportional representation the Labour Party would have gained 180 seats instead of 209, the Conservatives 277 instead of 297 and the Alliance 166 instead of 23, for these seats would then be proportional to the votes cast for these parties (27.6, 42.4 and 25.4 per cent respectively).[35] Of course, a change in the electoral system would certainly change voting habits. A timely change in the electoral system under the French Fourth Republic in 1951 succeeded in its intention of weakening the legislative representation of the Communists and Gaullists and thus ensuring a longer life for the constitution. The government of Northern Ireland abolished the single transferable vote in 1929, possibly to weaken dissidents in the dominant Unionist Party, and the British government reintroduced it for the June 1973 elections to increase the number of non-Unionist representatives.

There is little doubt that the electoral system does affect various aspects of the party system. The 'first-past-the-post' system helps the successful parties and distorts the relationship between votes and seats. A second ballot certainly reduces the number of seats held on a minority vote, and it increases the power of the local party organisations against the central organisations because of the need to bargain with other parties at local level before the second ballot.[36] The list system will increase the power of the parties over the candidates since the party decides the order of the candidates on the party list, but there is no evidence for countries such as Sweden or Italy that the list system encourages party splits or increases the number of parties. STV tends to make the voter concentrate on the individual candidate rather than the party label of the candidate and it makes it easier for smaller parties to gain representation in the assembly. In terms of the numbers of parties, a two-party system is more likely with the British and American system, multi-party systems are more likely with PR.

Thus the electoral system is an important factor in the character of the party system whether it distorts electoral opinion or whether it is a passive reflector of opinion. It has some influence on the degree of discipline parties can impose on their legislative representatives, and whether the parties reflect national or local interests and opinions. Yet the electoral system is only one factor. Canada has a similar electoral system to that of New Zealand but federalism and ethnic politics produce more political parties at national level. Eire, with STV, had only two parties before 1939 in the Irish parliament, although this electoral system tends to result in many parties. It is interesting to note that the Irish Fianna Fail party has twice been unsuccessful, in 1959 and 1968, in its attempts to change the electoral system, a change it was hoped would further strengthen Fianna Fail and weaken the electoral chances of the Labour Party, the third strongest in the legislature.

The arguments over the consequences of electoral systems are firstly factual ones; whether a particular system has certain effects, and the relevance of these effects to other social, economic and historical factors, in regards to the nature of the party system. Secondly, there are evaluative considerations such as whether stability of governments is a more desirable aim than an attempt to faithfully represent public opinion.[37]

References

1. J. A. Schumpeter, *Capitalism, Socialism and Democracy* (London, 1961) p. 279.
2. Sir Lewis Namier, *The Structure of Politics at the Accession of George III* (London, 1959), has strongly argued for the rejection of the party labels of Whig and Tory in the mid-eighteenth-century Houses of Parliament.
3. Edmund Burke, *Thoughts on the Cause of the Present Discontents*, in *Works* II, 82.
4. See S. Neumann, *Modern Political Parties* (Chicago, 1956) pp. 395–400.
5. See S. Henig (ed.) *Political Parties in the European Community* (London, 1979) ch. 4. for an outline of this feature of French political parties.
6. A. Bullock, *Hitler. A Study in Tyranny* (London, 1952) pp. 64–5.

7. See L. Binder, 'Political Recruitment and Participation in Egypt', in *Political Parties and Political Development*, ed. J. LaPalombara and M. Weiner (Princeton, NJ, 1966).
8. R. A. Dahl, *Democracy in the United States*, 4th ed. (Boston, 1981) p. 207.
9. See H. McClosky et. al., 'Issue Conflict and Consensus Among Party Leaders and Followers', in *American Political Science Review*, LIV, 406–27. Ogden Nash's observation has some relevance in this context:

   Between the parties Republican and Democratic
   The Feud is dramatic
   But except for the name
   They are exactly the same
10. See B. Chubb, *The Government and Politics of Ireland*, 2nd ed. (London, 1982) p. 104.
11. See P. H. Williams, *Crisis and Compromise*, 3rd ed. (London, 1964) pp. 310–313.
12. For a description of the Portuguese system, see T. C. Bruneau, 'Continuity and Change in Portuguese Politics: Ten Years After the Revolution of 25th April, 1974', *'West European Politics*, 7, 2, April 1984. pp. 72–83.
13. See F. J. Sorauf, *Party Politics in America*, 5th ed. (Boston, 1984) pp. 388–414.
14. M. Duverger, *Political Parties*, 2nd ed. (London, 1962) pp. 17–40.
15. See G. Smith, *Democracy in Western Germany*, 3rd ed. (London, 1986) pp. 97–104, and A. R. Ball, *British Political Parties*, 2nd ed. (London, 1987) pp. 200–210.
16. Duverger, *Political Parties*, p. 37.
17. See B. Wildavsky, 'A Methodogical Critique of Duverger's *Political Parties'*, *Journal of Politics*, XXI (1959) pp. 303–18, and Klaus von Beyme, *Political Parties in Western Democracies* (Aldershot, 1985) pp. 159–253.
18. J. Blondel, 'Mass Parties and Industrialised Societies', in *Comparative Government*, ed. J. Blondel (London, 1969) p. 121. The political party with the most members per head of population is to be found in Zaire, where 'every Zairian becomes a member of the M.R.P. at birth': S. E. Finer, 'The Morphology of Military Regimes', in *Soldiers, Peasants and Bureaucrats*. ed. R. Kolkowicz and A. Korbonski (London, 1982) p. 295.
19. See G. Smith, *Politics in Western Europe*, 4th ed. (London, 1982), pp. 18–26, for a discussion on the role of religion in Western European party systems.
20. For a discussion of the reasons for the failure of Mosley's fascists see R. Benewick, *A Study of British Fascism, Political Violence and Public Order* (London, 1969). Also R. C. Thurlow, *Fascism in Britain: a History 1918–1985* (Oxford, 1987).
21. See Ball, *British Political Parties*, pp. 37–39, 63–4, 102–4, 150–1, 187–9, for a brief history of the National Union.
22. See J. LaPalombara and M. Weiner, 'The Origins and Development of Political Parties', in LaPalombara and Weiner, *Political Parties and Political Development*, pp. 8–21.
23. See C. P. Potholm, *Four African Political Systems* (Englewood Cliffs, NJ, 1970) ch. 5 for an outline of the Tanzanian political system. See also R. J. Hill and P. Frank, *The Soviet Communist Party*, 3rd ed. (London, 1987).
24. After the July 1987 election the distribution of seats in the lower house was: Liberals 43; National Party 19; Labour Party 86.
25. The Wilson government did not have an overall majority between the February and October elections of 1974, and the Callaghan government lost its overall majority as a result of by-elections between 1976 and 1979.

26. See A. H. Thomas, 'Social Democracy in Scandinavia', in *The Future of Social Democracy*, ed. W. E. Paterson and A. H. Thomas (Oxford, 1986) pp. 172–222.
27. See W. N. Chambers, 'Party Development and the American Mainstream', in *The American Party System. Stages of Political Development*, eds. W. N. Chambers and W. D. Burnham, 2nd ed. (New York, 1975).
28. See Ball, *British Political Parties*, pp. 82–4, for a discussion of the reasons for the Liberal Party's decline in the early years of the twentieth century.
29. The December 1923 election result was as follows: Conservative 285 seats, Labour 191 seats, Liberals 158 seats.
30. See D. Butler and D. Kavanagh, *The British General Election of 1983* (London, 1984). The Belgian party system changed rapidly in the 1970s when as a result of ethnic friction nearly all the parties divided into two along the Flemish–Walloon dimension.
31. See V. Bogdanor, 'Conclusion: Electoral Systems and Party Systems', in *Democracy and Elections*, eds V. Bogdanor and D. Butler (Cambridge, 1983) pp. 247–61.
32. See D. Goldey and P. Williams, 'France', ibid pp. 71–83. The Socialist government of 1981–5 changed the French electoral system from the second ballot to the list system in an attempt to reduce the size of the Right's victory in the 1985 elections, and the Chirac government have reversed that decision for the next election.
33. See P. W. Campbell, 'European Experience. Electoral Systems and Coalition Governments', in *Adversary Politics and Electoral Reform*, ed. S. E. Finer (London, 1975) pp. 143–51.
34. P. G. J. Pulzer, *Political Representation and Elections in Britain*, 2nd ed. (London, 1972) pp. 55–6.
35. Butler and Kavanagh, *The British General Election of 1983*, p. 359.
36. See V. Wright, *The Government and Politics of France*, 2nd. ed. (London, 1983) pp. 154–8.
37. See particularly S. E. Finer in the introduction to *Adversary Politics and Electoral Reform*, pp. 3–32 for a rather emotional discussion of the relationship between stable government and electoral reform. The book strongly recommends a change to some form of PR in Britain. There was support for the introduction into Britain of the mixed West German electoral system in *The Report of the Hansard Commission on Electoral Reform*, June 1976. For some of the advantages of the present British electoral system see, J. A. Chandler, 'The Plurality Vote: A Reappraisal', *Political Studies* xxx, 1 (March 1982) pp. 87–94; A Maude and J. Szeemerey, *Why Electoral Reform? The Case for P.R. Examined* (London. 1982); P, Hain, *Proportional Misrepresentation. The Case Against PR in Britain* (Aldershot, 1986).

6

Pressure Groups

Pressure group analysis

'Pressure groups are social aggregates with some level of cohesion and shared aims which attempt to influence the political decision-making process.'[1] Of course, this brief definition raises certain problems. Farmers' organisations, trade unions or civic amenity groups can be readily identified as pressure groups, but some groups do not conform to the definition as easily. Thus government agencies such as the civil service may seek to influence the policies which they themselves implement and so possess many pressure-group characteristics. Pressure groups sometimes contest elections to gain representation in the assembly and so are similar to certain types of political parties, especially those that concentrate on one issue, never seeking or hoping to realise government office; many nationalist parties fall into this category.[2] Yet in spite of these complications pressure groups can be identified in all political systems. Some pressure groups devote all or most of their activities to influencing government policy; thus the Anti-Saloon League was formed solely to persuade the American government to introduce and maintain alcohol prohibition in the early years of this century.[3] Other groups may only rarely seek to influence governments and they concentrate mainly on other activities, for example a local nudist group seeking permission to use a stretch of the coast for its activities.

There is much dispute among academics over the problem of terminology and definition; various terms are used, such as lobby, political group, organised group, pressure group, interest group.[4] None the less, it is useful to use the term *pressure group* as the broad generic term and sub-divide pressure groups into interest groups and attitude (or promotional) groups. Thus interest groups can be said to be those groups whose members share attitudes resulting from common objective characteristics, for example all the members of the group are farmers, business people or plumbers, while the members of an attitude group hold certain values in common irrespective of their objective background, for example all the members dislike cruelty to animals whether they are business people or trade unionists. The distinction can be useful in terms of analysing the membership, the intensity of group solidarity, cross-pressures on members and the degree of political influence wielded by the group.[5]

Pressure groups are certainly not a new phenomenon in politics, but the academic recognition of pressure groups is more recent. The first systematic study was Arthur Bentley's *The Process of Government*, published in 1908, but widespread academic interest really dates from 1945, and now the study of organised groups has been incorporated into wider analyses of the distribution of power and the nature of the state.

We have already noted in Chapter 2 that pluralist approaches place particular emphasis on the role of pressure groups in liberal democracies. The pluralists argue that competing group interaction determines the outcome of many political conflicts, provides wider avenues of political participation and ensures a wider distribution of power. The state is sometimes regarded as neutral, holding the ring for the contending groups. Some pluralists argue that the state intervenes on behalf of the weaker or less privileged groups.

Marxists also agree that organised groups are important. However, the Marxist view holds that the state is far from neutral and that there are great imbalances in terms of political power between the groups. Thus not only will the state in liberal democracies favour business interests against those of organised labour, but there are also wide disparities of resources between the two; this is what Miliband calls 'imperfect competition'.[6]

A third view of the role of pressure groups is held in different variants by both Marxist and non-Marxist writers. They argue that many liberal democracies are at least partially characterised by corporatism. Thus Schmitter argues:

> Corporatism can be defined as a system of interest representation in which the constituent units are organised into a limited number of singular, compulsory, hierarchically ordered and functionally differentiated categories, recognised or licensed (if not created) by the state and granted a deliberate representational monopoly in exchange for observing certain controls on their selection of leaders and articulation of demands and supports.[7]

Liberal corporatism, however, should not be confused with the fascist concept of the corporate state. The main argument of those who apply the corporate thesis to liberal democracies is that increasing state interventionism, especially in the field of economic management, has led to the need to incorporate certain essential groups into the decision-making process. Thus the state needs the co-operation and advice of certain crucially placed groups such as business and labour.[8]

The emphasis, then, is on the functional representation of certain important groups in the policy-making process, and in return for easier access to this process the state gains greater social control, using, for example, the trade-union leadership to curb any militancy from the rank and file.[9] Few corporatist theorists would see liberal democracies as full-blown corporatist societies, but many regard corporatism as a useful tool of analysis for dealing with organised groups in political systems. Panitch and Jessop, for example, both argue that although there are many barriers to corporatism, cyclical resurgence or development of corporatist forms can be expected in most liberal democracies.[10]

Determinants of pressure group methods

Methods used by pressure groups in liberal democracies to realise their aims vary according to:

1. The political institutional structure.
2. The nature of the party system.
3. The political culture.
4. The nature of the issue.
5. The nature of the group.

The institutional structure affects the activities of pressure groups in various ways. For example, Britain has a unitary system of government with concentration of political power at the centre and in the hands of a relatively strong executive, and therefore pressure groups will deservedly regard their efforts as more successful if they gain access to ministers and their civil servants than if they are only able to influence MPs in the House of Commons. France under the Fourth Republic had a 'parliamentary'–centred structure, and although influence at the administrative level was regarded as important, there were many more opportunities to frustrate hostile policies and legislation at the parliamentary level than is the case in Britain. America has a bicameral legislature in which the Senate and the House of Representatives are of roughly equal political importance, and with the doctrine of the separation of powers, pressure groups can aim at the administration and the legislature, playing off one or sections of one against sections of other institutions. Moreover, the existence of a strong committee system in the United States Congress makes these a focus of attention for various pressure groups. This division of power between different centres may increase the opportunities to groups, but it may emphasise the opportunities to frustrate, not to propose. The constitutional changes brought about in France by the Fifth Republic of 1958 have tended to shift the attention of the pressure groups from the National Assembly to the administration. French prime ministers are now much stronger in relation to the legislature, and need not discuss certain matters there at all; thus pressure groups are now more eager for direct consultation with the administration.[11]

Federalism provides another interesting example of the effects of different political structures on pressure group activity. American pressure groups can operate at state level to defeat federally entrenched rivals, or concentrate at federal level to win concessions denied to them in the states. Small retailers successfully fought state by state to impose numerous state taxes on the larger chain stores in the 1920s and 1930s in spite of powerful chain store influence in Washington,[12] and there is the example of the National Association for the Advancement of Coloured People by-passing the influence of the strong white segregationist elements in the states and winning concessions at federal government level.

Relations between pressure groups and political parties and the effect on pressure group activity of different party systems provide other variables in pressure group politics. The largest British trade unions are formally affiliated to the Labour Party, and they provide the Party with the bulk of its money and membership.[13] However, the link between groups and parties in the United States is much weaker although the AFL–CIO (American Federation of Labour–Congress of Industrial Organizations) has close ties with the Democratic Party and expects better treatment when the Democrats control the presidency or Congress. A 1974 law limited the size of contributions to American political parties and this has led to the growth of political action committees (PACs) through which money is channelled to the parties. French pressure groups illustrate how close the ties between groups and parties can be. French trade unions are divided into three main sections depending on whether they support the Communists, Socialists or are independent of party. The most powerful union, the CGT *(Confédération Générale du Travail),* is an excellent example of a close relationship of a pressure group to a political party, in this case the Communist Party. This has had important repercussions on the strength and influence of French trade unions, since not only are they divided ideologically but the strongest is a satellite of a political party that has been effectively excluded from power for most of the period since 1947 . The Roman Catholic church provides an example of these ties between parties and groups: the church has had close links with the strong Christian Democratic Parties in West Germany and Italy.

The type of party system and the structure and ideology of the parties have significant effects on pressure group activity. American Congressmen, given the weakness of party structure, lack of party discipline and the absence of strong ideological differences between the parties, are easier targets for pressure groups, especially if those groups are based in the legislator's own constituency: Congressmen are very sensitive to local pressures. The two-party system in Britain, with the absence of comparable local pressures, allows greater resistance to group activities. Cross-voting is rare in the House of Commons, so groups must pay heed to party alignments. Multi-party systems provide a more fertile field for pressure group activity, especially at legislative level, even if the emphasis here is on preventing what is disliked rather than on encouraging what is preferred.[14]

The third variable is the political culture. American political attitudes show a greater political tolerance for pressure group activity than is the case in European liberal democracies. There may be greater hostility shown to particular types of group activity in certain countries: trade unions are usually regarded with more suspicion than their counterparts, employer associations, and much trade union activity is directed towards persuading their own members of the wisdom of certain policies and towards improving the image that trade unions have with the general public in order to better their bargaining position *vis-à-vis* the government. Direct action and resort to violence may be more common in some political cultures. French farmers have a well-established reputation for blocking roads with farm produce and machinery to support their demands against the government. The activities of the French students and trade unionists during the political troubles of May 1968 provide further examples of French attitudes. The tradition of the authoritarian state in West Germany may explain the weaknesses of attitude groups there.[15] The religious divisions in Northern Ireland have made it difficult for pressure groups to act independently of either religious group; the civil rights movement from its beginnings in 1968 became increasingly identified as pro-Catholic; this made it more difficult to influence the Protestant-based Unionist government. Thus in various ways the political culture determines the shape, intensity and direction of pressure group activity.

The nature of the issue is another factor in the analysis of pressure group methods. Pressure groups have to respond differently in particular circumstances although the aims of the group may be unchanged. British industry has long acted through such groups as Aims which undertake extended campaigns of educating the public and attempt to ensure the return of Conservative governments. However, dissatisfaction with the Conservative government's economic policy led the leader of the Confederation of British Industry (CBI) to threaten 'a bare-knuckle fight' with the government in 1980, a rare breakdown of business–government relationships in British politics.[16]

The fifth factor that influences the methods used by pressure groups is the nature of the group itself. Thus the aims of the group will affect how the group attempts to realise those aims. Groups with aims hostile to important aspects of the existing political system cannot hope to exert influence on the administration and legislature in the way that legitimised business groups would do. Thus the John Birch Society attempts to realise its aims through influencing the selection of candidates in the American Republican Party and educating public opinion through its publications. The type of sanctions that the group possesses will affect its methods. Those groups with powerful sanctions will not have to resort to national campaigns and programmes of civil disobedience. Governments will need the active co-operation of some groups if policies are to be implemented; a refusal to co-operate would be a powerful weapon in the hands of the group in any negotiations with the government. The medical profession provides a good example of a group whose co-operation is often needed in the carrying out of government policies.[17] Trade unions are often regarded as being very powerful in liberal democracies, but the number and strength of their sanctions is often over-estimated: trade unions are usually forced to spend a great deal of their resources in creating a more favourable climate of public opinion because of the political weaknesses of the unions. Sanctions include not only the ability to withhold co-operation from governments, but could rest on the number of votes the group can influence in a general election. The emphasis on sanctions does tend to exaggerate the power relationship of governments and groups, but it is important to remember that both groups and governments generally seek co-operation in preference to conflict.

There are other aspects of the group itself that will affect the methods used by the group. The nature of the group's organisation, whether it has a large and permanent bureaucracy, what type of leadership the group enjoys and the degree of internal democracy are all factors that will influence the ways in which a group operates. Membership is very important; here one should examine the degree of commitment of the members, the size of the membership in relation to the potential membership, and the type of members in regard to such factors as class, age, sex and perhaps heterogeneity. Finally, the wealth of the group will have an important bearing on the methods used by the group.

Levels of pressure group activity

Pressure group methods in liberal democracies are mainly concerned with influencing the decision-making processes at the executive and the parliamentary levels. and the attempted emphasis at a particular level will partly depend on the three variables of the political institutions, the party system and the political culture. As a general rule, with the increase in executive power and area of responsibility in the twentieth century at the expense of the legislatures, pressure groups will attempt to concentrate their activities at administrative levels, but obviously activity at one level does not preclude activity at another.

It is the most powerful economic interest groups that are more likely to have access to governments and their civil servants, although the Howard League for Penal Reform in Britain is an example of an influential attitude group which has regular channels of communications with ministers. It is co-operation that should be stressed at this level of consultation: governments want advice, technical information and most of all co-operation from strong interest groups. In America the administrative agencies (equivalent to British ministries) have varying degrees of independence of the president and Congress and are therefore targets of pressure group influence, but the groups can and are used by the agencies in their conflicts with other agencies, other pressure groups and Congress. The American Farm Bureau, representing the wealthier farmers, is an interesting example of agency–clientele relationships. The Bureau was formed indirectly out of federal government initiative in 1919, and its successfully close relations with the Department of Agriculture have generally allowed it to overshadow its rivals, the National Farmers Union and the Grange.[18]

This co-operation between governments and organised groups is institutionalised in Britain through a wide variety of permanent advisory committees on which sit group representatives alongside civil servants, e.g. the National Advisory Council on the Training and Supply of Teachers. In France pressure group representation has been institutionally organised for some groups at this level since 1924 and now include Chambers of Commerce and Industry, Chambers of Agriculture, Chambers of Trade and the Social and Economic Council, which is composed of trade unionists, employers and government representatives. However, emphasis on formal relations should not lead to an underestimation of informal contacts, and pressure group spokesmen are often selected for their ease of contact with government representatives.[19]

Pressure group activity at parliamentary levels is generally more spectacular and less secretive, but it is doubtful whether the publicity it receives is always commensurate with its importance. This is particularly true at Congressional level in the United States; the Congressional lobbyists are more professionalised than their British counterparts, and the previous emphasis on personal contacts with legislators has given way to a greater reliance on public relations campaigns and electoral assistance to sympathetic candidates. Technical advice and information are less important to American legislators than they are to European legislators, who are poorly served with legislative aids. Groups at parliamentary level try to establish contacts with individual representatives to gain their support, but usually the representative is already sympathetic to the aims of the group. The British Conservative backbenchers wishing to end the BBC television monopoly between 1951 and 1954 were not only active on the party's Broadcasting Policy Committee but had close links with the industries that would benefit from the introduction of commercial television.[20] However, the secrecy that accompanied the activities of that particular lobby was one reason for its success; the more publicised attempts to influence legislators by mass lobbying and bombarding representatives with petitions, letters and telegrams tend to bear out the generalisation that noise accompanies political weakness. A good example in Britain was the attempt to defeat the Abortion Bill of 1967.[21] The attempt failed partly because of these mistaken tactics by the bill's opponents.

Bribery is still used at legislative levels. The Natural Gas Bill of 1956 was defeated in the American Senate because of bribery allegations. In the 1970s about a hundred large American corporations are reported to have made improper payments over several years to governments and representatives of foreign legislatures. When the most notorious of these payments were revealed, those by Lockheed, Gulf and Exxon, several governments and political parties were shaken by the allegations. Means of preventing this sort of influence are being implemented by the American Congress.[22]

National campaigns are the most conspicuous method of pressure group activity, and unless accompanied by activity at other levels are an indication of political weakness. The Campaign for Nuclear Disarmament illustrates this point. However, although public campaigns may fail to stop particular pieces of legislation or the implementation of certain policies, they may have significant influence over the longer time period. The British Road Haulage Association failed in the 1940s to prevent road haulage nationalisation by the Labour government, but their campaign may have helped to ensure denationalisation by the Conservative government which came to power in 1951, and may have contributed to the growing hostility in many quarters to other nationalisation proposals. The American Medical Association's successful defeat of President Kennedy's medicare proposals in 1961 again shows that nationally mounted campaigns are not always ineffective, and the moderation of similar legislation by the administration of President Johnson in 1965 was probably due in part to the past successes of AMA campaigns. Nevertheless, public campaigns often indicate total and open hostility to government policies, and there lie the seeds of failure.

One other important area is open to pressure groups: in America, unlike other liberal democracies, pressure groups have more opportunities of attempting to influence the judiciary. American federal constitutional courts have wide constitutional powers to overrule the executive and the legislature and to interpret the meaning of legislation in more politically significant ways. Pressure groups will attempt to influence the selection of judges who usually have a politically active background; they can also use test cases and undertake public campaigns to influence particular decisions. They can offer the courts technical services and use the device known as the *amicus curiae*, which allows a party not involved directly in a case before the court to present legal arguments because it can claim that a decision would affect it in some way. But although American courts, and especially the Supreme Court, are firmly part of the political process, the traditions of the courts, the security of tenure of judges and their non-accountability to an electorate provide some defence against pressure group activity. Moreover, it could be said that federal courts tend to favour poorer and minority groups such as the Blacks.[23]

Pressure group activity in the liberal democratic sense is almost absent from autocratic and socialist systems. In some autocratic systems it is the low rate of economic development, poor communications and lack of technological advances that are strong barriers to pressure group activity. In some the emphasis on nationalism often brings embryo pressure groups into a nationally, not sectionally, orientated value system, and of course there is the emphasis on coercion. It is interesting to note the role of the military in autocratic systems, since in many developing countries the army is often composed of the best educated and technically competent elements. Given the nature of autocratic systems it is difficult to ensure the legitimisation of pressure group politics, and groups not completely subservient to the government are forced to take a more hostile attitude towards the very basis of the regime.

However, in recent years political scientists have devoted greater attention to what is sometimes called the 'bureaucratic pluralism' of the socialist regimes.[24] This approach focuses on the competition of groups within institutional structures, such as the party itself, the state administration and the military establishment. It also emphasises the reliance of the policy-making élite on the technical expertise of varied occupational groups, ranging from economists and physicists to jurists and teachers. Although pluralist models have been criticised, they do illuminate features of such political systems which static 'totalitarian' models ignore.

Determinants of pressure group influence

It is difficult to measure precisely the influence exerted by pressure groups,[25] but some generalisations can be made. The government's policy will be an important factor, especially the emphasis that particular policies receive from the policy-makers. But governments and pressure groups operate within a web of political values and attitudes and these provide other variables to determine group effectiveness. In Britain groups to promote the welfare of animals will have more public sympathy than, say, a society advocating some form of euthanasia. Nevertheless, the nature of the sanctions a group can use and the usefulness of the group to governments and legislatures are very important factors which make interest groups generally more powerful than attitude groups. The nature of the group's organisation, the identification of the rank and file with the initiatives of the leaders, the degree of participation by the members, the size of the group's purse are other variables. Thus the Roman Catholic Church is the dominant religious institution in many political systems, but there are divisions between the Church leadership and followers on matters of abortion, birth control and divorce. As a result of these internal divisions the Church is often defeated by its opponents. The lack of internal democratic procedures often prevent more liberal values being articulated within the organisation.[26] These may be factors tending to offset the large membership of the organisation. Money is another important factor in the success or failure of pressure groups, especially in view of the emphasis placed on public relations campaigns, but the example of the wealth and large membership of the West German DGB (Federation of German Trade Unions) not being translated into commensurate political influence is a warning that they are only two variables.

The degree to which a group maximises its potential membership and the extent to which similar interests are divided between rival organisations are important variables. The National Farmers Union has nearly 80 per cent of all farmers in England and Wales as members, but we have noted the three major divisions of farmers in the United States. Miners' trade unions often display a near-maximum membership, a result of geographical concentration which strengthens their position in other ways, i.e. influencing elections and ensuring that a miners' representative is returned to the legislature.

There are important barriers to pressure group effectiveness besides the faults of the groups' own internal organisation and lack of political skill. Group activity takes place in a wider political society, and to maximise its influence a group will try to identify its aims with what is described as the national interest. No group can be successful and still be identified with the ruthless pursuit of its own aims. However, this view of countervailing societal pressures must be treated carefully. Some groups are identified with national values and yet are pursuing aims as 'self-centred' as their opponents'. Thus business interests may claim that a strike by trade unionists is damaging the country's valuable export drive, and so disguise their disquiet at the damage done to their interests as businessmen.[27] It is possible, of course, to feel that the two are inseparable – 'What is good for General Motors is good for America.'

Perhaps a more important obstacle to pressure group influence is the overlapping membership of groups which may moderate the sectionalism of their demands, but again this is more relevant to Anglo-American pressure group politics, where groups, especially attitude groups, are more numerous and may be less ideologically orientated. This limitation on pressure group effectiveness would partly depend on the degree to which the leadership is representative of the members, and on the efficiency of the communications within the group. The overlapping membership of the pressure group leaders may be far more important in reducing the sectionalism of group demands. On this point of unrepresentative leadership, trade unions are particularly criticised because representative democracy is expected of such organisations, but the same criterion is not applied to all groups: no one expects the same degree of participation by all members of the Roman Catholic Church, and therefore the legitimacy of the group's demands is not affected.

The secrecy surrounding much pressure group activity is an aspect contributing to suspicion and exaggeration of the power of pressure groups. This is sometimes a factor allowing one group to infiltrate another and disguise its real demands. This may be relatively open, as with the 'anti-cruel sport' element in the British Royal Society for the Prevention of Cruelty to Animals, but it may be far more sinister, as when the American Asphalt Company infiltrated the American Farm Bureau in the 1930s, a move that was disclosed in 1935 by a Congressional committee investigating the Farm Bureau's campaign for better roads.

The American Federal Regulation of Lobbying Act of 1946 was an attempt to curb and publicise the activities of groups lobbying the American Congress. It stipulates registration, declaration of sources of funds and a list of the legislation that the lobbyists were employed to oppose or support, but its application is limited and even such a powerful group as the National Association of Manufacturers has not registered. There have been no major equivalents in other liberal democracies.

The permanent civil service, competing parties and the desire of governments for electoral success may balance the unrepresentative aspects of pressure groups. The British Conservative government after 1983 enacted regulatory restrictions on financial interests in the City of London in spite of Conservative links with these financial institutions. The government is often the only countervailing force against farming interests, which are not effectively balanced by direct opposing interests. Moreover, by encouraging wider political participation, pressure groups are said to extend the liberal democratic concept of representative government, and in some instances groups provide the only source of opposition to the united front of the political parties.

References

1. A. R. Ball and F. Millard, *Pressure Politics in Industrial Societies* (London, 1986) pp. 33–4.
2. See A. R. Ball, *British Political Parties*, 2nd ed. (London, 1987) p. 3.
3. For an account of the Anti-Saloon League, see P. Odegard, *Pressure Politics: The Story of the Anti-Saloon League* (New York, 1928).
4. For a discussion on the problems of definition see G. Wootton, *Interest Groups* (Englewood Cliffs, NJ, 1970) pp. 1–5.
5. For alternative methods of classification, see G. Wootton, *Pressure Groups in Contemporary Britain* (Lexington, Mass.,1978) ch. 2.
6. R. Miliband, *The State in Capitalist Society* (London, 1973) ch. 6.
7. P. Schmitter, 'Still the Century of Corporatism', *Review of Politics*, 36 (Jan. 1974) pp. 93–4.
8. See Ball and Millard, *Pressure Politics in Industrial Societies*, pp. 21–3.
9. See L. Panitch, 'The Development of Corporatism in Liberal Democracies', in *Trends Towards Corporatist Intermediation*, ed. P. Schmitter and G. Lehmbruch (London, 1979) pp. 119–46.
10. See Panitch, ibid, pp. 86–7. Also L. Panitch, 'Trade Unions and the Capitalist State', *New Left Review*, 125 (Jan.-Feb. 1981) pp. 21–43; and B. Jessop. 'The Transformation of the State in Post-War Britain', in *The State in Western Europe*, ed. R. Scase (London, 1980) pp. 23–93.
11. V. Wright, *The Government and Politics of France*, 2nd ed. (London, 1983) p. 242.
12. See H. Zeigler, *Interest Groups in American Society* (Englewood Cliffs, NJ, 1964) pp. 44–6.
13. See M. Pinto-Duschinsky, *British Political Finance, 1830–1980* (Washington, 1981) chs 6, 8.
14. See P. Williams, *The French Parliament, 1958–67* (London, 1968) pp. 85–9 for an excellent little case study of the French *bouilleurs de cru*, owners of fruit trees, defending their right to distill alcohol, a defence that was partially successful between 1954 and 1965 as a result of party manoevring in the National Assembly in both the Fourth and Fifth Republics.
15. Wolfgang Hirsch-Weber, 'Interest Groups in the German Federal Republic', in *Interest Groups on Four Continents*, ed. W. Ehrmann (Pittsburgh, 1964) p. 103.
16. Generally groups have better success by co-operating with government and maintaining a good public image. Thus the American Medical Association changed its tactics in the mid-1970s from trying to halt objectionable legislation to that of 'nudging them 5%', i.e. changing small parts of the bill. In 1978 the AMA only completely opposed one of the thirty bills concerned with health. See R. W. Rhein, *Medical World News* (12 Jan. 1978) pp. 77–81.
17. See M. Foot, *Aneurin Bevan, 1945–1960* (London, 1973) chs 3 and 4, for an account of relations between the Labour Government and the doctors at the time of the setting up of the British National Health Service.
18. See G. K. Wilson, *Special Interests and Policy Making. Agricultural Policies in Britain and the United States, 1956–70* (New York, 1977) pp. 76–80.
19. See W. Grant, 'The National Farmers Union: The Classic Case of Incorporation?', in *Pressure Politics. Interest Groups in Britain*, ed. D. Marsh (London, 1983) pp. 129–43.

20. See H. H. Wilson, *Pressure Group* (London, 1961).
21. See K. Hindell and M. Simms, *Abortion Law Reformed* (London, 1971).
22. See G. K. Wilson, *Interest Groups in the United States* (Oxford, 1981) pp. 62–4.
23. See M. Schapiro. 'The Supreme Court from Warren to Burger', in *The New American Political System*, ed. A. King (Washington, 1978) pp. 179–211. Public Enquiries of a quasi-judicial nature are also important in many political systems. For information on the role of these Enquiries in the field of environmental pressure group activities see Ball and Millard, *Pressure Politics in Industrial Societies*, pp. 183–8.
24. For a discussion on pressure groups in the Soviet Union and the Eastern European socialist systems see Ball and Millard, *Pressure Politics in Industrial Societies*, pp. 37–9. Also see H. G. Skilling and F. Griffiths (eds) *Interest Groups in Soviet Politics*, (Princeton, NJ, 1971.); H.G. Skilling, 'Interest Groups and Communist Politics Revisited', *World Politics*, vol. 36, no. 1, October 1983, esp. pp. 1–4.; W. Odom, 'A Dissenting View on the Group Approach to Soviet Politics', *World Politics*, vol. 28, no. 4, July 1976, pp. 542–67; A. Brown, 'Pluralism, Power and the Soviet Political System: A Comparative Perspective', in Susan Solomon (ed.), *Pluralism in the Soviet Union* (London, 1983) pp. 61–107.
25. For a discussion of this see Wootton, *Interest Groups*, ch. 5.
26. See Ball and Millard, *Pressure Politics in Industrial Societies*, pp. 235–9.
27. For a discussion of the dominant ideology that supports the demands of business groups in liberal democracies see C. Lindblom, *Politics and Markets* (New York, 1977).

7

Representation, Elections and Voting Behaviour

Theories of representation

We have seen that political parties and pressure groups represent interests, attitudes and values in the political system, but there is often confusion over what is meant by the term 'representation'. Adolf Hitler once said that he had the greatest claim to be called representative of his people, and this claim must be based on different grounds than those of liberal democratic systems which demand periodic and competitive elections. The British House of Commons is said to be a representative assembly, but this does not mean that it mirrors the geographical, class, sex, age and religious distribution of the British population.[1]

Direct democracy is difficult in modern states, and some form of representative system is found in all states with the exception of some conservative-autocratic systems. Naturally, there are wide variations in the form of representative government and the selection processes of the representatives: President Hastings Banda of Malawi claimed that he did not have to submit to re-election because the people 'selected' him to be president for life. However, most of these political systems share two basic concepts of representation: first, that sovereignty lies with the people and therefore the government is responsible to the people; second, that the will of the majority is more important than that of minorities. Neither of these two concepts has any real meaning until they are amplified and applied to different political systems, and neither has any meaning unless expressed in terms of particular structures. But we shall see that basically they provide the foundations of modern systems of representation.

Yet there are the problems of defining the 'people' and deciding how their will should be expressed. Rousseau's answer was direct participatory democracies in small decentralised states:

> Sovereignty, for the same reason as makes it inalienable, cannot be represented; it lies essentially in the general will, and does not admit of representation: it is either the same, or other; there is no intermediate possibility. The deputies of the people, therefore, are not and cannot be its representatives: they are merely its stewards, and can carry through no definite acts. Every law the people has not ratified in person is null and void – is, in fact, not a law. The people of England regards itself as free; but it is grossly mistaken; it is free only during the election of members of parliament. As soon as they are elected, slavery overtakes it, and it is nothing.[2]

The European medieval basis of representation was locked in the concept of corporate hierarchies. The 'people' were not individuals but groups in society, these groups being based on occupation and status. Thus medieval representative assemblies were assemblies of estates, each with reponsibilities, duties and rights and arranged according to a natural order of authority: the early English parliament had three estates of peers, church and commoners, of which the House of Lords and the House of Commons survive. The secularisation of western European societies and the rise of personal powerful monarchies saw the decline in some areas of the medieval assemblies, and the king was to become the representative of the people according to God's law. James I, the English king, summarised the basis of these views in one of his many lectures to parliament:

> The state of monarchy is the supremest thing upon the earth; for kings are not only God's lieutenants upon earth and sit upon God's throne, but even by God himself, they are called Gods. ...[3]

The Levellers were to make the earliest, clearest English demand for popular sovereignty during the revolutionary period in the mid-seventeenth century. The government was to rule with the consent of the people, and this consent was to be secured by the right of people other than those with property to take part in the election of MPs; a Colonel Rainboro put forward the claim, observing: 'I think the poorest he that is in England hath a life to live as the richest he.'[4] The claims were limited and were soon to be completely utopian with the return of the Stuart monarchy.[5]

These older views on representation are important because the break with the past is not a dramatic one, and many of these older theories remain, intertwined with modern theories of representation. Emphasis on intermittent lines of continuity is necessary for understanding. Thus the American revolutionaries rejected the sovereignty of the British crown and the British parliament, and were willing to quote John Locke as frequently as their opponents, but they only reluctantly placed that sovereignty in the hands of the people, and then only with massive conservative institutional safeguards.[6] In fact it is difficult to talk of theories of representation with the two underlying concepts of popular sovereignty and majority rule in modern terms before the nineteenth century. It will be convenient to group modern theories under two broad headings for further examination: (1) liberal democratic theories of representation; (2) collectivist theories of representation. Neither category can be completely isolated from the other, for as we shall see they both have common intellectual origins, and moreover we shall find several different approaches under these common headings.

Liberal democratic theories of representation

There are a number of alternative theories that can be grouped under this heading;[7] however, it is possible to isolate the essentials of liberal democratic theories of representation. Firstly, there is the emphasis on the importance of individual rights, especially the inviolability of the individual's property, and the neccessity of limiting the powers of government to protect those rights. The justification for these individual rights was to be found in the theories of natural rights, rights that were beyond the competence of any government interference. Thus the famous American Declaration of Independence of 1776 claimed 'We hold these truths to be self evident that all men are created equal, that they are endowed by their Creator with certain inalienable rights, that among these are Life, Liberty and the pursuit of Happiness.' Thus liberal democracy implies not only an extension of the franchise but an equality of voting rights. The representative represents individuals, their opinions and their interests, and therefore he is elected according to geographically demarcated constituencies, not according to classes, occupational distinctions or distinct interests. Secondly, there is in liberal democratic theories of representation a rationalist strand. Man is a creature of reason; he can identify his own interests and his own opinions, and is aware of the wider claims of the community. He will therefore use his vote in an intelligent fashion and is consequently entitled to share in the selection of representatives. Thomas Jefferson laid clear emphasis on the importance of an educated majority as a prerequisite for American representative government,[8] and this view was echoed by the classic English liberals of the mid-nineteenth century. Human reason is superior to historical tradition or hallowed custom, therefore political institutions and practices are to be judged empirically. This leads to the third characteristic, that of the sovereignty of the people, which was to be expressed through universal suffrage. The British reformist tradition in the nineteenth century measured its success by the successive Reform Acts which increased the size of the electorate, attempts to equalise the size of constituencies, the introduction of the secret ballot, the attack on corrupt electoral practices, and the weakening of the unrepresentative House of Lords in 1911.

One can see that in this framework the representative has a particular role to play: he is responsible to his electorate but he is not its delegate; he represents a geographical collection of opinions, but is not required to surrender his own. Liberal democracy emphasises the role of the representative assembly as a protection against the encroachment of executive power, especially encroachments on the liberties of the individual. However, there is the problem of the tyrannical majority, for if the representative assembly reflects the opinions of the electoral majority, can that popular majority interfere with the 'inalienable rights' of individuals? The problem was outlined be Alexander Hamilton during the debates on the American constitution in 1788: 'Men love power ... Give all power to the many, they will oppress the few. Give all power to the few, they will oppress the many. Both therefore ought to have power, that they may defend itself against the other.'[9] The extension of the British franchise aroused similar fears of mob democracy amongst the liberals. John Stuart Mill, fearing the uneducated majority, suggested limiting the vote to the literate and increasing the vote of the people with certain superior qualities.[10] The pessimism of the liberal doubters seemed to have been justified with the extinction of liberal democracy in Germany in the 1930s. The majority of the electorate rejected liberal democratic candidates pledged to support the Weimar Republic to vote for totalitarian parties intent on destroying German liberalism.

The potential conflict between the sovereignty of the majority and the protection of the rights of the individual may be seen in terms of Robert Dahl's concepts of Madisonian and populistic democracy.[11] Dahl defines the first in the following way:

> What I am going to call the 'Madisonian' theory of democracy is an effort to bring off a compromise between the power of majorities and the power of minorities, between the political equality of all adult citizens on the one side, and the desire to limit their sovereignty on the other.[12]

It is this that Dahl applies to the American political system with its constitutional checks and balances. His definition of populistic democracy is 'that it postulates only two goals to be maximised – political equality and popular sovereignty'.[13]

There are other variations within the representative theories of liberal democracy: the utilitarian demand for representatives to constitute an exact social mirror of the electorate presents one enduring aspect of these theories; the English idealists' partial reaction against nineteenth-century individualism in their belief that the system of representation should allow common interests to emerge after a process of discussion is another strand.[14] However, these representative theories, taken as a whole, have managed to accommodate themselves to the rise of the mass party and the growth in executive power. They have done this in two ways: first by the emphasis on the doctrine of the mandate, i.e. that the government programme is the implementation of election promises that have received the consent of the electorate. This is a partial reiteration of the rationalist element in liberal democratic representative thought, and as we shall see later it is difficult to sustain in view of what knowledge we have of the way in which voters decide which party to vote for. Therefore there has been a falling back on the theory that at election times voters are deciding which competing team of political leaders to support, and representative liberal democracy must be compatible with the existence of political élites.

Collectivist theories of representation

Collectivist concepts of representation were developed in modern form by the nineteenth-century European socialists.[15] These were to reject the individualism underpinning representation of the liberal theorists and to emphasise the importance of class conflict within society and the middle-class liberals' use of the state as an instrument of class oppression. Therefore, the socialists argued that assemblies should be representative, not of individuals and opinions, but of the majority class whose interests have been subordinated by middle-class parliaments. Here we find an emphasis both on the sovereignty of the people and on the will of the majority. Thus the *Communist Manifesto* of 1848 states: 'All previous historical movements were movements of minorities. The Proletarian movement is the self-conscious, independent movement of the immense majority, in the interests of the immense majority.'[16]

The most thorough rejection of parliamentary liberalism was achieved by the Bolshevik Communist Party under Lenin. The Soviet state claims to be a higher form of democracy than the form found in capitalist states. The basis of the claim is that social equality and the absence of economic exploitation is the yardstick of a genuine democracy, that Soviet society is united with the elimination of exploiting classes, and that there is full acceptance of popular sovereignty. The monopoly of the Communist Party is justified on the grounds of the absence of class conflict, a conflict that would necessitate competing parties, and by the historical role of the party in the building of communism.

Functional and vocational representation was abandoned in the new Soviet constitution of 1936, and replaced by the more traditional form of territorial representation.[17] However, Soviet theories still claim the superiority of their representative institutions on the gounds that there is wider participation and that representatives mirror more faithfully the social backgrounds of their constituents. L. G. Churchward has summarised some of the similarities and differences between Soviet and liberal democratic concepts:

> ... while Soviet and Western theories of democracy share a common historical origin the contemporary theories (and of course practice) differ widely. While Soviet theorists still define democracy as majority rule and place considerable emphasis on individual rights they do not recognise minority rights except in peculiarly circumscribed conditions as within a primary party or social organisation. Secondly, Soviet theory rejects many theoretical concepts found in Western theory of democracy, such as 'separation of powers', 'division of powers', 'ministerial reponsibility', 'the rule of law', etc. These principles are of course largely derived from the practice of parliamentary government or from English common law. Thirdly, while Soviet theory includes principles of electivity and accountability and removability of office holders, it couples the concept of 'direct democracy' to the concept of 'representative democracy'.[18]

Functions of elections

Elections are a means of choosing representatives. However, although elections are held in the majority of political systems whether they are termed liberal democracies, socialist democracies or authoritarian oligarchies, their purpose and importance vary from system to system.

Elections certainly allow the electors to participate in the choosing of their representatives, but even in competitive elections held in liberal democracies we have already noted the distorting effect of the various types of electoral system; the successful candidates may be the choice of the minority, the system may give the parties control over which candidates are presented to the electorate. Voters under the single transferable vote have a greater choice over which candidate should represent a particular political party than voters under the British electoral system. Voters in some socialist states have only the choice of voting for or against a single candidate, there being no opportunity for voting for an alternative representative. Yet in other socialist systems, voters are allowed to choose between candidates, as in Poland and Hungary. Similar reforms were initiated in the USSR in 1987. Even in some one-party states of Africa, such as Kenya, voters can and do vote for alternative candidates of the only party. Thus a crucial question in all political systems that hold elections is: how do the party or parties select their candidates and what are the opportunities for the electors to influence that choice? In the United States with frequent elections and a multiplicity of elected offices there are primary elections to choose the party candidates in open elections which serve to undermine party control of the nominating process.

However, choosing a representative does not mean that the elected representative is responsible to or controlled to any degree by the voters. Elections are rarely fought over one issue; therefore the failure of the elected representatives to fulfil their promises to their voters on one issue may be blurred by the claims of success on other promises. Governments are seldom elected on one particular issue.

Of course, referendums are a means of allowing voters to directly influence the decision-makers in terms of specific policies. Thus referendums have been held in Sweden on alcohol; in Italy, Spain and the Irish Republic on divorce; on cutting taxes in California; on immigration in Switzerland, on membership of the Common Market in the United Kingdom, on the powers of the President in France, on the defence budget in Romania. However, referendums are not necessarily the populist democratic device that their supporters sometimes claim. Referendums are not always binding on the government and the timing and the nature of the question or questions asked are important. The discrepancies in the resources of competing groups in a referendum campaign may prevent equal presentation and dissemination of competing opinions. Generally, referendums are conservative devices and the results tend to uphold the status quo.[19]

Elections do not necessarily decide which government takes office. In single-party systems the result is a foregone conclusion even though the electorate may influence the composition of the government by preferring one candidate to another from the same party. No African government outside South Africa has lost office as a consequence of an election. Even in liberal democratic states of Western Europe, the relative strength of the political parties in coalition government decides the nature of the government, and the bargaining of the parties is as important as the election that produced the varying party strengths. Governments in West Germany have been the consequence of the decision of the Free Democrats whether to support the Christian Democrats or the Social Democrats.

We have already noted that electoral corruption may distort the people's choice both in terms of which representative is elected to the assembly and which government takes office. The corruption may be mildly amusing, as in a Corsican election when a Socialist alliance polled 4965 votes and the Gaullists polled 4260 votes with only a total registered electorate of 4303,[20] but it becomes more serious when it is claimed that Kennedy's victory over Nixon in 1960 was achieved by the manipulation of vital votes in the Democratic stronghold of Cook County, Chicago.[21] The Watergate disclosures revealed many election abuses practised by the organisation supporting Nixon, the Committee to Re-elect the President (CREEP), in the 1972 presidential election.[22] The corrupt practices of President Marcos of the Philippines led directly to his fall from power in 1986.

Yet elections have other functions than those concerned with the choice and accountability of representatives or governments. Elections allow a degree of communication between the rulers and the ruled; the latter can educate the former on what are perceived as the main political issues. Above all, elections are a means of legitimising the right of the rulers to govern. Even in one-party regimes with little choice available to the voter, the authorities seek to maximise the turn-out and often exaggerate the actual number who take part in the election.[23] This legitimising process both mobilises the people for support of the regime and helps to engender positive attitudes amongst the governed, and in the process of legitimising the status quo, produces a degree of political stability constantly sought by those who hold political power.

Voting behaviour

We have already noted the role of political parties and the electoral system in deciding the result of general elections in all those political systems that hold elections, whether competitive or non-competitive. Another important area of inquiry is the field of voting behaviour. Obviously, this is more important in those political systems in which the voter has some sort of choice, no matter how limited. Unfortunately for the student of politics, there is little agreement among political scientists on the reasons why voters prefer one individual or party to the alternatives. Therefore, we are faced with numerous, though not always conflicting, theories and models concerning electoral behaviour. In part, these disagreements stem from political change which may make former interpretations outdated. Thus, increasing secularisation of society may lessen the impact of religion on voting behaviour, or the class structure may change over a period of time to complicate theories on the relationship between membership of a social class and voting preferences. However, there are important methodological problems in the analysis of voting behaviour. At first glance voting behavioural studies appear more susceptible to a scientific approach given the vast amount of quantifiable data the political scientist has at hand, yet the acquisition of these data is beset with numerous problems. Firstly, every elector cannot be asked questions concerning past and future intentions and therefore the sample must be chosen with care; for example, if surveys are conducted by telephone, compensation must be built into the sample, since working-class people are less likely to possess telephones at home than the middle class. Secondly, the nature of the questions asked is very important. Potential support for the Alliance in the 1987 British general election was higher in those opinion polls that prompted the respondent by naming the Alliance than in those polls that simply asked which party the elector intended to vote for. Thirdly, there are problems involved in the interpretation of the material. This is very important in cross-national comparisons, for if there are different conceptual uses of key terms such as social class, floating voter or church membership, then the conclusions are seriously flawed. Fourthly, the answer of respondents may be flawed. Voters may tell deliberate lies or possess faulty memories of how their vote was cast in the last election. Thus in attempting to account for the electoral failure of the British Labour Party in the 1987 general election, given the Party's popularity on several key issues such as health and education, one analyst was forced to the conclusion: 'When answering a survey on the most important issues respondents think of public problems; when entering the polling booth they think of family fortunes.'[24]

Within this complex arena of voting behaviour studies, three broad approaches stand out: first, the party identification model; voters cast their vote primarily out of long-term loyalty to a particular political party; secondly, the rational choice approach, with the electorate rationally deciding which way to vote on the performance and promises of the candidates or parties; thirdly, the sociological approach which emphasises the correlation between voting behaviour and the voter's class, religion or age, etc. None of these broad approaches provide a complete explanation of voting behaviour, and there are many divergent currents within each of them. However, each approach may be briefly examined.

The party identification model was the most popular interpretation of voting behaviour in the 1950s and 1960s. In most liberal democracies stability, not change, characterised the behaviour of the electorates and surveys revealed a high level of allegiance to specific political parties. Changes occurred as a result of the behaviour of small sections of the electorate, often labelled 'floating voters'; but stability was the outstanding characteristic of voting patterns. Whether this stability reflected relative economic prosperity, or whether the investigatory methods were deficient is not too clear. However, in the 1980s, it is obvious that voting behaviour based on loyalty to political parties is no longer a persuasive explanation. Political scientists now speak of 'partisan dealignment', that is the weakening of the voters' loyalty or attachment to specific parties. Electorates in industrial liberal democracies are now more volatile; they are now more likely to change their voting behaviour in each election. There has been the rise of the Independent voter particularly in American elections; these independent voters are not necessarily the politically ignorant or apathetic voters, but those who vote independently of party labels and may vote for candidates with different party labels for different political offices on the same day; this is termed 'ticket splitting'.[25]

This is not to imply that parties are not important in patterns of electoral behaviour. The personality of the candidate, particularly in French and American presidential elections, is significant, and although party control of the nomination process has weakened in American elections, parties are generally crucial in this respect. The presentation of issues, the mobilisation of the vote and the organisation of election campaigns are of the utmost significance; the inept electoral performance of the British Labour Party in 1983 certainly increased the Conservative majority.

The second approach, stressing rational choice, was supported by Downs' influential work published in 1957.[26] Downs likened political choices to economic choices; in the market place, the consumer will compare products in terms of costs and quality and purchase those goods which it is economically sensible to buy. Likewise, in the political market place, the voter will cast his or her vote for the party that is most likely, given the information available, to serve the ends of the voter. Social position or party loyalty are less important factors than the rational search for the party or candidate that will best serve the individual interests of each voter. This approach is not necessarily incompatible with party loyalty, but it does emphasise the importance of issues in elections. Electors may deem certain issues such as defence or education to be of such importance that it determines the direction of the vote. The importance of certain issues may lead to continual voting for the same party:

> For many electors ... certain issue areas will be very important, regardless of what macro-issues dominate the campaign. ... Such electors as a result of their permanent preoccupations will vote for the same party all the time – often as part of a cohesive social group concerned with the same issue.[27]

Thus in a wider sense, this approach may allow aspects of the party loyalty and sociological approaches to be included within its explanation. The rational choice approach allows the voter to vote on the record of the government, making a retrospective judgement, and thus to ignore the promises of candidates and parties. Certainly, there is strong evidence that the state of the economy at the time of the election is a powerful determinant of electoral behaviour; the American presidential election of 1984 and the West German and British elections of 1987 all appear to underline the importance of the economy. Moreover, there is evidence from many liberal democracies that issue voting is on the increase.[28]

The sociological approach has more supporters among students of voting behaviour, but it should not be forgotten that divergences within this approach are many and the arguments diverse. Broadly, the sociological approach stresses the group membership of the voter and gives prominence to the voter's social class, religious adherence, regional or ethnic loyalities and the age and sex of the voter. Of course, these may overlap, e.g. the voter may be a middle class, church-going female voting in Italian elections, or they may conflict, e.g. a middle class, Catholic, Irish immigrant voting in England. It is important to remember that the sociological approach merely finds correlations between social cleavages and voting behaviour; it does not claim that there is a causal connection.

There is no doubt that class is a powerful indicator of voting intentions. Generally, the working class is more likely to support a left-of-centre party and the middle classes more likely to vote for a right-of-centre party. It matters little to this explanation that for most of the electorate the terms 'right' and 'left' have little meaning. What is important is that there is a strong correlation between class and voting behaviour.[29] Thus in the French presidential election of 1981, two-thirds of businessmen, professionals and farmers voted for the conservative candidate, Giscard d'Estaing, while two-thirds of the manual working class voted for the Socialist candidate, François Mitterrand.[30] Even in the United States where voting along class lines is less pronounced, blue-collar workers were more likely to vote for the Democratic Party nominees in the 1980 and 1984 presidential elections whilst Reagan, the Republican candidate in both, won proportionally more support amongst the white-collar workers.[31]

However, if all social classes voted along class lines, conservative parties, particularly in Western Europe, would be in permanent opposition since the working classes generally outnumber the middle classes. The British Conservative Party has enjoyed long periods of dominance because sufficient numbers of the working class have refused to vote along class lines. Thus in the 1987 election it was estimated that only 35 per cent of skilled manual workers voted Labour, while 42 per cent supported the Conservatives. At the same election it was estimated that 13 per cent of middle-class voters supported the Labour Party.[32]

In all industrial liberal democracies, there has been a weakening of the relationship between class and voting over the last twenty years, and this has produced an argument among political scientists as to whether this weakening correlation is the result of voters simply ceasing to vote along class lines (class dealignment) or whether the class structure itself in these societies is in a process of change. Certainly, the traditional manual working class has declined in industrial liberal democracies and there has been a significant growth in white-collar occupations. This in turn has affected the nature of trade union membership, which in the past was associated with voting for left-of-centre parties.

The British general election result of 1983 led many observers to use social class in a different way. The working class were more likely to vote Conservative if they owned their own houses as opposed to renting them from the local council; working-class employees in state employment, whether white or blue-collar workers, were more likely to vote for the Labour Party than employees in the private sector; those dependent on the State such as pensioners or social security recipients were more likely to vote Labour.[33] Of course, the definition of social class that is used in the investigation of voting patterns is of crucial importance.[34]

The correlation between social class and voting behaviour may be reinforced or weakened by the other factors. Thus if one class predominates in a particular geographic area, it is plausible to argue that there is greater conformity in voting patterns; in a white-collar suburb, white-collar workers would have their conservatism reinforced, while the tendency of manual workers in this suburb to vote socialist would be weakened. Studies of European Communist parties have drawn attention to the party sub-culture in explaining the underlying solidarity of the Communist vote: the working-class family transmitted communist values to the children and these values were reinforced by membership of leisure and social groups which were organised by the Communist parties themselves. Thus communist sub-cultures were established among certain sections of the electorate, illustrated by the famous 'red belts' in areas of Italy and France.[35]

Religion is still an important indicator of voting patterns although its impact has declined. In predominantly Catholic countries such as Italy there is strong support for the Christian Democrats and even in the Netherlands and West Germany, where Protestantism is as important as Catholicism, there are clear correlations between religious allegiance and voting for religious or confessional parties. However, cross-cleavages are important; thus in the Anglo-Saxon democracies such as

Australia, Britain and America, Catholics are more likely to vote left-of-centre as a result of ethnic and class disadvantages. In the United States Jews voted 66 to 32 in favour of Mondale, and white 'born-again' Christians voted 80 to 20 in favour of Reagan in 1984. However, there is the problem of defining membership of a church, for different churches may define their membership in various ways, i.e. regular attendance, baptism, family membership, etc.[36] Moreover, membership of a church, whatever the method of calculation, may strongly correlate with social class status; thus Anglicans in England, and Episcopalians and Unitarians in the United States are more likely to be middle class, whilst Baptists in both countries and particularly in the United States are more likely to be lower middle and working class.

Women are more likely to be regular church attenders than men, but independently of religious adherence, women have traditionally tended to support right-of-centre parties. However, this correlation appears to be weakening, and this trend is more pronounced in the more secular liberal democracies of Britain and America than in those with a Catholic heritage such as France, Italy and West Germany.[37]

Age, too, is a complex variable. Older people clearly have a tendency to vote for conservative parties but one has to take care that this tendency is not partly a result of predominance of women or even the middle class amongst older voters as a consequence of demographic trends. It may be the case that conservative voting does not necessarily dramatically increase as the voter gets older, but that the voting patterns of the elderly may be a consequence of the hardening of voting habits that were formed in a different historical period. Thus a seventy-year-old American Democratic voter in the 1980s is reflecting an attachment for the party, an attachment established during the economic depression of the 1930s when the individual voted for the first time and voted Democratic.[38]

There are other variables in the sociological approach to studying voting patterns. There are many regional and nationalist parties throughout Europe in systems with competitive elections such as the Scottish and Basque nationalist parties or the Tyrolese separatist parties of Italy. In some political systems, the majority parties split along ethnic or linguistic lines, reflecting English–Boer animosities in South Africa or Walloon–Flemish differences in Belgium. In the United States, black voters give their support overwhelmingly to Democratic candidates, but here one must note a correlation between colour and economic deprivation.

Thus approaches to studying why people cast their votes in the way they do are varied and complex and subject to many qualifications. However, as we have seen, the different approaches are not necessarily exclusive of contrasting approaches. All the approaches have to struggle with methodological problems, especially those of defining concepts; and the societies they analyse are not static. Long-term structural changes and sudden crises such as war or economic depression complicate the area of study; there may be more volatility within the electorate than the aggregated figures betray. It is a field where excessive dogmatism should be avoided and all conclusions must be tentative.

The role of the mass media

One factor of increasing importance in the determination of election results is the role of the mass media, and especially that of television. However, there is little agreement on how important the effects of the mass media really are. The question is undoubtedly of great importance to students of politics, since there is now general agreement that in industrialised liberal democracies the major source of political information is the mass media, and that the importance of this source is growing.

Newspapers used to be the chief source but with the growth of television their relative importance has declined. Yet newspaper readership is still very high in most systems with competitive elections. This is particularly true of West Germany and Great Britain where over half the adult populations read the political news in a newspaper every day.[39] Ownership of newspapers tends to be very concentrated; Axel Springer owns nearly all the Sunday newspapers in West Germany and the ownership of British newspapers is similarly in few hands, with Rupert Murdoch increasing his share of readers over the last decade both in terms of the number of newspapers and in terms of the number of readers.[40] Even in the United States where there are fewer national newspapers, syndicated columns by well-known journalists partly bring the United States into line with Britain and Germany.

Newspapers in liberal democracies show clear political bias and this political bias is increasing. In 1983 only two of seventeen British national newspapers gave any support to the Labour Party and the political partisanship was even more pronounced in the months before the June 1987 election. The West German Springer empire consistently supports the right-of-centre parties. However, the Australian Liberal and Nationalist parties complained bitterly of the pro-Labour stance said to have been shown by the majority of newspapers and television stations in the 1987 election.

Television strives to take a more neutral stance in regards to political issues, partly because outside the United States it is more likely to be controlled by public corporations, and even where privately owned, is subjected to more controls than the newspapers. In West Germany, the Constitutional Court in its supervision of television has successfully resisted private ownership. In countries such as Britain where television is partly in private hands and in the United States where the public service is minute, there is often an overlap between ownership of television stations and newspapers.

Television now takes the major share in political advertising and election campaigns are increasingly fought through the television screens. This makes any accusation of political bias all the more sensitive. Television, whilst striving to be politically objective, does, in fact, provide less political information than the newspapers. It stresses personalities and images to the detriment of informed political analysis. Television because of its increasing pre-eminence in the dissemination of political information becomes more open to political interference on the part of governments. The bias in favour of the government of the day shown by French television has long been the subject of comment, and the splitting up of the monopoly public corporation into six regions and the attempted reforms proposed by President Mitterrand in 1982 have failed to significantly change the situation. British governments increasingly attempt to force television to provide a more favourable image of the party in power. These attempts became more overt and less subtle when Norman Tebbit became Chairman of the Conservative Party in 1985; the BBC was forced to pay heavy damages to two Conservative MPs in 1986 following a programme on right-wing infiltration into the Party.

Yet despite this heavy reliance on the media and especially television for political information on the part of the electorate, there is no agreement among observers on the effect of the media on political attitudes or voting behaviour. It is argued by some that the media merely reinforce existing party loyalties and political opinions. It is the more politically committed that spend more time reading, watching or listening to analyses and comments on political matters. Others argue that the media influence opinion and importantly set the political agenda; they decide what political issues are to be important.

Those holding the first view claim that the media merely increase political awareness and do not significantly affect views formed or reinforced by that increased awareness. Thus an analysis of the television debates between Carter and Ford in the American 1976 presidential election claimed that the effect on viewers was less than imagined. Of course, presidential election debates are different from news coverage of political events and in Britain, the Glasgow Media group studies of television reporting of political issues claim to have detected persistent bias against groups such as trade unions and in favour of established political élites.[42]

Yet even if the political effects of media distortion of political messages are slight, whatever bias there is becomes more important given the increasing electoral volatility in liberal democracies. If voters are no longer as firmly anchored to party loyalties and if class and religious membership become less significant in terms of identifying electoral trends, then the media and particularly television become more important. Even if the evidence for short-term influence, such as influencing votes in a particular election, is difficult to obtain, there is the importance of long-term formation of political attitudes. The media cannot be ignored as significant political actors.

References

1. See A. H. Birch, *Representative and Responsible Government* (London, 1964) pp. 13–17 for a discussion on the different usages of the term.
2. *The Social Contract* (Everyman's Library ed., London, 1913) p. 78.
3. Quoted in S. H. Beer, *Modern British Politics*, 2nd ed. (London, 1969) p. 5.
4. Quoted in A. D. Lindsay, *The Essentials of Democracy*, 2nd ed. (Oxford, 1935) p. 12.
5. For a fuller account of the demands of the Levellers, especially those contained in the debates with the army leaders in 1647, see A. S. P. Woodhouse (ed.), *Puritanism and Liberty* (London, 1938).
6. See B. Bailyn, *Ideological Origins of the American Revolution* (Cambridge, Mass., 1967) chs 6 and 7.
7. See Birch, *Representative and Responsible Government* for an outline of British theories of representation. For the development of the American liberal consensus, see L. Hartz, *The Liberal Tradition in America* (New York, 1955).
8. See R. Hoftstadter, *The American Political Tradition* (London, 1962) pp. 26–32.
9. Quoted in R. A. Dahl, *Democracy in the United States* (Chicago, 1976) p. 73.
10. J. S. Mill, *Representative Government* (Everyman's Library ed., London, 1910) pp. 280–90.
11. R. A. Dahl, *A Preface to Democratic Theory* (Chicago, 1956).
12. Ibid. p. 4.
13. Ibid. p. 50.
14. An example of the work of the English idealists in the twentieth century is to be found in Lindsay, *The Essentials of Democracy*.
15. For an account of these early socialist theories, see G. Lichtheim, *The Origins of Socialism* (London, 1968).
16. The *Communist Manifesto* (Penguin Books ed., Harmondsworth, 1967) p. 92.
17. G. Ionescu, *The Politics of the European Communist States* (London, 1967), points out that in theory 'communist states are said to be *direct* and not *representative* democracies', but that 'in practice it has not worked out at all like that' (p. 29).
18. L. G. Churchward, *Contemporary Soviet Government*, 2nd ed. (London, 1975) pp. 226–7.
19. See D. Butler and A. Ranney (eds), *Referendums. A Comparative Study, Practice and Theory*, (Washington, 1978). The Polish government's defeat in the 1987 referendum provides a dramatic exception.
20. *Time Magazine*, 16 February 1970.
21. See L. Lewis *et al.*, *An American Melodrama* (London, 1969) pp. 230 and 509.
22. See T. H. White, *Breach of Faith. The Fall of Richard Nixon* (London, 1975). Also G. Liddy, *Will* (London, 1980); John Dean, *Blind Ambition*, *The White House Years* (London, 1977).
23. See M. Harrop and W. L. Miller, *Elections and Voters. A Comparative Introduction* (London, 1987) pp. 21–4.
24. I. Crewe, 'Tories Prosper From a Paradox', *The Guardian*, 16 June 1987.
25. See M. P. Wattenburg, *The Decline of American Political Parties 1958–80* (Harvard, 1984).

26. A. Downs, *An Economic Theory of Democracy* (New York, 1957).
27. I. Budge and D. Farlie, *Explaining and Predicting Elections* (London, 1983) p. 41.
28. For American evidence see N. Nie *et al.*, *The Changing American Voter* (Cambridge, Mass., 1974). There is a wealth of new studies of voting behaviour particularly in Britain: see A. Heath *et al.*, *How Britain Votes* (Oxford, 1985); R. Rose *et al.*, *Voters Begin to Choose* (London, 1986); P. Dunleavy *et al.*, *British Democracy at the Crossroads* (London, 1985); D. Robertson, *Class and the British Electorate* (Oxford, 1984). See also H. Himmelweit *et al.*, *How Voters Decide* (London, 1981) for some support for the rational voter approach. For an overview see Harrop and Miller, *Elections and Voters*.
29. For a discussion of perceptions of 'left' and 'right', see D. Butler and D. Stokes, *Political Change in Britain*, 2nd ed. (London, 1974) pp. 323–37.
30. See V. Wright, *The Government and Politics of France* (London, 1983) 2nd ed.. Appendix 8.
31. See E. C. Ladd, 'On Mandates, Realignments, and the 1984 Presidential Election', *Political Science Quarterly*, 100, 1 (Spring, 1985) pp. 1–25.
32. ITN/Harris Exit Poll, *The Independent*, 13 June 1987.
33. See P. Whiteley, *The Labour Party in Crisis* (London, 1983) pp. 94–107. See also, Dunleavy et al., *British Democracy at the Crossroads*, pp. 121–46.
34. See Heath *et al.*, *How Britain Votes*, pp. 13–44.
35. See A. Kriegel, *The French Communists. Profile of People* (Chicago, 1972). Of course, both the 1985 French elections and the Italian elections saw a weakening of the support for the Communist parties, the French far more seriously than the Italian.
36. See A. R. Ball and F. Millard, *Pressure Politics in Industrial Societies* (London, 1986), pp. 211–16, for a discussion of the problems of calculating and defining church membership.
37. See D. McKay, *American Politics and Society*, 2nd ed. (Oxford, 1985) p. 105. Also see C. T. Husbands, 'Race and Gender', in *Developments in British Politics*, 2nd ed., H. Drucker *et al.* (eds) (London, 1986) pp. 304–13.
38. For a discussion of 'age cohorts', see Butler and Stokes, *Political Change in Britain*, p. 62.
39. L. G. Edinger, *West German Politics* (New York, 1986) p. 114.
40. See K. Newton, 'Mass Media', in *Developments in British Politics*, pp. 314–17.
41. See A. Abramowitz, 'The Impact of a Presidential Debate on Voter Rationality', *American Journal of Political Science*, 22 (August 1978) pp. 680–90.
42. See Glasgow University Media Group, *Really Bad News* (London, 1983). This is the third book in the series, the first being published in 1976. See also P. Dunleavy, 'Fleet Street: its Bite on the Ballot' *New Socialist*, January 1985, pp. 24–6.

PART THREE

Structure of Government

8

Assemblies

The nature of assemblies

Previous emphasis on constitutional law in the study of politics has tended to confuse the discussion of assemblies, with the result that there has been exhaustive accumulation of detail on procedural matters, but less consideration of the wider relationship with the total political system. The usual term 'legislature' is one indication of the exaggeration of the law-making function of assemblies. This function is important in some political structures, but historically assemblies have emerged from the executive's need for advisory bodies, a need which in the example of the British parliament later provided a means of limiting the power of the executive.[1] Legislative functions were neither historically anterior to nor are they more politically important than other functions of modern assemblies. The emphasis on the doctrine of the separation of powers in liberal democracies provides a useful guide to the distribution of legislative and executive powers, but interpreted too rigidly and applied universally, it leads to misconceptions rather than enlightenment.

There are wide variations in status, powers and functions even between states whose constitutional frameworks lead to expectations of conformity rather than difference. At one extreme we find the Supreme Soviet of the USSR, a bicameral assembly which has wide powers according to the 1977 constitution but which reaches its decisions by unanimous votes and only meets a few days each year, and despite its extensive network of committees, its role as an independent political actor is slight.[2] At the other end of the spectrum, the

United States Congress exercises real power in respect to various decision-making processes, and it offers a far more potent political challenge to executive power than its counterpart in the Soviet Union.[3]

These differences among assemblies depend on several variables. The constitutional structure of the state may provide for a federal structure and this, as in the case of the American Senate, may exalt the importance of a second chamber. The transition from a parliamentary to a more presidential type of government by the French under the Fifth Republic reduced the power of the National Assembly.[4] British governments, with majority party support in the House of Commons, have been immune from major adverse votes of confidence in the House since 1885.[5] The party system also provides an important reason for the insignificance of the Supreme Soviet, while the political importance of the Italian parliament is enhanced by the confused party system. The system of representation leads to many variations; we have seen in Chapter 7 that socialist states reject the liberal democratic view of representation but that even in liberal democratic systems there are significant differences. Thus the American Congressmen with their identification with local constituency interests offer a contrast to the British MPs, who can afford to take a wider national view of political priorities and who are not so tightly tied to local interests. There are other variables which affect the position of assemblies in the political process. The level of socio-economic development and the importance of regional differences are significant for the functioning of the national assembly. The political culture and the historical development of the political institutions in a given political system are other important variables.

To examine these functions more systematically, we may classify them under the following broad heading:

1. Relations with the executive.
2. Legislative functions.
3. Representative functions.

Assembly–Executive relations

In parliamentary types of governments the political chief executive is selected by the assembly in that the strongest party in the assembly provides the necessary political support for its leader to emerge as prime minister, chancellor, etc., and to select the majority of the members of his government from his party represented in the assembly. Of course, the process differs according to the type of party system that exists in the parliamentary regime. In two-party or dominant party systems the process of selection is straightforward, and the next prime minister is known immediately after the general election: Disraeli was the first British prime minister to offer his resignation immediately after his election defeat instead of awaiting defeat in the House of Commons. In multi-party systems the process may be more complex, and the difficulties of the bargaining procedures between the parties may lead to further splits, so that individual members may find their political position enhanced outside the party structure.

The period of British political history 1845–67 provided an interesting example of what has been referred to as 'the golden age of the private member'. As A. H. Birch has observed: 'it was in this period that writers with liberal sympathies laid stress on the supremacy of Parliament in the British Constitution. Gladstone described the House of Commons as the "centre of our system" and said that the supremacy of the Commons administration was "the cardinal axiom of the constitution".'[6] It was in this period that the House of Commons could 'make ' and 'unmake' governments with frequent ease. The French Republic of 1946–58 has been described as a 'deputy-centred Republic'[7] because of the ability of the National Assembly to limit the lives of successive governments. Between 1947 and 1958 the National Assembly defeated twenty-one governments. The Italian parliament since 1946 has succeeded in restricting the average life of Italian governments to nine months.

In presidential systems the chief executive is usually elected directly by the mass electorate, yet in some the assembly shares the powers of executive appointment. In the Philippines, the

Congress must confirm any presidential nomination of a vice-president in the event of a mid-term vacancy and the nominee must be a member of Congress. The American Senate can veto certain 'political' appointments of the president, and although it cannot 'defeat' the president even in the theoretical terms of parliamentary governments, it may use the power to impeach a president. In 1974 the start of impeachment proceedings in the House of Representatives led to the resignation of President Nixon. Yet the constitutional power of the Senate to 'advise and consent' on the appointment of judges to the Supreme Court, for example, does provide an opportunity for the legislature to influence the policy of the executive at federal level. The Senate rejected the two Nixon nominations of Haynesworth and Carswell, as well as Reagan's nomination of Robert Bork.

This power to influence executive policies is more important than the power to appoint and remove the political head of state. In the example of Italy, the power to defeat governments so frequently is essentially a negative power, to prevent not to promote, the politics of 'immobilism' as it has been called. Influencing the decision-making process may be achieved in various ways. Debates and questions may have some effect on the government and certainly serve to inform the government as to opinion in the assembly. Even in the most stable party-dominated assemblies they may set a chain of events in motion which leads to a change of government, as with the famous May 1940 debate in the British House of Commons on Chamberlain's handling of the war.[8] But even without these drastic consequences, the knowledge that in parliamentary regimes a government will have to explain and defend some of its policies in the assembly does lead to some circumspection, especially on the part of the permanent civil service. This is true of countries where the government cannot be brought down by an adverse vote in the assembly: in Switzerland the federal council cannot be forced to resign in this way, but a clash with the assembly does lead to a modification of government policy. The American president frequently consults Congressional leaders to secure support and prevent adverse criticism. In 1964 President Johnson obtained Congressional approval for his actions over the Gulf of Tonkin incident, and he used this to escalate the Vietnam war: although the president was not believed to be constitutionally bound to approach Congress on this matter, yet he was aware of the political implications.[9]

Assemblies conduct investigations into government policies, and these serve to act as a brake on the government motor. These investigations may be carried out by committees of the assembly: the House of Commons Select Committee on Public Accounts provides an example consisting of fifteen members and chaired by a leading member of the Opposition. The Committee has no executive power and merely reports back its findings to the House of Commons, but it has acquired a fearsome reputation and governments dread adverse reports. Committees of investigation have been developed more thoroughly in the American Congress; the Senate Ervin Committee, investigating the Watergate affair, and the Senate and House committees investigating the supply of arms to Iran by the Reagan administration are examples of this.[10]

Supply of money for government spending has been a traditional weapon in an assembly's arsenal in seeking to exercise some control over government policies, in fact the English House of Commons owes its origin to the need of medieval kings to tax their wealthier subjects. The supply of money may be broken down into several stages, such as the assembly's authorisation to raise revenue, permission to spend money, and as we have seen with the Select Committee of the House of Commons on Public Accounts, inquiries into how the money was spent. It is a mistake to concentrate too much on the detailed procedure of financial control; the real importance of these powers is found in their use to influence the policies of the government that necessitate the spending. Again the United States Congress provides the extreme example of this form of control and influence, as it was not until 1921 that it gave the president full responsibility for preparing the federal budget. Congress has been able to influence extensively American defence policies by its control over appropriations. Congress limited further American government aid by these powers to the rebels in Nicaragua in 1987.

Yet the restrictions on influencing policy by means of financial control are obvious even in the most independent of assemblies. Complexity of procedure, the amount of money involved in modern government spending, the lack of time and specialised information and the inability of assemblies to match executive speed of action and united leadership, all these militate against much effective influence. These observations on financial control also have a wider bearing on assembly–executive relations: the increasing power of executives to initate and realise their own policies is a fact of the twentieth century, and this is particularly true in the field of foreign policy. The United States Senate's constitutional powers in regard to the declaration of war have been eroded by the simple failure of the government actually to declare war in the last two major conflicts, Korea and Vietnam, although the War Powers Act of 1973, passed partly as a result of Nixon's misuse of power in illegally invading Cambodia in 1970, is an attempt to reassert more power over the president. Of course there is nothing incompatible between strong government and the increased ability of assemblies to influence the government:[11] it may be argued that the French Fifth Republic was not so much an attempt to establish a more dictatorial executive against a democratic National Assembly, as a search for a more balanced legislative–executive relationship in place of the ineffective and self-stultifying powers of the Assembly in the Fourth Republic.

It must also be borne in mind that many assemblies in liberal democratic systems lack the procedural weapons of even the British House of Commons. Questioning the executive on the floor of the assembly is rare in most European parliaments; the French National Assembly introduced immediate oral answer questions for the first time in April 1970. Some assemblies, such as the West German Bundestag, rarely make use of the committee of inquiry and there is no provision for votes of confidence.[12]

However, it is impossible to consider the relations between the assembly and the government without emphasising the importance of the party system. Even in the United States Congress, with less party discipline than most of its European counterparts, party membership still remains the most reliable indicator of Congressional voting. Contrary to many fears expressed at the time of the appearance of mass parties at the end of the nineteenth century, power has remained with the parliamentary wings of the parties in liberal democratic systems, not with the mass organisation outside the assembly. Therefore the advent of mass parties has not weakened the power of assemblies as it was assumed it would, and this has allowed parliamentary representatives to behave more in conformity with the liberal democratic ideas of representation that were discussed in the last chapter. Thus the key to the power structure in most modern assemblies lies in the party system in the assembly itself: this is where the parliamentary leadership and executive support emerges, and this determines the degree of control and influence the assembly exercises.

Legislative functions

The law-making functions of assemblies may be seen as an extension of the function of influencing the executive. In this area, again as a consequence of administrative complexity and party organisation, the government's initiative is large. In Britain all important and controversial legislation emanates from government sources, and the very few exceptions to this rule need pronounced government support. There is provision for private members' legislation, but this is severely restricted and may, as in the period 1945–51, disappear completely.[13] In the 1979–80 session of parliament 71 government bills were successful, but only ten of 152 private members' bills received the royal assent. In the United States Congress almost 80 per cent of the bills considered come from the executive, and the fact that the presidential initiative has now become permanent and institutionalised is illustrated by a chairman of a House committee who said to a member of the administration in 1953: 'Don't expect us to start from scratch on what you people want. That's not the way we do things here – you draft the bills and we work them over.'[14]

The legislature may, in addition, be consitutionally barred from making laws on certain matters: Article 34 of the French 1958 constitution defines the subjects on which the National Assembly can make laws, and those which are the prerogative of the executive. But it is usually the more fundamental constitutional laws that are placed beyond the legal competence of the assembly, and most states provide special procedures for constitutional amendments; for example Belgium requires the election of a special assembly to consider constitutional revisions.

Executives are often armed with powers to veto legislative proposals; this is really only of importance in presidential systems such as the United States where presidential vetoes are rarely overridden by Congress.[15] There is in parliamentary regimes the threat of the dissolution of the assembly, but this is rarely used to discipline the assembly, especially in the more stable party systems of Britain and Scandinavia, and was a dead letter throughout the history of the French Fourth Republic. Most European governments survive for the whole life of the parliament, the main exceptions being those of Italy and Finland.

Most assemblies have provisions for bringing discussions on bills to an end. Closures, guillotines and adjournments are devices which can be used to prevent undue delay and obstruction by opposition parties, although recognition is given to the rights of minorities to criticise.[16] These devices are firmly entrenched in the constitution of the French Fifth Republic, and they are used quite extensively in the crowded timetable of the British House of Commons. However, they are not universal: the Netherlands, Sweden, Denmark and Norway either have no provision for them at all or they are not used. The United States Senate provides a good example of unlimited discussion: here it requires the difficult process of petition of sixteen Senators backed by two-thirds of those Senators present and voting to end a debate.

In spite of these various obstacles, the legislative activities of assemblies are important. The procedures are a fundamental means of the legitimisation of rules in a society, they provide for some oversight of government activities and they allow interest groups to operate through their parliamentary representatives. Of course, the extent of the assembly's power in the rule-making process will depend on the strength of the government, the scope of its legislative programme and the immediacy of a general election, but in most liberal democracies it is rare for a government to emerge from the legislative process with its programme unscathed. The British Labour government had many difficulties after it came into office in 1974. It was successful in 1975 in pushing the Industry Act through Parliament relatively unscathed, but had to amend its Community Land Bill of 1975 quite drastically to ensure its passage. Of course, the government suffered from temporary absences of a majority in the House of Commons, but even the Conservative governments after 1979 suffered setbacks in spite of large majorities; in 1986, for example, 70 Conservative MPs voted against the government's Shop Bill to ensure its defeat.[17]

Representative functions

Walter Bagehot once described the functions of the House of Commons as elective (maintaining the government), expressive, teaching, informing and legislative,[18] and it is the expressive, teaching and informing functions that are most relevant to the representative aspects of modern assemblies. There are elections in the vast majority of modern states, and although the resulting representative assemblies differ in status and power, they share, in varying respects, the function of providing some form of link between government and governed. They are one means of channelling demands from below and providing information and explanation from above. Bernard Crick has enlarged Bagehot's description of the functions of the House of Commons: 'The most important actual function of Parliament does not (and normally should not) consist in the threat to overthrow governments or of passing, refusing or amending legislation, but in the need to put relevant facts and fancies before the electorate which does sit in judgements upon governments.'[19] Samuel Beer has developed this line of argument, claiming that strong governments are a fact and that they should be helped in their tasks by the constant 'mobilisation' of consent of the electorate, a job which the House of Commons amongst other 'communicating' agencies should perform, and that this should be a task not limited merely to periods of elections.[20] There is little doubt that the representative function is by far the most important function of the Supreme Soviet.

The seemingly meaningless rituals of much of the procedure in representative assemblies in the passage of legislation, or the granting of money, is explicable not in terms of efficiency, but in terms of the roles that assemblies play in the legitimisation and authorisation of government policy, the resolution of conflicts between groups represented, and the need to speak to a wider audience than that of the assembly. These are important functions in the working of the whole political system and work towards the stability of the system. The communist parties in Western European assemblies may be denied participation in governing and in theory may be aiming at the overthrow of the parliamentary regime, but the fact of their being represented at legislative level in a number of political systems is a safety valve and is a support for the structural status quo. Congressmen in the United States may perhaps cynically work for the defeat of a bill by devious means to prevent their having to actually record a vote against the measure and thus anger interests in their constituencies, but what is significant here is the recognition of the link between the representative, his legislative activities and his electorate.

At a more individual level representatives reinforce these links by helping or advising particular constituents. This may only involve guidance in the field of administrative legal rights, but the 'social welfare officer' role does become more personalised when the representative seeks to satisfy patronage-seekers looking for government positions; in fact, certain rewards may have already been mortgaged to individuals as the price for supporting and furthering the representative's election to the assembly.

Internal organisation

The manner in which modern assemblies perform these tasks of influencing the executive, legislating and representing wider interests and opinions depends on their organisation and internal procedure. We have noted that efficiency may not be the goal of assemblies, in that they seek to implement more quickly government policies, especially in regard to legislation; therefore these three separate functions may conflict with each other, and this should be remembered when proposals of reform are mooted.

The number of times an assembly meets in a given period and whether the representatives regard their attendance as a full-time occupation or as an addition to some other form of employment, are important aspects of an assembly's effectiveness. The demotion of the French National Assembly under the Fifth Republic was underlined by a reduction in the length of its sessions. We have seen that the Supreme Soviet meets very infrequently, and in fact claims it as an advantage of the Soviet representative system that the members of the assembly are not set apart from their electorates. The British House of Commons attempted to extend morning sittings in 1967, but abandoned the experiment because of the hostility of certain MPs who argued that involvement in extra-parliamentary employment was a vital aspect of their role as representatives, and certainly the traditional view of the 'amateur' MP remains a significant part of parliamentary politics in Britain.

West European assemblies are still vastly inferior to the United States Congress in regard to sources of information and research facilities. This is partly due to American political life being less secretive, but American Congressmen are enabled to carry out their duties, especially that of influencing and controlling the executive, far more effectively because of their separate offices, library, Congressional professional staff and adequate funds to hire personal assistants.

The use of committees may be vital aspects of the internal organisation of assemblies. Committees have the advantages of division of labour, with its speed and specialisation, a lower degree of formality and a mitigation of the sometimes unreal party conflicts that take place on the more publicised floor of the assembly. However, they provide a most controversial aspect of assembly organisation because the arguments over the advantages and disadvantages of an extended committee system are at the heart of the discussion of what the proper functions of assemblies and the relations of the assembly with the executive are.

Committees, in the main, have two broad functions: that of assisting (in some cases dominating) the legislative process, and that of inquiring into particular problems. Both functions of committees have been developed more thoroughly in the United States than in any other assembly. The committees in the Senate and the House of Representatives monopolise the legislative procedures: bills begin in committee, are discussed and examined there and can be killed in committee without the inconvenience of a formal vote on the floor of either house. The investigatory powers of committees are of great importance; we have noted the power of the Ervin Committee on Watergate, and the House of Representatives Committee on Internal Security, formerly the House Un-American Activities Committee, was solely concerned with investigations until its abolition in 1975.[21] The committees specialise in a particular field such as foreign affairs, finance, defence, armed services, membership varying according to which party has the majority of members, the largest party always supplying the committee chairman and a majority on the committee. These committees, however, have increased their influence *vis-à-vis* the once very powerful committee chairmen. Developments in the 1970s, such as the weakening of the seniority system as a basis for the selection of chairmen, have tended to fragment further the distribution of power in Congress.[22]

The considerable power of Congressional committees results from the lack of Congressional party unity, the absence of centralised leadership and the immense local pressures exerted on Congressmen from their constituencies, but while critics base their arguments on the lack of speed and the inefficiency of the legislative process, and the ability of Congressional minorities to frustrate majority wishes, it should be remembered that the present committee system is ideal for the reconciling of conflicting interests in American politics.

Committees have emerged as power centres in the West German Bundestag: all the important legislative work of the assembly is done in committee, and committees have developed some of the specialisation of their American counterparts. However, a cabinet system (ministers and civil servants have the right to attend committee meetings), the existence of disciplined parties, the lack of information and professional staff, and the failure to develop investigatory powers, have prevented these Bundestag committees rivalling the powers of Congressional committees. French legislative committees are weaker now than under the Fourth Republic and their investigatory powers have almost disappeared. H. W. Ehrmann has made the following comment, which is still relevant:

> At present their proceedings are strictly regulated. Committees can at all times exclude press and public from their hearings and do not need to publish their findings. Moreover, the majority is able to determine the membership at will, which makes the committees meaningless to the opposition. All this has meant that only a few trivial matters have been made the subject of investigation.[23]

The committee system of the British House of Commons may also be seen in contrast to that of the American Congress. The committees lack specialisation and are involved in only a limited part of a bill's progress through the House.[24] There have been various attempts since the 1960s to strengthen the committee system of the House of Commons. Following the 1979 election, fourteen select committees were added to the main survivor of the old system, the prestigious Public Accounts Committee. These new committees were an innovation in that they paralleled existing government departments; thus there are now committees on Agriculture, Defence, Transport, etc., and they were given increased powers to hire staff and to call witnesses. It is still too early to judge how successful these committee reforms are, but they have certainly increased the amount of valuable information to MPs and thus strengthened the Commons in its role as watchdog of the executive. Critics of the new system point to the extra burden on the civil service, and there are still the old fears that specialised committees interfere with ministerial responsibilities. It is difficult to point out where the committees have influenced particular government decisions, even if they do contribute to the climate of informed opinion. The old attitudes are still illustrated by a former Labour Minister of Supply: 'The floor of the House of Commons, in open debate, is the only place that the mind of the people can effectively influence policy.'[25]

The argument over committees in representative assemblies is basically that of deciding what the main functions of assemblies are. If members are to rival the executive's sources of information, detail and speed and seek to pierce the secrecy of the increasingly complex machinery of the administrative process, it would seem that the development of an effective committee system is the only answer. But if the emphasis is on the electoral battle, on publicity rather than on direct policy influence, and on the legitimisation of government directives, then the development of committee systems in modern assemblies is not necessarily the first priority.

Second chambers

So far we have discussed the functions and organisation of assemblies without particular emphasis on whether they are bicameral or unicameral. Most modern assemblies have two chambers, the most prominent exceptions being New Zealand, which abolished the upper house in 1950, and Denmark, which did likewise in 1954, while Sweden followed in 1970.[26] The defence of second chambers rests on two foundations. Firstly, that a second chamber widens the basis of representation, and secondly, that an additional chamber may prevent hasty action by the first, acts as a conservative stabiliser and assists the first in its many duties.

The argument based on widening the representative basis of the assembly may be readily seen in federal states: the American Senate has two representatives from each of the fifty states, irrespective of population; the Australian Senate has ten members from each of the six states, and the same pattern is followed in other federal states such as the USSR and Switzerland. However, it can be seen from an examination of the power of second chambers in federal systems that a presidential system of government is necessary as well as less disciplined political parties to implement fully an effective system of state representation in the federal assembly. The Republic of Ireland has a second chamber, in theory based on a type of functional representation, members being elected by different occupations and professions, but the Irish party system modifies this type of representation. In most unitary and parliamentary regimes the second chamber is either appointed or elected indirectly; in Belgium it is elected on a different type of electoral system from the first and in Norway a single elected chamber divides in two to form a bicameral legislature.[27]

However, widening the representative basis of assemblies in this way is only valid if the second chamber has sufficient power and utility in regard to its supposed functions; but as the Abbé Siéyès once remarked: 'If the second Chamber agrees with the first it is unnecessary: if it disagrees it is pernicious.' The lower house is usually the more representative chamber measured by the yardstick of majority rule, and it is usually given the predominant role, being allowed ultimately to overrule the obstruction of the second chamber, but given executive control of the bulk of legislation this obstruction is aimed more directly at the government. Certainly second chambers can assist the lower house with the legislative programme, initiating and amending bills, but the real basis for a defence of second chambers is political: second chambers act as a more conservative force in the political system, and must be seen as indicating a fear of liberal representation in the populistic sense. Ironically, the United States Senate, which was not elected directly until the early years of the twentieth century, being previously elected by the state legislatures, has become less conservative than the more directly representative House, which is elected *en bloc* every two years, but this has mainly been due to the failure until recently to reform the outdated constituency boundaries of the House of Representatives, and there is no necessary connection between liberal policies and a more efficient reflection of popular feeling.[28]

With the major exception of the United States Senate, which is the constitutional equal and indeed has more political prestige than the House, most second chambers are politically unimportant, and attempts to increase their powers, as with the Senate in the French Fifth Republic, have failed. There are occasions when the pattern of power in the political system will increase the political importance of the second chamber in parliamentary systems. The power of the House of Lords increased after 1974 because the relative strengths of the parties in the British House of Commons had been significantly altered, i.e. no party has a strong independent majority over all the others.[29] The Australian political crisis of December 1975 illustrated this latent power of second chambers; the Senate's opposition to the Labour government's budget led to the Governor General's dismissal of the government and the ultimate defeat of the Labour Party in the ensuing general election. However, these occasions are rare, and, indeed, second chambers are often an embarrassment in that efforts to reform their composition and powers inevitably raise the question of representation and for what purpose second chambers need certain political powers. It would seem that in the absence of the development of some effective form of functional representation, a federal structure provides the greatest relevance for second chambers.

Decline of assemblies

With the development of mass disciplined parties and the increasing scope and complexity of executive powers in the twentieth century, it is fashionable to talk of the decline of assemblies. However, it must be asked whether the development of parties and the increased power of modern governments have been at the expense of assemblies. Professor Beer has argued convincingly that in Britain there must be sharp qualifications to the view of an increasingly powerful executive. He sees the growth of a form of functional representation alongside the traditional representative system, and it is this which seriously limits the government's power; and he points out that it is 'pluralistic stagnation' that is the danger, not the efficiency of modern governments. Governments may not be strong enough to resist the various group pressures, and they need parliament to establish links with the electorate.

Part of the problem is the rosy view of nineteenth-century liberal representation and the myth of the sovereignty of assemblies, political, if not legal as well. The history of the French Fourth Republic, like that of the Third, illustrates that this may not mean so much control of the executive, but 'immobilism': the ability to prevent anything happening. Assemblies have never 'governed', and therefore a discussion of their supposedly decreasing powers can only take place within an agreed framework of what their functions are. We therefore return to the representative functions of assemblies and their role as links between governments and governed. J. Blondel has pertinently argued that: 'While the "decline of legislatures" may be apparent to some – limited – aspects of rule making, the decline of assemblies as communicating mechanisms can scarcely be substantiated.'[30] It is a question therefore of whether assemblies can become more efficient in this communicating process.

References

1. See K. R. Mackenzie, *The English Parliament* (London, 1959) for an account of the origins of the English parliament.
2. See S. White, 'The USSR Supreme Soviet: a Developmental Perspective', in *Communist Legislatures in Comparative Perspective* eds D. Nelson and S. White, (London, 1982) pp. 125–59.
3. See M. Green, *Who Runs Congress* 4th ed. (New York, 1984) pp. 161–220.
4. See J. R. Frears, *Politics in the Giscard Presidency* (London, 1981) pp. 161–6.
5. See J. P. Mackintosh, *The British Cabinet*, 3rd ed. (London, 1977) ch. 23.
6. A. H. Birch, *The British System of Government*, 4th ed. (London, 1980) p. 37.
7. P. Avril, *Politics in France* (London, 1969) ch. 2.
8. Mackintosh, *The British Cabinet*, pp. 430–1.
9. The Gulf of Tonkin incident was an alleged attack by North Vietnamese torpedo boats on two American destroyers off the North Vietnamese coast in 1964. President Johnson, as a result of the publicity this incident received, sought and got a free hand to use American forces wherever he chose in Vietnam. The resolution was repealed in June 1970. Johnson's successor, Nixon, defended himself over his handling of the war on the grounds of his constitutional position as commander-in-chief of American forces, not on the grounds of this Resolution.
10. The full title of the Ervin committee set up in February 1973 was the Senate Select Committee on Presidential Campaign activities. The numerous committees investigating the Iran–Contra affair were finally reduced to two, one in the House and one in the Senate, by 1987.
11. See B. Crick, *Reform of Parliament*, 2nd ed. (London, 1966) ch. 1.
12. See G. Smith, *Democracy in Western Germany*, 3rd ed. (London, 1986) pp. 63–6.
13. See P. A. Bromhead, *Private Members' Bills* (London, 1956).
14. Quoted in R. Neustadt, 'Presidency and Legislation', *American Political Science Review*, XLVIII (Dec. 1955) p. 1015.

15. In the 94th Congress, President Ford vetoed sixteen Congressional Bills and Congress, with a large Democratic majority, was able to override only three of these Presidential vetoes. See D. W. Rhohde and D. M. Simon, 'Presidential Vetoes and Congressional Response: A Study of Institutional Conflict', *American Journal of Political Science*, 29.3 (August 1985) pp. 397–427. Also G. W. Copeland, 'When Congress and President Collide; Why Presidents Veto Legislation', *The Journal of Politics*, 45, 3 (August 1983) pp. 696–710.
16. Closure is a means of bringing a debate to an end at any stage if enough members agree. It was first applied in the British House of Commons in 1881 after a debate lasting 41½ hours; it needs the support of 100 members and the permission of the Speaker. The 'guillotine' allows a specific time period for each section of a Bill.
17. See D. Coates, *Labour in Power?* (London, 1980) pp. 149–54. Also see I. Burton and G. Drewry, 'Public Legislation: 1981/2 and 1982/3', *Parliamentary Affairs*, 38, 2 (Spring 1985) pp. 219–52,
18. Walter Bagehot, *The English Constitution*, (London, 1963) pp. 150–4. Also see J. Obler, 'Legislatures and the Survival of Political Systems', *Political Science Quarterly*, 96, 1 (Spring, 1981) pp. 127–39 for a criticism of the functional approach to the study of legislatures.
19. Crick, *Reform of Parliament*, p. 238.
20. S. Beer, 'The British Legislature and the Problems of Mobilising Consent', in *Essays on Reform*, ed. B. Crick (Oxford, 1967).
21. See W. Goodman, *The Committee* (London, 1969) for a history of the Un-American Activities Committee.
22. See S. C. Patterson, 'The Semi-Sovereign Congress', in *The New American Political System*, ed. A. King (Washington, 1978) pp. 160-3.
23. H. W. Ehrmann, *Politics in France*, 4th ed. (Boston, 1983) p. 315.
24. The stages that a Bill passes through in the House of Commons are the formal First Reading, the Second Reading concerned with the general principles of the Bill, then either a Standing Committee or a Committee of the Whole House for the committee stage, a Report Stage and finally a formal Third Reading.
25. G. R. Strauss, 'The Case Against Specialised Committees', *The Times*, June 1966.
26. The Gambia is an example of an African state with a unicameral legislature. In 1987 the Poles were considering the possibility of introducing a second chamber.
27. For a brief discussion of the constitutional aspects of second chambers, see K. C. Wheare, *Legislatures*, 2nd ed. (Oxford, 1968) ch. 8.
28. For comments on the Senate and representation, see R. A. Dahl, *Democracy in the United States*, 4th ed. (Boston, 1981) pp. 113–26.
29. The 1974 Labour Governments suffered severely from defeats in the Lords, but even the Conservatives endured important setbacks from the Upper House. See D. R. Shell, 'The House of Lords and the Thatcher Government', *Parliamentary Affairs*, 38, 1 (Winter, 1985) pp. 16–22.
30. J. Blondel, *An Introduction to Comparative Government* (London, 1969) p. 390. Also, see J. Blondel, *Comparative Legislatures* (Englewood Cliffs, NJ, 1973) pp. 140–2.

9

Organisation of Government, I

Area of study

Although assemblies have many functions, including those of law- or rule-making, we have argued that their main function is that of providing a link between governments and governed. When we turn to governments we find similar overlapping functions ascribed to particular parts of the governmental machine. Traditionally distinction has been made between making policy and putting that policy into operation, rule-making and rule application, and it has been customary to distinguish between different roles of the political executive and the professional administration. Thus according to liberal democratic theory the minister made policy and was responsible to the parliament for that policy-making and also for the policy implementation of his department, while his civil servants, although not necessarily anonymous, were certainly not politically reponsible to the assembly in this way, only indirectly through the minister.

The distinction between the executive in this political sense, and the administration in the permanent sense, is difficult to sustain. It does point to some important differences of status and functions, but even in political systems where the dividing line between politicians and civil servants is clearer, it is impossible to see top civil servants without any degree of policy initiative, especially given the increasing complexity and scope of the policy-making process in modern 'welfare' states. Civil servants have a far greater degree of independence and wider powers of policy initiation than constitutional myths will allow; they are as firmly a part of the political process as are parties and pressure groups.[1] The breakdown of the traditional allocation of functions in the political system has gone further in that not only are bureaucrats seen to trespass into the judicial field, as we shall see later with administrative courts, but the judiciary itself is equally part of this rule-making and rule application process.

In some states the distinction between politicians, responsible ultimately to an electorate and owing their political position to a process of party recruitment, and civil servants, trained and selected on the basis of special skills, and ready to implement the commands of their political overlords, is very thin indeed. Unlike British civil servants, their French counterparts are allowed to take part in political party activities, and are less concerned to avoid party labels. In the French Fourth Republic over half the ministers came from civil service backgrounds and the number of Ministers without parliamentary experience is still quite high compared with governments of the Fourth Republic. The number without this experience was large between 1958 and 1962, and again increased in the mid-1970s, with a third of the Cabinet in 1976 coming from outside the National Assembly, and this has not changed.[2] In the Soviet Union the distinction between 'politician' and 'bureaucrat' is even more difficult to define at the top levels of Soviet government. The administration is the party's servant, and the party becomes a bureaucratic machine itself in the effort to parallel other rival power structures in the Soviet system of government. As Merle Fainsod has pointed out:

> Soviet public administration is one-party administration. The conception of the politically neutral civil servant who serves his successive political masters 'with equal fidelity and equal contempt' is utterly foreign to the Soviet scene. Soviet public administration is suffused with political content.[3]

The dividing lines between political policy-making and bureaucratic implementation are confused in developing countries. Policy implications are present in all significant administrative behaviour, and in political systems where the development of party systems and other coherent power centres may be lacking, the bureaucrats are less likely to be the passive pawns of political leaders, especially as there may be strong cultural differences between the nationalist politicians and the ex-colonial trained civil service.[4]

The extent to which civil servants have trespassed into 'political' areas even in stable liberal democracies has been emphasised by Richard Rose in relation to British government.[5] He has argued that British political parties do not attempt to monopolise the important positions in the machinery of government, and that there is a lack of continuity in the positions that are occupied by party politicians. British government, he says, does not provide the politician with the necessary expertise and experience to rival the permanent administrator, nor with the encouragement to develop long-term political solutions: the result, argues Professor Rose, is government decision-making by civil servants.[6]

Thus it is difficult to make clear-cut distinctions between the bureaucracy and the political executive of prime ministers, chancellors, presidents and their cabinets in regard to their functions. Nevertheless, some distinctions can be made, and even at the risk of methodological confusion, it is convenient to separate a discussion of political chief executives of state and their bureaucratic assistants.

Chief executives

Terminology presents certain difficulties in discussing chief executives. The terms 'prime minister', 'chancellor' and 'president' mean different things in different political structures: there are significant variations in the political significance of the presidents of France, the United States and West Germany in relation to the distribution of political power in their respective countries. In some political systems there is a distinction between the political head of state and the ceremonial head of state; there is always the division in liberal democratic parliamentary regimes, but in presidential systems such as the United States the roles are fused in one person.

Chief executive powers may not be vested in one person, but dispersed between two or more individuals. In the Soviet Union, since the fall of Khrushchev in 1964, power has been collectively exercised by the top leaders of the Communist Party of the Soviet Union. The Fifth French Republic allowed the president to exercise more real power than the prime minister, but with the same constitution, the 1985 election forced President Mitterrand to concede more power to prime minister Chirac. Constitutional frameworks often hide more than they illustrate about the distribution of political power with regard to chief executives. Richard Neustadt has illustrated the possible divorce between constitutional rights and political power with the anecdote of President Truman contemplating the election of General Eisenhower as his successor in 1952: 'He'll sit here', Truman would remark (tapping his desk for emphasis), 'and he'll say, "Do this! Do that!" *And nothing will happen.* Poor Ike – it won't be a bit like the army. He'll find it very frustrating.'[7]

The generalisation is often made that the twentieth century has seen an increase in the power of chief executives, but even allowing for some historical distortion, we are back to the question asked in the second chapter, power in relation to whom or what? Governments and administrations may not be synonymous with the power of chief executives, and we may be in danger of crediting modern governments with a more monolithic nature than they in fact possess. Nazi Germany, far from being a hierarchical pyramid of power relationships, dominated by Hitler, resembled in fact a feudal regime in which the barons fought and intrigued against each other for the attention and favours of the Führer, and the power to cultivate their own private empires away from their leader's interest.[8]

Chief executives in liberal democracies may be divided into prime ministerial and presidential types, although there are exceptions, such as Switzerland with its Federal Council. In presidential systems both the political and ceremonial functions of head of state are vested in one man. The American president is elected for a four-year term of office and is limited to only two successive terms by the Twenty-Second Amendment to the constitution. He is elected directly by the people (by means of the Electoral College), not by Congress, and is not responsible to Congress in any formal manner. Although Congress may control the supply of money, veto nominations and investigate aspects of government machinery and policy, the office of president is far from the Jeffersonian concept of the president as chief servant to implement the will of Congress.

The president and Congress are elected by different constituents at different times, and often a different party controls the presidency and the legislature with no serious consequences for American government. Advisers and cabinet members are chosen with a large degree of political freedom by the president, and modern presidents show an even greater tendency to choose their executive assistants from outside Congress. It has been estimated that whereas in the period 1861–96 37 per cent of cabinet appointments were from Congress, between 1941 and 1963 this figure had dropped to only 15 per cent.[9] Carter and Reagan continued this tendency to recruit from non-political backgrounds. The overwhelming majority of their Cabinets came from universities, business and law; few had ever won elective office.[10]

A president or a hereditary monarch may be the ceremonial head of state in parliamentary-cabinet systems of government. The British monarchy monopolises the prestige as formal head of the executive but has a minimum and decreasing degree of political power. The Conservative Party's decision to elect its leader and potential prime minister, a method first used in 1965, is a further obstacle to the monarch exercising the initiative of seeking a prime minister who would gain the support of a majority in the House of Commons, a task which constitutes a major function of other formal heads of state such as the Italian president. The Labour party's selection of James Callaghan as party leader and therefore PM in April 1976 illustrates how firmly the selection process is at present in the hands of the parties with a parliamentary majority.

The British prime minister is elected to the House of Commons in the same way as any other MP; he or she must obtain a majority in the lower chamber before forming a government, and that government is, with few exceptions, chosen from amongst members of both Houses of Parliament. The prime minister and cabinet are 'responsible' to the House of Commons, that is, they must explain and defend their policies in the Commons,[11] and if the Commons withdraws its support of the government, the prime minister either resigns or advises the monarch to dissolve parliament in order to seek fresh support through a general election. The British prime minister dominates the House of Commons far more effectively than the American president does Congress, but the reason may lie only partly in the formal constitutional differences and owe more to the differences in the British and American party systems.

If we take the Soviet Union as an example of an executive in a non-liberal democratic state, we find that the ceremonial functions of state are performed by the Presidium of the Supreme Soviet, which under the constitution is elected by both houses of the Supreme Soviet. The Presidium convenes and dissolves the Supreme Soviet, appoints and dismisses cabinet ministers, and the chairman of the Presidium is regarded as titular head of the Soviet Union. Executive and administrative authority is vested in the Council of Ministers, whose chairman may be regarded as the Soviet prime minister. In theory, this body is responsible to the Supreme Soviet and the Presidium, but its members are not always drawn from those bodies. However, because of the size of the Council of Ministers, decision-making is carried out by an 'inner cabinet', the Presidium of the Council of Ministers. It is this body that provides the all-important connecting threads between the apex of the Communist Party, the Politburo, and the organs of government, since the top leadership of the Party is reflected in this executive arm of state. In spite of historical examples, executives in socialist or fascist systems are not necessarily characterised by the domination of one individual such as a Stalin or a Hitler, and the present collective leadership in the Soviet Union is an example of this dispersal of power. It is the fusion and overlapping of executive and legislative powers in the Politburo that is the most outstanding characteristic.

Autocratic systems present more difficulties in the attempts to discuss executive heads. Conservative autocracies such as Saudi Arabia illustrate the exercise of executive chief of state functions by a hereditary monarch, although certain offices common to other systems may exist, such as a prime minister.

The relationship between these types of ruling monarchs and their prime ministers resembles the British system in the eighteenth century or that of Bismarck and the German emperor at the end of the nineteenth century; the prime minister or chancellor is dependent on the support of the monarch, not of any representative assembly, for his continuation in office even where elections take place. Of course, the concentration of executive power in one man may be legitimised through elections; the domination of France between 1851 and 1869 by Louis Napoléon is a most interesting European example of plebiscitary dictatorship. The Portuguese dictator Salazar monopolised executive power between 1932 and 1968 holding only the office of prime minister.[12]

Military juntas provide a different type of executive structure, and the former Greek dictatorship of the army colonels, 1967–74 is an example of this type of political executive operating within the former formal constitutional structures. Usually the leaders of successful coups or revolutions wish to legitimise the new power structure: the Spanish dictator Franco re-introduced the monarchy in an attempt to stabilise the existing structure after his death. The Brazilian army which seized control in 1964 suspended certain constitutional rights, but secured the election of successive generals as Brazilian presidents, and in the face of opposition passed an emergency act in December 1968 closing Congress and giving almost limitless discretionary power to the president. The Portuguese military junta held a series of elections after the coup of April 1974 to legitimise the new regime in an apparently genuine desire to find an alternative form of government.

Origins and stability of chief executives

Chief executives, whether constitutional monarchs, civilian presidents or military dictators, are rarely representative in that they reflect the numerically dominant social classes, ethnic groups, etc., in society. They are produced by powerful groups such as the church or the army, or they are recruited by the political party machines. Armies supply the chief executives in many developing political systems not only because of their monopoly of physical force, but also from the concentration of technical and administrative competence in the armed forces, and sometimes their ability to cut across tribal divisions. Archbishop Makarios, president of Cyprus, provided an interesting example of one source of recruitment, not as common in modern states; and the origins of South African prime ministers, especially since 1948, have been determined by the political dominance of one of the two white minorities. But usually, political parties on a wide franchise have forced traditional élites in society to widen the avenues for political promotion. In socialist systems the political party becomes the sole source of recruitment, and these states have been more successful than other authoritarian regimes in resisting army coups.[13]

In liberal democracies executives are recruited from established political élites working through the political parties. Thus in Britain Labour prime ministers often have an almost identical social background to that of Conservative prime ministers, and Ramsay MacDonald may be said to have been the only prime minister of working-class origins, although Wilson, Callaghan, Heath and Thatcher were lower middle class in origin. A similar position is found in West Germany, although without the same concentration on a few schools and universities as in Britain. The West German top political leadership continues to come from the top social strata.[14] The United States provides one of the best examples in liberal democratic system of recruitment of chief executives outside the ranks of the political party professionals. President Eisenhower, who was sought after by both political parties as a presidential candidate, and who is credited with the remark that he did not in fact like politics, joins the long list of American presidents who were nominated and elected on the basis of non-political achievements.[15]

The processes of achieving the position of chief executive are varied. In socialist regimes the emphasis is on the manoeuvring within the single party: Stalin achieved supreme power by his control of the party bureaucracy and his subsequent ruthlessness in dealing with Party rivals.[16] In liberal democracies not only is the intra-party battle usual, but there is also the necessity of defeating rival political party leaders in competitive elections, if not always to gain power, at least to retain it. There are also what can be termed the various extra-constitutional means of achieving chief executive power, such as coups and civil wars and perhaps imposition by a foreign power. However, it is difficult to classify some means of achieving executive control as constitutional and others as not. General de Gaulle was invested with chief executive powers in 1958 by the president of the Fourth Republic, but the potential army revolt in Algeria could not be ignored. Hitler was invited to become German chancellor by President Hindenburg in 1933, but since 1930 successive governments had been ruling by emergency decrees, and although the strict letter of the constitutional laws was observed with Hitler's succession, the political situation in Germany made it something of an academic question.

The stability of the chief executive varies. Lord Bryce once remarked that 'the problem of constructing a stable executive in a democratic country is indeed so immensely difficult that anything short of failure deserves to be called a success',[17] and this was Bryce's view of the office of American president. The term of office of a president of the United States has only been interrupted by the death of the president, with one exception, Nixon's resignation, and furthermore the nomination for a second term of office of an incumbent is seldom denied to him by his political party. Presidents Truman and Lyndon Johnson refused to accept renomination on the grounds that they would be unlikely to win the ensuing presidential election. However, there are signs that the former stability is being threatened by electoral volatility. Ford, in 1970, was the first president since Hoover, in 1932, not to be returned to office by the electorate, although he was not originally elected to the presidency, and Carter was decisively defeated in 1980.

In regard to parliamentary liberal democracies, the examples of France and Italy have been frequently quoted to illustrate the instability of executive leadership, but Sweden, and to a lesser extent Australia, show not only the long domination of government by one party, but the stability of the governments those parties have supported. In Britain since 1945, Attlee in 1951, Home in 1964, Wilson in 1970, Heath in 1974 and Callaghan in 1979 have suffered reversals in general elections while holding the office of prime minister, although Thatcher's dominance after 1979 emphasises the stable elements in British cabinet government. In British Government the governing party's support for its leader and prime minister is very consistent. No Labour prime minister has been forced out of office by his party. The Conservative Party, which has enjoyed office for longer periods, also reflects this basic stability of executive power, and it could be argued that only Balfour in 1905 and Neville Chamberlain can be said to have lost office through declining support in their own party. In one sense it could be said that Chamberlain resigned in 1940 more on account of the Labour Party's refusal to join his wartime coalition, and even the loss of the customary loyalty of some Conservative MPs was due to abnormal conditions. Both Eden in 1956 and Macmillan in 1963 resigned as a result of ill health, not as a result of their own party's hostility.[18] In the twentieth century only four prime ministers, Balfour, Asquith in 1916, Lloyd George in 1922 and Chamberlain, can be said to have been forced out of office through difficulties within the government party or parties, and only MacDonald in 1924 and Callaghan in 1979 have held general elections following parliamentary defeats.

Of course, it is very difficult to discuss the stability of chief executives in liberal democratic systems without reference to the party system and the electoral system.[19] Furthermore, the degree of stability of all these various governments is very similar when compared to the durability of chief executives in authoritarian regimes. Salazar, Mussolini and Hitler held power for thirty-six, twenty-one and twelve years respectively, and Franco ruled for over thirty years.

The Soviet Union provides an illustration of stability and change in socialist systems. Stalin died in 1953 after having monopolised all sources of executive power of the Party and the state. His immediate successor Malenkov became both chairman of the Council of Ministers, the equivalent of prime minister, and chief secretary of the Central Committee of the Communist Party,[20] the most influential position inside the Party. In the ensuing struggle for power with Khrushchev, Malenkov relied on the state executive machinery as opposed to the control of the Party, and his replacement as first secretary of the Party in October 1953 by Khrushchev was followed in 1955 by Bulganin, Khrushchev's ally, replacing Malenkov as chairman of the Council of Ministers. The seal was put on Khrushchev's victory by the expulsion of Malenkov and other opponents from the governing bodies of the Party, the Central Committee and the Presidium, in 1957. In 1958 Khrushchev replaced Bulganin as chairman of the Council of Ministers, and appeared to have followed Stalin's example of concentrating Party and state sources of executive power in his own hands. Khrushchev was successful in his leadership struggle because his political abilities and his career within the Communist Party apparatus enabled him to secure support within the top levels of the Party hierarchy.

Two further points are worthy of notice in this post-Stalinist power struggle and that of 1964 when Khrushchev was replaced. Firstly, defeat in the political power struggle did not have the disastrous consequences of the Stalinist period, when possible opponents were killed: among the top leaders only Beria, head of the political secret police, was murdered in the 1953 struggle. Secondly, policies followed by the Soviet government seem to play an increasingly important part in determining the distribution of political power. Khrushchev was replaced by Brezhnev as first secretary and by Kosygin as chairman of the Council of Ministers as a result of his failures in economic and foreign policy, his leniency to critics of the Soviet political system, his inability to satisfy consumer demands and his many administrative reorganisations; there was also the factor of his personal idiosyncracies. Gorbachev's accession in 1985 as General Secretary of the CPSU, after Chernenko's death, emphasised orderly succession and maintained the division between State and Party leadership.

Functions and powers of chief executives

Putting on one side the ceremonial functions of the formal head of state or the formal functions of the political executive, the most important function of the chief political executive is that of providing policy-making leadership to the government, and this gives rise to definitional boundary problems. The traditional areas of executive action, such as foreign policy, defence and internal policing, have been joined by the crucial roles modern governments play in the management of the economy and in attempting to satisfy demands for social welfare. It is these additional functions that have added to the complex nature of the decision-making process and increased the size of modern bureaucracies, with the political executive having to ensure co-ordination throughout the whole government machine. A nineteenth-century British prime minister such as Robert Peel could participate in all the decision-making of central government, but modern chief executives must delegate in ways that allow, for example, such an important piece of modern legislation as the 1944 Education Act to weave its way through the House of Commons without once being considered by the cabinet.

The increased scope of modern governments has been partly the result of technological changes, but a significant factor in the twentieth century in major political systems has been the totality of modern wars. As A. J. P. Taylor has pointed out: 'Until August 1914 a sensible law abiding Englishman could pass through life and hardly notice the existence of the state beyond the post office and the policeman.'[21]

One area in which the chief executive is most active is that of foreign policy. The degree of freedom in this sphere is due partly to reduced electoral considerations and partly to the need for speed and secrecy of action. The Cuban missile crisis of 1962 is an illustration of the speed of response and personal decision-making by Kennedy and Khrushchev. There was little opportunity to consult and win approval of other power centres in the American system on the part of President Kennedy, although he was constantly explaining his actions in public. The episode underlined the comments of Woodrow Wilson in 1908, four years before he became American president: 'One of the greatest of the President's powers ... [is] his control which is very absolute, of the foreign relations of the nation.' The power of the American president in 1962, or in relation to the Vietnam war, can be paralleled in parliamentary systems by the power of the British prime minister during the Suez and Falklands crises of 1956 and 1982.[22]

A significant area of chief executive responsibility is that which demands emergency action in the constitutional sense. All modern executives have developed a degree of freedom in defining emergencies and an increase of power to deal with them. The British government was granted dictatorial powers by the Emergency Powers Act of 1940, which passed through all its parliamentary stages in a single day, and gave unlimited power in practice to the government over citizens and their property. Article 16 of the French constitution of 1958 reads:

> When there exists a serious and immediate threat to the institutions of the Republic, the independence of the Nation, the integrity of its territory or the fulfilment of its international obligations, and the regular functioning of the constitutional public authorities has been interrupted, the President of the Republic takes the measures required by the circumstances, after consulting officially the Prime Minister, the Presidents of the Assemblies and the Constitutional Council.

This article could institute a period of presidential dictatorship, and is similar to the clause in the German Weimar constitution which allowed the president to abrogate civil rights and pass legislation by decree, and which was invoked frequently between 1930 and Hitler's assumption of powers in 1933.

Chief executives and the political process

The claim of decreasing control of governments and increasing scope of administrative activity is not necessarily to be equated with the increased power of governments or chief executives. Certainly presidents, prime ministers and chancellors are at the centre of government activity and their power to appoint the rest of the members of the government is a very real power indeed. However, as Richard Neustadt has observed in a perceptive analysis of the power of the American presidency, the process of influence must go further than the mere power to appoint and dismiss; it must be a continual ability to personally affect the behaviour of those he has appointed. Thus President

Truman's dismissal of General MacArthur during the Korean War, far from being an example of presidential power, was in fact a confession of weakness: Truman had failed to influence events by other means, and the dismissal of such an important figure as MacArthur, with the severe political consequences that it entailed, was a last resort on the part of the president.[25]

Chief executives rarely have a free hand in the selection and appointment of members of their governments; electoral considerations, the party balance of power, and the danger in leaving outside the government prominent rivals who could become a centre for discontent, act as restraints. The ability to survive is not a true indication of executive power, but the number of concessions that have to be made to ensure the support that makes survival possible. Harold Macmillan dismissed a third of his cabinet in 1962, and this, it could be argued, was an illustration of the power of the British prime minister, but the dismissals were partly dictated by the fall in the electoral popularity of the government, they lessened the scope for further changes, and they may have been connected with the willingness of Macmillan to resign in 1963. Certainly the struggle over the succession to Macmillan as Conservative prime minister did little to enhance the political strength of Home, although he only narrowly lost the 1964 election.[24]

The office of chief executive, whether prime minister, president, etc., does invest the individuals concerned with authority that they do not possess as politicians, and this strengthens their position against potential rivals. Moreover, the publicity and the opportunities to exploit the mass media are important factors: de Gaulle was a master in the utilisation of television, and his carefully staged press conferences were designed to create the impression of aloof royalty unsullied by the real world of political bargaining and compromise. With political recruitment falling more and more into the hands of political parties, it is rare for a head of government to reach the top position without the ability and personality for political advancement: political parties in both socialist and liberal democratic systems provide thorough selection processes, and the party is the key to executive stability in these systems.

An important aspect of the power of chief executives is the relationship with other members of the government. The British prime minister's relations with his cabinet have led to discussions about whether the British system of government can be called cabinet government any longer, and whether we should speak of prime ministerial or even presidential government.[25] A significant aspect of the chief executive's position *vis-à-vis* other members of his government is the growth of the leader's personal secretariat, which is drawn from outside the ranks of the party and the professional civil service. It provides individual advisers and a barrier between the leader and the rest of the government. There is the President's Office in France[26] and the Prime Minister's Office in Britain, but the most developed is the American president's White House Office.

The American president has a formal cabinet which since the Eisenhower presidency has infrequent full meetings. Far more important is the Executive Office of the President, created in 1939, of which a principal part is the White House Office. It consists of personal advisers who are directly responsible to the president and who assist with co-ordination within the administration, relations with Congress, speech-writing, press relations and policy advice. This 'praetorian guard', as it has been called, is successful in even protecting the president from his own cabinet; the careers of Haldeman with Nixon and Regan with Reagan provide good examples of this protection.[27] However, the danger of any personal body of advisers is that they may insulate the leader too effectively from outside political pressures, which may result in party or electoral disaster.

There are various bases that a modern government leader must secure to ensure his retention of office: the distribution of power in the political party, relations with the assembly, electoral considerations and the co-operation of powerful pressure groups, such as business, labour or the church. The loyalty of the armed forces is a factor in some political systems. But apart from these 'external' considerations, the most difficult problem is to ensure oversight of the whole administrative structure of government; this is the most subtle, and the hardest to paint in black and white. A leader can organise and reorganise the structure of the administrative machine and the political controls, and he may have full constitutional powers of appointment and dismissal and wide opportunities for patronage, but the complicated machinery of the modern state may still defy him. Richard Neustadt has summed up aspects of this approach to executive power when commenting on the power of the British prime minister:

> The P.M.'s hold on ministers at most times is so great that he can have his way with them in matters of this sort if he is determined to. On the other hand his hold on civil servants is tenuous, and that's the real separation of power in the British system, as I understand it.[28]

The organisation and the nature of the political controls over the bureaucracy are, therefore, important aspects of government structure, and it is to this side of the government machine that we will now turn our attention.

References

1. Richard Crossman has many interesting points to make about the power of the civil service in Britain; see *The Diaries of a Cabinet Minister*, vol. I (London, 1975) and vol. II (London, 1976). Also B. Sedgemore, *The Secret Constitution. An Analysis of the Political Establishment* (London, 1980); and P. Kellner and Lord Crowther-Hunt, *The Civil Servants* (London, 1980).
2. See V. Wright, *The Government and Politics of France*, 2nd ed. (London, 1983) p. 87.
3. M. Fainsod, *How Russia is Ruled*, 2nd ed. (Harvard, 1963) p. 387.
4. See J. LaPalombara, 'An Overview of Bureaucracy and Political Development', in *Bureaucracy and Political Development*, ed. J. LaPalombara, 2nd ed. (Princeton, 1967) pp. 3–33.
5. R. Rose, *The Problem of Party Government* (London, 1974) pp. 379–426. See also R. Rose, *Do Parties Make a Difference*, 2nd. ed. (London, 1984).
6. See H. Wilson, *The Labour Government, 1964–70* (London, 1971); Marcia Williams, *Inside Number 10* (London, 1972). These illustrate the reactions to the power of the civil service during the Labour administrations of 1964–70.
7. R. E. Neustadt, *Presidential Power*, 2nd ed. (New York, 1964) p. 22.
8. For an account of the Nazi regime, see Robert Koehl, 'Feudal Aspects of National Socialism', *American Political Science Review*, LIV, 4 (Dec. 1960) pp. 921–33.
9. S. P. Huntington, 'Congressional Responses to the 20th Century', in *Congress and America's Future*, ed. D. B. Truman (Englewood Cliffs, NJ, 1965) ch. 1.
10. H. Heclo, 'Issue Networks and Executive Establishment', in *The New American Political System*, ed. A. King (Washington, 1978) pp. 87–124. Also see N. Polsby, 'Presidential Cabinet Making', *Political Science Quarterly*, 93 (1978) pp. 15–25. Also, J. W. Riddlesperger and J. D. King, 'Presidential Appointments to the Cabinet, Executive Office, and the White House Staff', *Presidential Studies Quarterly*, XVI, 4 (Fall, 1986) pp. 691–9.
11. For a discussion of ministerial responsibility, see J. P. Mackintosh. *The British*

Cabinet, 3rd ed. (London, 1977) pp. 529–36; and A. H. Birch, *Representative and Responsible Government* (London, 1964) chs 10, 11.

12. See Antonio de Figueiredo, *Portugal: Fifty Years of Dictatorship* (London, 1975).
13. See Chapter 12. In Poland the Communist Party in effect abdicated power to the military authorities in December 1981.
14. See L. Edinger, *West German Politics* (New York, 1986) pp. 127–34.
15. See M. Cunliffe, *American Presidents and the Presidency* (London, 1972).
16. See I. Deutscher, *Stalin* (Oxford, 1967) chs 7, 8, 9.
17. James Bryce, *The American Commonwealth*, 3rd ed. (New York, 1928), vol. 1, p. 72.
18. There has been some dispute as to the circumstances of Macmillan's resignation in 1963; for an account of these differences, see R. T. McKenzie, *British Political Parties*, 2nd ed. (London, 1963) p. 594, and J. P. Mackintosh, 'A Rejoinder', in *The British Prime Minister*, ed. A. King (London, 1969), pp. 191–210. See also H. Macmillan, *At the End of the Day, 1961–63* (London, 1973) pp. 486–519. See also, A. Howard, *RAB. The Life of R. A. Butler* (London, 1987) pp. 295–323.
19. The importance of the party system was underlined by the fall of the West German Social Democratic government in late 1982. The Free Democrats switched their support to the CDU, and Chancellor Schmidt was forced out of office.
20. The titles of First Secretary and General Secretary of the Party have been used at different times to denote the same office.
21. A. J. P. Taylor, *English History, 1914–1945* (Oxford, 1965) p. 1.
22. The best account of the Suez operation and the power of Eden, the Prime Minister, is that by a member of the government at the time, Anthony Nutting, *No End of a Lesson* (London, 1967). On the 1982 Falklands War see M. Hastings and S. Jenkins, *The Battle for the Falklands*, (London, 1983).
23. Neustadt, *Presidential Power*, pp. 22–32.
24. Interesting accounts by 'insiders' in the struggles for the succession in 1963 are to be found in Reginald Bevins, *The Greasy Pole* (London, 1965) and Iain Macleod, 'The Magic Circle', *The Spectator*, 14 February 1964.
25. Crossman, *The Diaries of a Cabinet Minister*, p. 198; Mackintosh, *The British Cabinet*, ch. 24. See also H. Wilson, *The Governance of Britain* (London, 1976) p. 8 for a curt dismissal of academic views on this subject.
26. See E. N. Suleiman, 'Presidential Government in France', in *Presidents and Prime Ministers*, ed. R. Rose and E. N. Suleiman (Washington, 1980) pp. 45–85.
27. See F. I. Greenstein, 'Change and Continuity in the Modern Presidency', in *The New American Political System*, ed. King, pp. 45–85. Also, D. A. Stockman, *The Triumph of Politics. Why the Reagan Revolution Failed* (New York, 1986).
28. R. E. Neustadt, '10 Downing Street', in *The British Prime Minister*, 2nd ed. (London, 1985) p. 150. Neustadt continues, however, to argue that the PM's control would be greater if the British developed the PM's Private Office on the lines of the American White House Office. See K. Berrill, 'Strength at the Centre – The Case for a Prime Minister's Department', *The British Prime Minister*, pp. 242–57. See also M. Holmes, *The First Thatcher Government, 1979–1983* (Brighton, 1985) pp. 29–34.

10

Organisation of Government, II

Scope of government administration

We have seen that it is difficult to draw a hard and fast line between the policy-making of governments and the implementation of these policies by professional administrators,[1] and that the increased functions of modern states have emphasised the roles and the size of modern bureaucracies.[2] The regulatory fields of public health and policing have been joined by welfare functions such as education, and by those functions concerned with economic regulation and control. In some states the increased supervision of large industries has taken the form of direct control of electricity, gas, railways, road and air transport, banking and other service and production industries, all of which has necessitated a large expansion of the public service. In the Soviet Union state control of economic aspects of society is in theory absolute, and bureaucratic controls extend into the cultural spheres: the all-embracing nature of the Soviet state drives all forms of political, economic and social activity under the administrative umbrella.

This is not to seize on some new aspect of human organisation and relate it to modern political developments: public administration is a continuing feature of all political structures, but the size and the capabilities of modern bureaucracies present differences in degree. Even in the United States, where federal government interference in the economic field is relatively low compared with other liberal democracies, there are now over two and a half million civil servants, and new areas such as space exploration are naturally dominated by government agencies.[3] In Great Britain there are over 596 000 civil servants,[4] and this does not include personnel employed by the nationalised industries.[5]

Professional administrators usually have a degree of permanence denied to the politicians in most political systems. Their expertise, career specialisation, ability to control sources of technical information, sometimes a group solidarity against their political masters, as well as hierarchical structures necessitated by their increased numbers and specialisation and division of labour, can create additional obstacles to political control. In some political systems the bureaucracy presents a degree of stability, coherence and continuity that is absent from other political structures: it is claimed that the economic strides made by France in the 1950s were the result of the excellence of the permanent administrators, in the face of numerous changes of prime ministers and general government instability.[6] In West Germany the administration inspires greater trust than the politicians,[7] and as in France before 1958, bureaucratic continuity has bridged the gaps between the many political upheavals of the twentieth century.

Structure

The degree of decentralisation is an important aspect of the administrative structure. As one would expect, in most federal systems the majority of civil servants are recruited and controlled by the state and provincial governments. However, decentralisation of this sort may vary: federal functions may be carried out by the state civil service under the supervision of the federal government, or there may be parallel structures with the federal civil servants operating at state level to implement the politics of the federal government. The constitutional division of functions between the central government and the smaller units may merely leave less important functions to the state or provincial governments.

Federalism is but one aspect of decentralisation; the federal system of the United States allows for many important functions to be performed at local and state levels, but the federal administrative structure itself is far from unified. It is less of a hierarchy than a holding company. There are few large departments responsible to the president, some independent regulatory commissions such as the Interstate Commerce Commission or the Federal Communications Commission created by Congress, and a whole host of agencies and bureaux which have either been created by an act of Congress or are subdivisions of existing departments, all of which have separate, particular purposes. There are two major reasons for this lack of unity. Firstly, the division of powers between the president and the legislature: Congress creates the agencies and controls their funds, and therefore they tend to act more independently of the presidency in favour of their own programmes, not as part of a coherent executive machine, and they can play Congress and presidency off against each other to forward their own ends, in fact behaving like other pressure groups in the American political system.[8] Secondly, the top appointments in the American administrative structure are given not to career civil servants but to political appointees of the president, and therefore there is less unity within departments, agencies and bureaux, or between them. Over two thousand posts may change hands with the change of president.

The British and French administrative structures are far more hierarchical and centralised than the American model, in spite of the problems of co-ordination and departmental rivalry. This is not to say that there is necessarily more political control over the bureaucracy or that there are not certain traditions and styles within different ministries, but that given the absence of a political civil service at the top, and a more standardised system of recruitment, there is in consequence more consistent self-regulation within the administration, and the various departments act less as independent, self-contained power centres. In both countries the regions are less important parts of the administrative system, although the socialist government of President Mitterrand began almost immediately to esablish a system of greater administrative decentralisation and to weaken the role of the prefects, traditionally the agents of central government in the departments. In Britain the most important functions are usually the monopoly of the central government, but even if they are shared, the local authority dependence on central financial assistance is but one of the controls the central administration may use.

The structures of bureaucracies cannot be classified into liberal democratic and non-liberal democratic categories; as Merle Fainsod has observed: 'The ways of bureaucracy elude totalitarian and nontotalitarian labels.'[9] The Soviet administrative structure is centralised, but the federal structure does allow some decentralisation. There are four categories of ministry: (1) the All-Union ministries, which exist only at USSR level, and whose local branches and offices are directly subordinate to the centre; (2) the Union Republican ministries, which exist at the USSR and Union Republic level, although certain ministries may not exist in all Union Republics, e.g. there is no Coal Industry Ministry in certain Union Republics; (3) Republican ministries, which exist only at Union Republic level with no corresponding body at USSR level; (4) Autonomous Republican ministries, with no equivalent body at Union Republic or USSR level. These four types are listed in descending order of the degree of central control.[10] In spite of official emphasis on the unity provided by the single-party system, there is competition between various sections of the administrative system, and this 'departmentalism' is continually criticised by the higher party officials.

Functions

We have seen that a rigid distinction between rule-making and rule application is difficult and that the policy-making process, even in liberal democracies where the division is possibly easier, has to be defined broadly. This blurring of functions is inevitable given the extent of governmental activity and the permanence and specialised skills of the civil servants. Yet it would be wrong to emphasise this policy-making function unduly: there are important external controls, and some bureaucratic systems develop traditions that inhibit the civil servants from straying too far into what is regarded as the political decision-making field. Besides, the degree of policy-making initiative left to top permanent administrators depends on the nature of the political leadership provided by the ministers. Some ministers and heads of departments are more pliable mouthpieces of their civil servants and may lack political support to challenge their own administrators, The British Ministry of Energy, in the late 1970s, successfully fought for the installation of the American type of nuclear reactor despite the opposition of the Minister himself.[11] The French Ministry of Education has always attracted more 'leftist' anti-clericals than other departments; the American State Department has had important influences on presidential foreign policy-making since 1945, especially in regard to relations with the USSR.[12] The American Central Intelligence Agency is credited with both a large degree of independence and a great deal of initiative in various fields of American defence and foreign policy, and was particularly saddled with the responsibility for the disastrous Bay of Pigs (the attempted invasion of Cuba) episode in 1961.[13]

Of course it is difficult always to distinguish political and civil service influences: a consistent departmental policy may reflect consensus amongst the political leaders as much as the ability of the civil service to impose its approach to certain policies. The consistency of British foreign policy, at least in its main outlines, reflects more a widely based agreement in this area of policy-making since 1945 than a developed policy imposed by the permanent administrators in the Foreign Office. There was a degree of conflict between politicians and the Foreign Office over the future of the Falklands Isalnds before the Argentine invasion in April 1982, and the Department was heavily criticised when the crisis broke.

Policy implementation at all levels and assisting ministers in their relations with their representative assemblies in such fields as briefing ministers for questions and parliamentary committees of investigation and drafting legislation are functions of the civil service. We have already noted[14] the growth of initiative in legislative activities on the part of the executive even in systems that emphasise the separation of executive and legislative powers. The importance of these law-making functions has been enhanced with the increased powers of governments to frame rules and regulations with less reference to the legislature than the normal rule-making process requires. In Britain these are referred to as 'statutory instruments': the government, under wide powers previously granted by the legislature, may propose and implement rules and regulations which, although supervised by parliament through a select committee and possibly requiring formal parliamentary consent, in practice give the executive great freedom of action. The definition of a 'legislative' sphere in the French Fifth Republic, reserving some areas to the executive, is a more ambitious attempt in the exercise of delegated legislative functions.[15]

Administrators also take part in the process of bargaining, consulting and negotiating with pressure groups, and we have seen[16] the important obstacles that the civil service may present to the groups' bargaining power because of the fact that fewer political sanctions can be applied to the permanent administrators compared with the politicians. Often the permanent officials, backed by a traditional pride in their own impartiality, see themselves as the main protectors of what they define as the 'national interest' between the conflicting political demands of rival groups in the political system.

This pride in the professional competence of the permanent civil servants may sometimes amount to a degree of condescension to the politicians, who are subject to the winds of electoral change or intra-party rivalries, and may play an important part in the civil servants' attitudes to the political process. The permanent administrators may feel that only they can judge what is in the general interest, and that they are more competent in the fields of initiation, implementation and supervision of policy. This emphasis on the rationality and objectivity of bureaucracies is identified with Max Weber: his ideal type of bureaucracy is one in which there is a hierarchical structure, fixed rules and a clear division of labour. All is orderly, objective, rational and therefore efficient.[17]

The bureaucracy, given such pride and self-respect, may become an important stabilising force within the political system. We have referred to the roles of the civil service during the political upheavals in France and Germany in the last half-century, and this may sometimes be an even more important function of bureaucracies in developing societies with tribal or ethnic divisions, poverty, lack of industrialisation and a weakly structured party system without effective pressure group activity on the wider scale of more developed countries. Ralph Braibanti has emphasised these functions with regard to Pakistan: 'It is assumed that in Pakistan for the foreseeable future the Bureaucracy will be the principal factor in determining, interpreting, and safeguarding the policy of the state'; and he speaks of the 'Platonic guardianship' dominant in the civil service.[18] This does not imply that bureaucracies always perform these functions in all political systems.

This stabilising function may be linked to the conservative role of bureaucracies in more economically advanced liberal democracies. The British civil service has been criticised for its timidity and fear of innovation in the government process: the British civil servant sees his function as an anonymous, impartial adviser and executor of ministerial policy, and unlike the French civil servant believes that it is not his responsibility to plan for the future, but to administer the present.[19] British higher civil servants may not take part in national politics, and certainly cannot become parliamentary candidates. French civil servants have far more freedom, and if they are elected to parliament, they are placed on leave; if defeated, they simply return to their posts in the administration.[20]

The bureaucracy in some systems may be an important source of patronage for parties and government leaders: posts in the civil service can provide rewards for political support. The 1854 *Report on the Organisation of the Permanent Civil Service*, known as the Northcote–Trevelyan Report, advocated competitive entry to the British civil service supervised by the Civil Service Commission, which was to be an independent body. Some of the criticisms of the report were based on the fear that the end of the patronage system would result in the collapse of the British party system. although patronage was already in the process of disappearing before the report. The United States combined patronage and merit for the selection of its top civil servants, and the number of posts directly under the control of the president is important for the promises of reward he can make as candidate to political supporters and backers in the electoral and party struggle for the presidency. However, patronage in the American political system is declining in importance even at state and local government level.[21]

A final important function of bureaucracies is that of their own internal management. This includes the improvement of the means of internal communication, administrative co-ordination within and between departments, and the important field of personnel management, training and recruitment. There are degrees of independence in these areas, but the larger and more complex the bureaucracy becomes, the greater will the trend be towards more independent internal self-management.

Control of the bureaucracy

The need for controlling bureaucratic discretion and power is apparent in every political system. This has been emphasised in liberal democratic systems because of the representative and responsible aspects of political leadership, but even in socialist regimes the party usually possesses more communication links with the mass of the governed than the bureaucracy does, and it is the 'political' element within a system, such as the political leaders, assemblies and parties, that are the legitimising forces, not the permanent administrators. However, there is a possible conflict between the need for more representative government and the administrative need for more efficient government. This clash is significant in systems with a strong established central administration and weak representative, participatory traditions. The demands for more extensive and standardised government services may gradually transform party government into more oligarchic patterns even in the more representative liberal democracies.

One form of protection is the development of a concept of public service, and it is the absence of this concept which presents difficulties in developing countries, particularly those where no effort was made by the colonial government before independence to encourage the development of an indigenous public service. There is a stronger consciousness of this spirit in British, French and West German civil services than in the United States, partly due to the pattern of recruitment. Yet even where this tradition exists, there still remain some important obstacles to democratic control, such as the permanence of many public servants, their expertise, and size, complexity and secretive nature of modern bureaucracies.

Oversight is necessary, not merely to ensure that the wishes of the governed, indirectly expressed with varying degrees of efficiency by parties and representative assemblies, are taken into account, but also to further efficiency, administrative co-ordination and the primacy of the political arm of government in the choice of political priorities. There are problems of protecting the individual from over-zealous public officials not accountable in the usual legal and political ways, and there is also the possiblity of corruption within the administrative machine itself. The controls may be divided into three broad divisions: internal, political and legal.

The internal machinery for controlling bureaucracies consists of the self-regulatory means within the administrative structure itself. These are aimed at internal co-ordination, self-discipline and a recognition of the hierarchical structure. In Britain, the Treasury regained the task of controlling the civil service in 1982, especially with regard to its size, pay and distribution; the Conservative government abolished the Civil Service Department, established in 1968 to co-ordinate the civil service. Recruitment, however, remains in the hands of the Civil Service Commission, which works closely with the Treasury in this area, but higher promotions rests heavily on the advice of the permanent secretary of the Treasury. The Office of Management and Budget, a part of the Executive Office of the American president, exerts some degree of influence similar to that exerted by the British Treasury, by virtue of the fact that all the American administrative agencies, no matter what their degree of independence, have to clear their budgets with the Office before they are submitted to Congress.[22] The position of the Soviet Ministry of Finance in budgeting 'gives it strategic leverage as a control agency'.[23] Other departments, such as the various economic ministries, the former DEA in Britain and the former Ministry of Economic Affairs in France, were also potential conflict-resolving institutions. The methods of recruitment and training and the social background of the civil servants are other factors.

In the second category of controls, the supply of money is also important. It is the key to the oversight exercised over the administrative agencies by the American Congress, especially bearing in mind the rivalry between Congress and the presidency. Yet even where assemblies lack the independence of the American Congress, they often have various opportunities to act as watchdog over the bureaucracy. The Public Accounts Committee of the British House of Commons seeks to investigate government expenditure with the assistance of the Controller and Auditor General. It is one of the most powerful and prestigious committees of the House but it does have the disadvantage of investigating only *past* expenditure.[24]

The power to appoint civil servants is an important means of executive control; this may have to be shared with the legislature, as it is in the United States. The co-operation of the assembly may also be necessary to provide an increase in statutory powers of departments, and in 1962 President Kennedy was frustrated by Congress in his attempt to create a new department of urban affairs. Generally, the 'political' executive, supported by the stronger political party or parties, and possessing the prestige that goes with governmental authority, can exert greater controls over the bureaucracy than the assembly. We have seen[25] that chief executives are furnished with some form of personal staff which is independent of the assembly and the rest of the administrative machine, and which is responsible to the president or prime minister. Yet if the administrative machine is fragmented, and if there is competition for control from the legislature, this provides opportunities for different parts of the bureaucracy to resist the controls of the government leader, and pressure groups are able to exploit this fragmentation. The American president has his Executive Office, which includes not only the White House Office, but the Office of Management and Budget, the Council of Economic Advisors and the National Security Council; but this machinery has to be co-ordinated and controlled by the president before he can use it for wider controls. Some presidents have preferred the regularity of formal meetings, as did President Eisenhower, whereas others, such as President Kennedy, opted for a more informal, personal means of supervision. President Nixon was in the process of reforming the administrative machine before his resignation.

Administrative subservience to political demands is most complete in the Soviet Union. The control is exercised through the Central Committee of the Party or, more precisely, the secretariat of the Central Committee. The Party structures parallel the administrative structures perhaps even at the cost of inefficiency, and there is both Party penetration of the bureaucracy and overall control. However, there are factions within the Party, and the bureaucracy is not as monolithic as theory suggests.[26]

The third area of control is legal/judicial. This includes the machinery and procedure for dealing with administrative corruption as well as controls to ensure impartial and efficient administration. These controls are also directed at administrators exceeding the authority that has been granted to them. These controls may be exercised through the ordinary legal channels, the civil servants being responsible to the criminal and civil courts for failure to carry out his proper functions and for the misuse of his authority. The Soviet Union in 1962 included capital punishment as a possible punishment for bribery by state officials. The highest official known to have been executed for bribery was the Deputy Fisheries Minister, in 1982.

However, the ordinary law courts may not provide an adequate degree of control of civil servants, since the dividing line between corrupt and inefficient administration is not a rigid one. A special commissioner, the ombudsman or parliamentary commissioner, has been introduced in many states, to examine complaints of maladministration. His functions and powers vary; in Britain he can report back to parliament, having no executive power of his own. The Soviet Constitution establishes the institution of the procuracy with supervisory powers over the administration. According to Smith, 'the percentage of satisfied cases is very high in procurational supervision. More than 96 per cent of all protests and representations are accepted by administrative organs, economic enterprises and social organisations in the first instance'.[27]

Some states have gone further and recognised a different code of administrative law, with separate administrative courts to adjudicate. Britain has a system of administrative tribunals, a halfway house between executive and judicial supervision,[28] but West Germany and France have distinct administrative legal systems. At the apex of the French administrative courts is the Council of State, which as well as acting as a form of protection for civil servants against the political leaders, exercises a general supervision over all forms of French administration. It can insist that civil servants justify particular actions they have taken and award damages if these have proved injurious to a citizen.[29]

Recruitment and training

Recruitment to the bureaucracy is now chiefly based on merit with selection being made through competitive exams. The West German civil service, for both the federal and regional services, demands for the higher administrative posts a university degree, usually in law, an entry examination, a rigorous three-year training period, and a second state examination. The French National School of Administration, established in 1945, an outstanding feature of the French administrative system, recruits and trains for the higher posts in the French civil service. There is open competition for two-thirds of the places, and an examination for existing civil servants to ensure the promotion of only the most intellectually able candidates. Candidates for the open places must have qualifications amounting in practice to a second university degree. The training course lasts for nearly two years; the students do not specialise for a particular branch of the civil service, but the best students are able to choose posts in the ministries with the greatest prestige. The system produces highly professionalised élites, and it is difficult to enter the civil service except at the start of one's career. The *École Polytechnique*, founded by Napoléon I, still produces top administrators with an engineering background.[30]

Recruitment for the higher civil service in Britain is similarly based on a competitive examination and a good university degree. Unlike France, there is more promotion for the middle ranks of the civil service, but these recruits to the higher civil service rarely reach the top posts. Another difference as compared with the French system is that the British examination requires a general interview, which, it is often alleged, produces distortions in the meritocratic basis of selection.[31]

Recruitment is controlled by the Civil Service Commission established in 1855, but the selection on merit was only gradually extended to the whole service and was not complete until the early years of the twentieth century. The basis of selection may be said to be still largely grounded on Macaulay's observation in 1854, a result of his experience of the Indian civil service:

> We believe that men who have been engaged up to 21 or 22 in studies which have no immediate connection with the business of any profession and of which the effect is merely to open, to invigorate and to enrich the mind, will generally be found in the business of every profession superior to men who have at 18 or 19 devoted themselves to the special studies of their calling.[32]

Even in spite of the reforms following the report of the Fulton Committee in 1968, [33] elements of this amateur basis of the higher civil service remain unbalanced by the pre-entry training of the French National School of Administration. However, the specialist classes of the British civil service, lawyers, scientists and doctors, who are recruited on the basis of existing specialist qualifications, are declining more slowly than the other classes in the civil service.

Entry to the United States civil service is distinguished not so much by political patronage at the top, as by the fact that the federal public service 'is basically job orientated, and is not a career service in the sense that the United Kingdom service is'.[34] Recruitment is mainly through open competitive exams managed by the Civil Service Commission. The Pendleton Act of 1883 first introduced selection on merit and it now extends to nearly 90 per cent of federal civil service posts, but entry is further distinguished from the British example by the absence of division into classes, and more so by the fact that entry is possible at any age. There is less of a rigid demarcation of the political and administrative areas than there is in Britain, although the barriers between permanent officials and political partisans are becoming less precise with the widening opportunities for patronage for British governments in public posts.[35] We have already noted the choice for cabinet posts of top French civil servants.

At first sight there appear to be less centralised recruiting procedures for public service in the Soviet Union: there is a body called the State Establishments Administration of the Ministry of Finance which is concerned with standardising jobs and regulating the size of departments and agencies, but recruitment would, in theory, be left to each ministry, with the emphasis on school records and close ties with special academic and training institutes, not on general competitive examinations. However, this is to ignore the system of the *nomenklatura*, which is a means of filling posts in the Soviet Union for all manner of public positions. It is a list of posts that cannot be filled without the special scrutiny and approval of special organs. Each organ has supervision over the recruitment to a given number of posts, the distribution depending on the importance of the post, some posts being reserved for the scrutiny of the Central Committee of the Party. The *nomenklatura* jobs are the most important and responsible ones, carrying large privileges and the system provides an efficient means of party control.[36]

A career-structured higher civil service and a competitive entry procedure appear to be synonymous with a preponderance of higher social class membership. The middle and upper-middle class provide the majority of the entrants to the higher public service in West Germany, Britain and France. Two-thirds of the higher civil servants in Britain were born into the upper or middle classes, with only 19 per cent being born to working-class parents. Two-thirds of those with degrees attended Oxford or Cambridge Universities, and over half attended private as opposed to state schools. As the Fulton Report observed, entry to the higher civil service in Britain is narrower than entry to most other professions and occupations.[37]

In France over 70 per cent of senior civil servants come from the upper and middle classes, with only 10 per cent coming from the manual classes, and as in Britain, the upper- and middle-class bias is even greater in regard to direct entry recruits as opposed to promoted civil servants. There is less social exclusiveness in the American federal service: nearly 25 per cent come from the working class, and a higher proportion from the lower-middle classes than in Britain or France.[38]

The social background of higher civil servants is important for a number of reasons. Firstly, an examination of administrative élites in comparison with other élites in the society is a vital indicator of the balance in prestige and power in the political process. We have noted the stability provided in German politics by the civil service, and the relative lack of respect for the political leaders. Secondly, the composition of the higher bureaucracy is a useful reflector of social forces in society: recruiting agencies are rarely in control of the type of civil servants they select; it is a process more dependent on the relationships of social class, education and the prestige of the public service. Thirdly, the existence and origin of common values and attitudes among higher administrators, given their importance in the policy-making process, has important bearings on how society is governed.

References

1. See Chapter 9.
2. I am using 'bureaucracy' in the general 'institutional' sense of public administration, and will be mainly concerned with higher level public administrators. The term 'bureaucracy' lacks a precise definition, but there are several alternative ones suggested in M. Albow, *Bureaucracy* (London, 1970) ch. 5.
3. The National Aeronautics and Space Administration Agency was established in 1958.
4. *Civil Service Statistics* (London, 1986) pp. 3–4.
5. See G. Fry, *The Changing Civil Service* (London, 1985).
6. See P. Avril, *Politics in France* (London, 1969) ch. 5. For a note of caution, see V. Wright, *The Government and Politics of France*, 2nd ed. (London, 1983) pp. 111–12.
7. See Chapter 4.
8. H. Seidman, *Politics, Position and Power* (Oxford, 1980) ch. 9.
9. M. Fainsod, *How Russia is Ruled*, 2nd ed. (Cambridge, Mass., 1967) p. 386.
10. See D. Lane, *State and Politics in the U.S.S.R.* (New York. 1985) pp. 173–206. Also see R. J. Hill, *Soviet Union* (London, 1985) pp. 108–16.
11. See B. Sedgemore, *The Secret Constitution* (London, 1980) pp. 108–125.
12. See G. Kennan, *Memoirs* (London, 1968). Kennan was an influential career specialist in the State Department in the years after 1945.
13. See A. Schlesinger, *A Thousand Days* (London, 1965) chs 9 and 10.
14. See Chapter 8.
15. See E. C. Page, *Political Authority and Bureaucratic Power* (Brighton, 1985) pp. 68–73.
16. See Chapter 6.
17. Max Weber, *The Theory of Social and Economic Organisations*, trans. A. M. Henderson and T. Parsons (Glencoe, Ill., 1947).
18. R. Braibanti, 'The Civil Service of Pakistan', in *Comparative Politics*, ed. R. R. Macridis and B. E. Brown, 3rd ed. (London, 1968) p. 470.
19. Of course this view of the British civil service is challenged. See, for example, P. Kellner and Lord Crowther-Hunt, *The Civil Servants* (London, 1980). Also see

R. Rose, 'The Political Status of Higher Civil Servants in Britain', in *Bureaucrats and Policy Making*, ed. E. N. Suleiman (New York, 1984) pp. 136–73.

20. See E. N. Suleiman 'From Right to Left: Bureaucracy and Politics in France', ibid., pp. 107–35.
21. See F. J. Sorauf, *Party Politics in America*, 5th ed. (Boston, Mass., 1984) pp. 88–92. In August 1970 the Postal Reorganisation Bill became law, and this freed the US Post Office from being the major source of presidential patronage by making it an independent agency.
22. See Page, *Political Authority and Bureaucratic Power*, pp. 77–9.
23. Fainsod, *How Russia is Ruled*, p. 409.
24. See L. Chapman, *Your Disobedient Servant* (London, 1978), Chs 8 and 9 for two case studies of the Committee at work.
25. See Chapter 9.
26. See R. Hill and P. Frank, *The Soviet Communist Party*, 3rd ed. (London, 1987) pp. 104–21.
27. G. B. Smith, *The Soviet Procuracy and the Supervision of the Administration* (Alphen aan den Rijn, 1978) p. 106.
28. D. Foulkes, *Introduction to Administrative Law*, 5th ed. (London, 1982).
29. For a comparative discussion of judicial control, see Page, *Political Authority and Bureaucratic Power*, pp. 121–9.
30. See Suleiman, *Bureaucrats and Policy Making*, pp. 109–18.
31. 'One senior Frenchman told us that he thought the British type of interview was an unfair and dishonest method of selection', *Fulton Committee Report, 1966–8*, CMND, 3638, vol. 1, 134.
32. Quoted in A. Sampson, *Anatomy of Britain Today*, (London, 1965), pp. 222–3.
33. For post-Fulton reforms, see N. Johnson, 'Change in the Civil Service: Retrospect and Prospects', *Public Administration*, 63, 4 (Winter, 1985) pp. 415–33.
34. *The Civil Service of North America, A Report of the Civil Service Department* (London, 1969) p. 39.
35. See Civil Service Department, *A Directory of Paid Public Appointments Made by Ministers* (London, 1978), for a list of the paid public appointments made by ministers.
36. See Hill and Frank, *The Soviet Communist Party*, pp. 85–9.
37. For the background of higher civil servants in Britain see Rose, 'The Political Status of Higher Civil Servants in Britain', pp. 144–5.
38. See I. Sharkansky and D. Van Meter, *Policy and Politics in American Government* (New York, 1975) ch. 10.

11

Judiciaries

The courts and the political process

The discussion in the last chapter illustrated the difficulty of confining bureaucracies to the function of implementing policy as opposed to policy-making. Likewise, in a discussion of the courts in modern political systems, it is impossible rigidly to distinguish between interpreting rules and making them, between rule-making and rule adjudication. It is sometimes convenient to separate different political structures, but this separation can be artificial, and it is often dictated by political patterns found in liberal democratic systems. Administrative courts and administrative tribunals have emerged increasingly in modern political systems,[1] and these institutions prevent an inflexible dividing line being drawn between administrative and judicial structures. This is also true of the whole legal system: judges and courts of law are significant aspects of the total political process, and a distorted view of that process would result if there were too crude a separation of functions. Robert Dahl has argued this point strongly: 'To consider the Supreme Court of the United States as a legal institution is to under-estimate its significance in the American political system. For it is also a political institution, an institution, that is to say, for arriving at decisions on controversial questions of national policy.'[2] The American Supreme Court was the pace-setter in the 1950s and 1960s on important political questions such as civil rights, with the presidency and the Congress alternating between periods of inaction and reluctant following of the political lead established by the Court in such controversial areas.

This is not to imply that all courts of law have the political independence of the American Supreme Court: there are wide differences between the American courts and those of the Soviet Union, where Party policy is recognised as superior to judgements of the courts. But it is important to recognise that legal adjudication is not a process far removed from the world of politics, and that there is an interplay between the legal structure, the political culture and the political and social values of the judges, which all bring the legal system firmly into the arena of choice, priorities and conflict.

There are two main reasons why this point, that the judicial system is part of the political process, has to be emphasised. Firstly, liberal democratic theory has traditionally put a premium on the necessity of protecting the citizen from a too powerful state, and has therefore emphasised the impartiality of the judicial process, to increase the independence of the judiciary, and to deepen the respect and confidence with which judicial decisions are received.[3] This semi-fiction is therefore a necessary aspect of the stability of many political systems. This is why there is disquiet in some liberal democratic regimes over the growth of administrative courts and quasi-judicial administrative tribunals. Secondly, it has led to the emphasising of aspects of the doctrine of the separation of powers, both to prevent too much concentration of political power in the hands of the government, and to guard against the 'excesses of democracy' or the tyranny of the majority.[4]

In socialist political systems, no lip service is paid to the doctrine of the separation of powers: the Party is considered the embodiment of the will of the people, and the courts are the servants of the people. It is not a difficult step to the conclusion that the courts, therefore, are subject to the directions of the Party, albeit not always in the form of explicit instructions. This distinction between socialist and liberal democratic attitudes to the legal system has important repercussions on the role of the courts in their respective political system, but it does not mean that the courts in liberal democracies are somehow divorced from the political process. If one were to examine, for example, the attitudes of the British courts to trade unions, one would find by looking at the Taff Vale decision of 1901, or the miners' strike of 1984–5,[5] that the courts, far from interpreting existing law, have on these occasions displayed distinct attitudes to the trade unions, attitudes which may have sprung from the values held by particular judges, or from more general societal pressures, probably from both.

To examine the role of judiciaries in the political process we need to focus on the following areas: (1) the nature of the law, and its relationship to political decision-making; (2) the structures of the courts and the selection of personnel; (3) the functions of the courts and the nature of the external controls; (4) the relation of the citizen to the legal process.

The nature of law and the political process

In liberal democratic systems the legal system is said to be characterised by such concepts as impartiality, consistency, openness, predictability and stability. All citizens, in theory, are equal before the law; the legal results of certain actions may be reasonably foreseen, and the legal procedure is known and will follow certain patterns. This is what is sometimes meant by the 'rule of law'. It is claimed that these aspects do not characterise the legal systems in socialist and autocratic states, and that the use of arbitrary powers by the police, absence of trials, secret trials, failure to publicise procedures and verdicts are the antithesis of liberal democratic systems.

However, the distinctions may be more relative than absolute. Liberal democratic systems can grant extra-ordinary powers to governments during emergencies, whether war or internal unrest, resulting in the abrogation of normal judicial procedure, and in 'normal' times the definition of internal security may be wide enough to give the police extra powers and special tribunals increased jurisdiction. We have already noted the impact of the administrative courts on the 'rule of law'. It is possible to have predictable legal rules and due processes of law in autocratic systems: the legal theories of the Prussian state and liberal democratic systems in nineteenth-century Europe seem to underline the fact that the differences are of degree rather than of kind.

In socialist systems the absence of such characteristics as impartiality and predictability may be true only of certain areas. Criminal and civil cases, involving cases of theft, slander, debts and such-like, may be conducted in a manner common in liberal democratic systems, but the uncertainty, discretion and the degree of bias are more characteristic of what are termed 'political' cases. In the Soviet Union there was a marked move towards stabilising judicial procedures after 1956–7.[6] But it is difficult to apply liberal democratic concepts to regimes whose dominant ideology is based on Marxist-Leninism. Socialists see the legal system of liberal democracies and non-Marxist totalitarian or autocratic states as instruments of class rule, and argue that the main functions of the courts in these systems are to legitimise and buttress the domination of the capitalist class. The Bolsheviks saw the temporary role of the courts, before the 'withering away of the state', not as a check on the executive, nor as a form of protection for minority rights, but as a means of enforcing the will of the majority as expressed through the ruling party.[7] There are various problems of this stage, in that all crime tends to become an ideological challenge and a possible indication of weakness of the political system. Moreover, the USSR has a wider range of crimes: they cover such categories as 'economic crimes', certain of which can be punished with the death penalty.

However, many of the different attitudes to the legal system and the role of the courts that British and American jurists find in socialist states are not the result solely of ideological differences but emanate from a contrasting development of legal procedures. East European socialist states have far more in common with continental European legal concepts than with Anglo-American. Thus pre-trial procedures, committal proceedings, the power of the state prosecutors as compared to that of the defence counsel, the role of the judge as an investigator, not an umpire, the absence of a jury system are common in many European legal systems irrespective of whether the regime can be described as liberal democratic, socialist or autocratic. These European procedures are termed 'inquisitorial' as contrasted with the Anglo-American 'accusatorial' procedures. This, of course, has important implications for the concept of 'the rule of law' which is essentially a product of British and American liberal democratic systems. This is not to imply that there are not important differences between the legal systems of socialist and liberal democratic regimes, but merely that departures from the Anglo-American legal pattern do not necessarily indicate the absence of legal concepts regarded as important in liberal democratic systems.

The West German Federal Constitutional Court provides an illustration of some of the difficulties of attempting to ideologically classify different legal systems. One observer has said of this court:

> The constitutional courts are not, nor were ever intended to be neutral, 'nonpolitical' instruments of the state in the sense of the positive tradition in German jurisprudence. Their judges are supposed to be nonpartisan in interpreting the constitutional principles of the prevailing order, but biased in favor of the regime. In other words, the constitutional courts and particularly the Federal Constitutional Court are quite explicitly judicial structures for legitimising and preserving the present political system.[8]

The Federal Constitutional Court has not hesitated to act in ways to preserve the West German political system. Article 21(2) of the 1949 Basic Law reads: 'Parties which according to their objectives or according to the behaviour of their members aim to threaten or to abolish the free democratic basic order, or to endanger the substance of the German Federal Republic, are unconstitutional. The Federal Constitutional Court shall decide on the question of unconstitutionality,' The Court, under the provisions of this article, accordingly declared a neo-Nazi party illegal in 1952 and outlawed the German Communist Party in 1956.

Legal structure and recruitment

Legal structures vary according to several factors. Federalism may necessitate parallel courts adjudicating on federal and state or provincial law. In the United States federal courts extend into every state alongside state courts, with the Supreme Court at the apex of both systems. Likewise, the Supreme Court of the USSR stands at the top of a pyramid of Supreme Courts in the Union and Autonomous Republics, with courts in area circuits and regions: at the lowest level are the people's courts in towns and rural areas. Canada has only one system of courts, although it is a federal state.

Some legal systems emphasise specialisation. In West Germany there are regular courts for civil and criminal cases, separate administrative courts and distinct constitutional courts. There are separate federal and state courts, but at the top they are integrated into a single hierarchy. In Britain there are no separate administrative and constitutional courts, but above the lowest courts there are, as in France, separate civil and criminal courts with separate courts of appeal. The highest court of appeal, the House of Lords, is unique in the sense that as well as forming part of the British legislature, it is the highest court of appeal, although by constitutional convention only members with the correct legal background may participate in these appellate functions. The Judicial Committee of the Privy Council acts as a court of appeal for some Commonwealth countries.[9]

The structure of legal systems is important for some of the functions of the courts, such as those concerned with the increasing powers of the central governments, and for the protection of administrative and civil rights, but for the wider range of functions the principles underlying the selection of the judiciary have more significance. The procedures for selecting and dismissing judges, and the background of the recruits are perhaps more crucial factors in assessing the degree of independence and in evaluating the political behaviour of judges.

Judges may be appointed by the government, elected directly or indirectly, or co-opted by fellow judges. The extent of their legal training and the nature of their qualifications also vary. West Germany and France provide the best examples of hierarchical career structures for judges. In both countries they are appointed by the government after acquiring a university degree in law, and having undergone a period of legal training culminating with a stiff competitive examination. They must choose a judicial career early in life, and are not recruited from among barristers as they are in Britain, and they have established security of tenure. The methods of recruitment and training mean that the recruits come from predominantly upper-middle-class backgrounds. In both countries they are imbued with a tradition similar to the civil service, that of impartial, dedicated service to their view of the state's interests.[10]

British judges, above magistrates, are selected from among barristers and likewise have a distinct upper-middle-class, conservative background. Also, as with other systems where some form of appointment by the government takes place, the legal profession itself has various formal and informal channels of access to influence the selection process.[11] Security of tenure of judges is another important aspect of the British legal system: judges of the superior courts may only be dismissed by both Houses of Parliament on the grounds of misbehaviour. Thus, as in France and West Germany, legal training, method of selection, security of tenure and the consequent prestige and respect given to higher court judges make them a significant conservative stablising force in the political system.

Election of judges may weaken this respect shown to them, but it may also make the judiciary more representative of the electorate or of the particular groups that direct the election. The election of judges for the lower courts in some states of the USA may make them more responsive to current political feeling in particular states, and may lead to conflict with the federal courts, especially on such issues as Black rights. In the Soviet Union all judges are elected directly or by the appropriate soviet, but in practice the recruitment of higher-level judges is carried out through the *nomenklatura* system; this provides another mechanism of Party control over the judiciary.

Constitutional courts and courts which have constitutional powers of adjudication as part of their functions are even more involved in overt political considerations as regards appointments. The Canadian Supreme Court, which was made the final court of appeal in 1949 in place of the Privy Council, must have at least three judges from Quebec to ensure ethnic and religious balance.[12] The judges of the Federal Constitutional Court of West Germany are elected by parliament, with six coming from the ranks of the career judges elected for life, and the other ten being elected from the most important groups in West Germany, such as the political parties, administration and other élite groups; these are not elected for life but only for eight years. The Constitutional Court of France, which is difficult to classify really as a court in the strict sense, but which has the power to examine the constitutionality of laws, has a different source of recruits from the regular and administrative courts. Its members are not professional judges but are past presidents of the republic, with three appointed for nine years by the president, the National Assembly and the Senate.

The American Supreme Court is nominated by the president with the consent of the Senate, and the selection, which is for life, is even more involved in political considerations than other courts with constitutional functions, or at least this aspect receives more publicity and emphasis in the United States than in the more circumspect procedures elsewhere. But these political factors involved in the appointment of American Supreme Court judges only reflect issue conflict within the American political system, they do not challenge it. As John Schmidhauser has pointed out,[13] class background in the appointment of American Supreme Court judges is important, 88 per cent coming from north-western European ethnic groups, which in American terms indicates roughly middle and upper-middle class. Nearly all the judges of the Court have had strong political commitments before appointment, but in spite of class background (or because of it) and varying political backgrounds and levels of political partnership, the Court has in recent years been more liberal on many matters, including civil rights and the race question, than other more representative parts of the American political process. Chief Justice Warren, appointed by President Eisenhower in 1953, was expected to reflect more conservatism in these areas, but instead, until his retirement in 1968, he became one of the champions of liberal issues. The difficulties of President Nixon in 1969 and 1970 in finding a replacement for Justice Fortas indicated the extent of the involvement in current political issues. The Senate's rejection of Haynesworth and Carswell,[14] only the second and third rejections in the twentieth century, forced Nixon to look outside the south to Blackmun of Minnesota, who was regarded as more moderate on many issues, including civil rights, than the two rejects. After his rejection by the Senate, Judge Carswell announced his intention of competing in the Republican Party primary in Florida for election to the United States Senate.

It should be remembered that security of tenure of judges may not necessarily indicate the independence of the judiciary from government or electoral pressures, but may be more of a sign of the underlying stability of the political system. It may also be an indication of the ability of the judiciary to underpin the authority of the more powerful élites in the political system. Robert Dahl has said of the American Supreme Court that it 'is inevitably a part of the dominant national alliance'.[15] This is a fact of all stable political systems, and the more obvious tampering with the judicial system in many developing countries is a sign of instability of the political system, not merely that the judiciary is more involved in the political process than in more developed systems.

Functions of the judiciary

The courts will have various functions to perform in the political system depending on the degree of specialisation involved. We have already noted the work of the administrative courts, and the regular courts involved in criminal and civil cases do not concern us in so far as they do not involve overtly political areas such as civil liberties. We will therefore concentrate on the functions of the constitutional courts, or on the constitutional functions of courts in systems where legal specialisation has not developed in this way. To examine this area of judicial responsibility we can look at the following four fairly distinct groups of functions: (1) judicial review and interpretation of the constitution; (2) arbitration between separate institutions in the political process; (3) general support for the existing political system; (4) the protection of individual rights.

The power to review the constitutionality of decisions and legislation varies enormously. In Britain the legal sovereignty of parliament and the absence of a codified written constitution force the courts to construe acts of parliament with the intentions of the framers of the legislation as the paramount considerations. This is far from the judicial power of review that has gradually been acquired by the Supreme Court of the United States. The famous case of Marbury *v.* Madison in 1803 established the Court's right to declare a law void if it is in opposition to the American constitution as interpreted by the Court. Generally, the Court has reflected the dominant forces in the American political process, and the right of judicial review did not provoke serious contradictions within the system until the 1930s, when the Court declared unconstitutional several of the legislative enactments of President Roosevelt's New Deal. The president did attempt to interfere with the Court to make it more amenable to what he regarded as the wishes of the majority of Americans, but although he was defeated in his attempts, the Court, after 1937, ceased to regard economic regulation by the federal government as a serious threat to the constitution, and this type of legislation has not been challenged since.

The Federal Constitutional Court of West Germany is the nearest equivalent to the American model among European states. The wide powers of judicial review were written into the 1949 constitution to protect the Federal Republic from the fate of the Weimar Republic, which allowed the rise of Hitler to power without serious infringement of the constitution. We have seen how this power has been invoked in regard to political parties of the right and left. Powers of judicial review have been granted to the Supreme Courts of Italy and Austria for similar historical reasons, but these courts lack the wide powers of the West German court.[16] The strengthening of the French Constitutional Council in 1958 (formerly the Constitutional Committee, established in 1946) marked a further move away from a republic dominated by the National Assembly, but its powers of judicial review are seriously limited by the necessity for the initiative to consider the constitutionality of legislation to come from other organs of government.

South Africa provides an interesting example of judicial review of legislation, and the government's reaction, which deserves some closer examination. In 1951 the Nationalist government introduced the Separate Representation of Voters Bill into the South African parliament; this was designed to remove coloured voters from the common electoral roll and put them on a separate roll which would elect white representatives to parliament, but at other times than general elections. As the coloured voting clause was one of the entrenched clauses of the constitution, it needed a special parliamentary majority to become law: a two-thirds majority vote of the two Houses of Parliament sitting together.

This special majority was not attained and so the South African Appeal Court, in March 1952, declared the act invalid. The government attacked the courts for political interference, and by a special bill in 1952 set up a special committee of parliament called the High Court of Parliament which was to have power to review any judgement of the Appeal Court which invalidated any act of parliament. This new Court reversed the decision previously reached by the Appeal Court. However, the Cape Provincial Division of the Supreme Court upheld the decision of the Appeal Court.

As the government could not gain the necessary two-thirds majority in parliament, it threatened various devices such as that of setting up a special Court of Constitutional Appeals. Finally, in 1955, the government, led by a new prime minister, J. G. Strijdom, won its long-drawn-out constitutional battle with the courts, firstly by appointing five new judges to the Appeal Court, and secondly by raising the number of judges required to sit on the Appeal Court when it is considering the validity of acts of parliament to eleven. The government also increased the size of the Senate to ensure the necessary two-thirds majority. New legislation was then passed, not only securing the coloured voters legislation which had initiated the constitutional conflict, but also reducing the entrenched clauses of the constitution and limiting the courts' rights to question the validity of any legislation other than the one remaining entrenched clause. The enlarged Appeal Court validated this legislation in 1956.[17]

All constitutional courts have the important function of arbitrating between various political institutions, whether between federal and provincial governments or between executives and assemblies. The early history of the American Supreme Court saw an insistence on the national government's rights as opposed to the powers of the states. In 1821 the Court ruled in McCulloch *v.* Maryland that the states had no authority to levy a tax which would challenge the right of Congress to establish a federal bank, and this continued insistence on the powers of the federal political institutions has been of great political importance in the growth of nationalising tendencies and the expansion of executive authority in spite of the economic liberalism of the Court before 1937.

Similar attempts to arbitrate between central and regional governments may be found in the short history of the West German Federal Constitutional Court. In a decision of 1958 the Court ruled that the Hamburg and Bremen atomic rearmament referenda cases violated the constitution, thus buttressing the power of the West German federal government.[18]

However, the decisions of constitutional courts are not always directed towards strengthening the central government in federal cases, nor do they automatically decide in favour of the executive arm of government when this is in conflict with representative assemblies. The American Supreme Court severely limited the powers of the presidency in regards to the concept of 'executive privilege' in 1974, forcing President Nixon to surrender the tape recordings of his White House conversations.[19] Yet because the movement in the twentieth century has been towards stronger and more complex functions being given to national governments, constitutional courts, as part of the political process, have tended to reflect this movement.

It may be seen that in this centralising tendency constitutional courts are performing one of their most important functions, that of stabilising and supporting the existing political system. The degree to which it is necessary for the courts to perform this task depends a great deal on the political culture within which the courts operate. In West Germany and Italy there is less agreement both on the ends and on the structure of government than there is in Great Britain, and therefore the need for the role the courts play is of greater political significance. Thus in spite of the courts' involvement in political decision-making, it is necessary to stress their political impartiality and to increase the respect given to the decisions of the courts. To return to the 1937 example of President Roosevelt's attempt to change the composition of the Supreme Court, he was defeated in spite of his massive electoral majority gained in 1936 because of the belief that the Court was above politics and that it was politically dangerous to the stability of American politics to tamper with it in the way the president proposed. The Court showed its political sensitivity by changing the policy that had given rise to the conflict. We have already noted the underlying purpose of the West German Federal Constitutional Court implicit in the method of selecting its members.

The courts are an important aspect of legitimising the outputs of governments, and it is a necessary feature that they should reflect conservative opinion. This does not mean that the courts are still anti-democratic in that they will not reflect the aspirations of the majority, but that the courts tread carefully in reflecting majority opinions. Since 1966 the American Supreme Court has been more cautious on segregation issues, not as a result of sudden changes in the composition of the Court, but because of the underlying uneasiness in American politics as the issue remained no longer one for the minority southern states alone, but became more important in the industrial states outside the south. The blows the Court received over the disclosures of Justice Fortas's financial involvements in 1968, leading to his resignation shortly after President Johnson had nominated him as chief justice, illustrate the sensitivity of the Court's relationship to the total political process, and that its power is closely related to the respect it can engender.

For these reasons constitutional courts tend to be cautious in the fourth category of functions, that of protecting individual civil rights. Lewis Edinger has noted that the West German Court 'has been more conservative than innovative, especially on socio-economic and civil liberty issues, and has sought to remain above partisan controversies'.[20] Donald Fouts has referred to the slightly anti-civil liberties tendencies of the Canadian Supreme Court.[21] Of course there are other means of protecting the civil rights of the citizen: in Britain there is no constitutional declaration of rights, and civil liberties have been established through judicial decisions interpreting the common law subject to the supremacy of statute law.[22] Soviet courts are often regarded as playing little part in the protection of civil liberties, although it should be remembered that the Soviet concept of human rights is rather different from the liberal emphasis on individualism; the Soviet view emphasises the protection of the collective rather than the individual and places greater weight on social and economic rights rather than on political rights.[25] However, in 1987 Poland established an Ombudsman for Civil Rights.

Civil rights have become one of the major areas of impact of American Supreme Court decisions since 1937. It has been estimated that since that date 45 per cent of the cases before the Court have involved civil liberties other than those of property rights.[24] The Court has ruled on such issues as whether it infringes the constitutional rights of citizens for their children to have to salute the flag, and whether prayers should be said in state schools.[25] There have been two major problems facing the Court: those of the concern for law and order, and the issue of internal security in the face of the alleged threat from communism. Thus in the Dennis case of 1951, the successful prosecution of a well-known American communist was upheld, and not until after the end of the McCarthy purges did the Court rule that threats to overthrow the American system of government without action was not sufficient basis for prosecution of individuals.

The aspect of civil liberties that has firmly brought the Court into the political process has been that of race. In the famous 1954 Brown case the Court ruled that the Fourteenth Amendment, guaranteeing equal protection of the laws, would not permit separate facilities for blacks, in this instance for education. The Court extended its rulings to cover other facilities, including the important field of voting rights. The presidency and the Congress have intermittently added their support to the liberal decisions of the Court, but as Robert McCloskey has remarked: 'In the decade 1953–63 the paramount innovations in public policy can be traced more to the Supreme Court than either the Congress or the President.'[26]

There are other functions of constitutional courts in addition to these four main areas, including those of ruling on disputed elections and electoral boundaries and advising the executive on the assumption of emergency powers. But these are clearly related to those we have discussed and can quite easily be fitted into our existing categories. The significant point that arises in the context of these functions is that within all these areas the courts function as important policy-makers. Their contribution is made in different ways from those of the traditionally identified policy-makers, but it is as crucial in understanding how the political system works. It is to limitations on this role that we must now turn our attention.

Control of the judiciary

Criticism directed at the degree of independence of the courts is often based on misconceptions of the role of the courts in the policy-making process, but it is sometimes, more realistically, directed at the political élite supporting anti-democratic orientations of the judiciary. The selection of the judges, their socioeconomic background, the anonymity of their decision-making, and their relative immunity from dismissal and other political sanctions often make them appear as an aristocratic intrusion on representative governmental processes.[27] Yet we have seen that the methods of their selection, their adherence to procedural norms, especially important in systems where case precedent (i.e. previous judicial decisions establishing a norm) is followed, and judicial sensitivity to political and societal pressures are important limitations on judicial independence. Moreover, legal professions themselves establish norms of behaviour that govern the relationship of judiciaries to the political process.

Beyond these are the more institutionalised forms of control. Legislatures may circumvent judicial opposition by new laws, and may share in the power to dismiss judges. Constitutions may be amended or rewritten. Specialisation of the courts may be developed to encourage greater sensitivity to political demands, as we have seen with constitutional and administrative courts, the development sometimes taking the form of quasi-judicial tribunals. Perhaps the most important controls are exercised through the executive. The procuracy in the Soviet Union exercises a general supervision over the courts as well as other areas of Soviet administration. It is closely tied to the top party leadership and is said to be second only to the Soviet secret police, the KGB, in its establishment of legal norms and control of judicial proceedings.[28] The new French constitution of 1958 gave the president increased disciplinary powers over the legal profession by decreasing the independence of the High Council (*Conseil Supérieur de la Magistrature*) in matters relating to discipline, promotion and selection. Ministers of Justice in all political systems are able to exercise considerable means of control over administrative matters relating to the judiciary, such as appropriations, initiating new laws, regulating punishments, as well as controlling appointments for the higher posts in the legal system.

The most important weapon in the hands of the executive is that without its co-operation judicial decisions cannot be implemented. In the 1954 Brown case the American Supreme Court ordered the desegregation of public schools, but given the hostility of the southern states, it needed enforcement by the federal government. President Eisenhower was reluctant to act, but, more importantly, the federal government had difficulties in enforcing such decisions on reluctant states. Several similar decisions by the Court followed, but until the 1964 Civil Rights Act gave certain sanctions, such as the withholding of federal funds, a president had limited powers of ensuring compliance with the Court's rulings.[29] Now that more sanctions exist, it is still dependent on the president whether they shall be used, and the desegregation battle in regard to southern schools is still being waged twenty-three years after the original court ruling.

These limitations on the power of the courts do not imply that the courts have little power in the policy-making process. This power will vary according to the political coalitions ranged for and against the courts on particular issues. The courts are part of the political process and one should stress co-operation as much as conflict. They interact with other parts of the political system, not as illegitimate outsiders but as part of the stable ruling political alliance. If they are not part of the 'successful coalition', their subordination to other political groups will be apparent.

References

1. See Chapter 10.
2. R. A. Dahl, 'Decision Making in a Democracy: The Role of the Supreme Court as a National Policy Maker', *Journal of Public Law*, VI (1958) p. 279. See also J. D. Casper, 'The Supreme Court and National Policy Making', *American Political Science Review*, LXX, 1 (March 1976) pp. 50–63.
3. In a debate in the House of Commons in reply to a criticism of the bias of the British judiciary in regards to an industrial relations decision, Margaret Thatcher stated: 'I have full confidence in the judiciary, which is independent of politics and must remain so', *House of Commons Debates*, Vol. 49. 1983/4. Nov. 21 – Dec. 2. p. 985.
4. See Chapter 7 on representation.
5. The Taff Vale decision of the House of Lords determined that the funds of a trade union were liable for damages inflicted by union officials, in this case by a railway strike which damaged the interests of a railway company. The decision, which was

reversed by legislation in 1906, would have prevented any successful strike action by unions. (See H. Pelling, *A History of British Trade Unionism* 4th ed. (London, 1987) pp. 123–4 for a brief note.) On the miners' strike of 1984/5 see B. Fine and R. Millar, *Policing the Miners' Strike* (London, 1985).

6. See F. C. Barghoorn, *Politics in the USSR*, 2nd ed. (Boston, 1972), ch. X.
7. For a fuller study of the basis of the Soviet legal system, see H. J. Berman, *Justice in the U.S.S.R.* (New York, 1963). Also, J. N. Hazard, *The Soviet Legal System* (New York, 1984).
8. L. J. Edinger, *Politics in Germany* (Boston, 1986) pp. 322–3.
9. For an outline of the English legal system see P. James, *Introduction to English Law*, 11th ed. (London, 1985). Also A Patterson, *The Law Lords* (London, 1982).
10. For a description of the French judicial system see J. E. S. Hayward, *Governing France*, 2nd ed. (London, 1983) pp. 132–49. For West Germany, see L. J. Edinger, *West German Politics* (New York, 1986) pp. 26–30.
11. See C. Neal Tate, 'Paths to the Bench in Britain', *Western Political Quarterly*, XXIII, 1 (March 1975) pp. 108–29. Also J. A. C. Griffith, *The Politics of the Judiciary*, 2nd ed. (London, 1981) pp. 17–34. Also, 'Judges on Trial', *Labour Research*, Vol. 76, No. 1. Jan. 1987, pp. 9–11.
12. See D. E. Fouts, 'Policy Making in the Supreme Court of Canada, 1950–60', in *Comparative Judicial Behaviour*, ed. G. Schubert and D. J. Danielski (Oxford, 1969) ch. 10.
13. J. Schmidhauser, *The Supreme Court: Its Politics, Personalities and Procedures* (New York, 1960) ch. 3. Also H. J. Abraham, *The Judicial Process* (New York, 1980) pp. 147–60. See also, S. Goldman, 'Judicial Selection and the Qualities that Make a Good Judge', *Annals of the American Academy of Political and Social Science, 4, 62* (July 1982) pp. 112–24. Also R. Hodder-Williams, *The Politics of the Supreme Court* (London, 1980) pp. 21–45.
14. See Chapter 8.
15. See R. A. Dahl, *Democracy in the United States*, 4th ed. (Boston, 1981) p. 160.
16. For details of these courts see Taylor Cole, 'Three Constitutional Courts: A Comparison', *American Political Science Review*, LIII, 4 (Dec. 1959) pp. 96–184.
17. See B. Bunting, *The Rise of the South African Reich* (London, 1964) pp. 125–9. In 1987 South African courts continued their partial opposition to executive decisions by declaring aspects of the State of Emergency illegal, for example, the banning of public reporting of clashes between demonstrators and police.
18. See G. Smith, *Democracy in Western Germany*, 3rd ed. (Aldershot, Hants, 1986) pp. 201–11.
19. See J. P. Frank, 'The Burger Court – The First Ten Years', *Law and Contemporary Problems*, 43. 3 (Summer 1980) pp. 101–35.
20. Edinger, *Politics in Germany*, p. 324. See also S. Cobler, *Law, Order, and Politics in West Germany* (London, 1978).
21. Fouts, 'Policy Making in the Supreme Court of Canada, 1950–60', pp. 268–73.
22. G. Peele, 'The State and Civil Liberties', in *Developments in British Politics*, 2nd ed., ed. H. Drucker *et al.* (London, 1986) pp. 144–74. See also D. G. Smith, 'British Civil Liberties and the Law', *Political Science Quarterly*, 101, 4, 1986, pp. 637–60.
23. See D. Lane, 'Human Rights under State Socialism', *Political Studies*, XXXII, 3 (Sept, 1984) pp. 349–68.
24. See H. J. Abraham, *Freedom and the Court: Civil Rights and Liberties in the United States*, 3rd ed. (New York, 1977).

25. For a discussion of the 1943 'saluting the flag' cases and the 1962–4 'prayer' cases, see F. J. Sorauf, 'Zorach *v.* Clauson: The Impact of a Supreme Court Decision', *American Political Science Review*, LIII (Sept. 1959) pp. 777–91.
26. R. G. McCloskey, 'Reflections on the Warren Court', *Virginia Law Review*, LI (Nov. 1965) pp. 1250–1.
27. This immunity from dismissal is certainly not absolute. In March 1981, nine senior Pakistan judges, including the Chief Justice, were dismissed by President Zia for not agreeing to an increase in presidential power.
28. See P. Juviler, *Revolutionary Law and Order: Politics and Social Change in the U.S.S.R.* (New York, 1976). Also see G. B. Smith, *The Soviet Procuracy and the Supervision of Administration* (Sijthoff and Noordhoff, Alpenaanden Rijn, The Netherlands, 1978).
29. For a discussion of the problems of federal enforcement of Supreme Court decisions, see D. McKay, *American Politics and Society*, Rev. ed. (London, 1985) pp. 265–6.

12

The Military and Politics

Characteristics of the military

The lengthy list of successful and unsuccessful direct interventions by the military[1] in Central and South America, the Middle East, the new African states, Asia and several European countries since 1945 creates the impression that seizure of political control by the armed forces, or the military ensuring the replacement of one civilian government by another, is the norm rather than the exception in modern political systems. Between 1960 and 1982 there were 25 coups in Africa, fifteen in Latin America, twenty in the Far East and fourteen in the Middle East (including Turkey). Latin America has been a particularly fruitful area for military intervention since the beginning of the nineteenth century. In Spain there were 43 successful and unsuccessful military coups between 1914 and 1923, culminating in the establishment of a relatively stable period of military dictatorship under Primo de Rivera, who maintained power until 1930.[2]

However, the relationship of the military to the political process is more complex than is indicated by the direct seizure of political power. In fact this type of intervention may sometimes indicate the inability of the armed forces to achieve their political goals by other means, and may be an indication of the nature of the political system that has given rise to such interventions. The political influence of the military stretches from direct assumptions of complete political control to complete subservience of the military to other political structures. There are intermediate stages between these two extremes, such as the power of replacing one civilian government by another civilian government, or simply acting as the main political support for a civilian government, or where the military behaves as one of the many pressure groups within the political system, using the methods and applying the sanctions acceptable within that system.

The armed forces have characteristic features which distinguish them from other groups in all political systems, and these characteristics would lead one to expect that the military would intervene more frequently than it does: they raise the question of what prevents direct military intervention, rather than the question of why it happens at all.[3] The structure of the armed forces is hierarchical and centralised, putting a premium on rapid communications. Discipline and obedience to higher commands are considered of fundamental importance, and here one should note the bureaucratic obedience, in Weber's sense, to the rank and not to the individual who holds that rank. The armed forces in varying degrees emphasise their separation from civilian society by separate barracks, distinctive uniforms and indoctrination of recruits in the history and traditions of that particular branch of the armed forces, resulting in a pride in that tradition and a distinct *esprit de corps*. Sometimes the military ensures for potential recruits a different type of education from an early age from that of civilian society. The consequent values held by members of the armed forces, especially the officers, may distinguish them from the rest of society in a way that is not true of other comparable groups such as police forces. Above all the military monopolises the chief instruments of violence in the political system.

Yet it should not be thought that these values and attitudes may be such that they inevitably lead to a belief in right-wing solutions for the ills that are judged to face society. There are many examples of military intervention to support radical policies of both the right-wing and left-wing varieties. But generally such values imply that in some way the military is above the sectional, vested interest conflicts in the political process, and that the military is the embodiment of the national interest, albeit an authoritarian, disciplined conception of the national interest.[4] It is true that military influence is used to protect the armed forces from civilian mismanagement such as a failure to expand them or equip them with the necessary modern weapons to carry out the important functions of protecting national territory from foreign aggression, and sometimes military pressure may result from junior officers being dissatisfied with their promotion prospects. None the less, these distinctive features do lead the military to the belief that it is the only body aware of what constitutes the true national interest, and that only the military is capable of implementing policies to protect that interest.

This is partly the consequence of the role that the military plays in the crises of war and the threat of foreign invasion, and it is often immaterial whether it has been successful and provided countless heroes, or whether it has been humiliated. Witness President Ebert, the Social Democrat, welcoming back the German army in 1918 after the German surrender: 'I salute you, who return unvanquished from the field of battle.'[5] Defeats can be blamed on convenient scapegoats such as ethnic or political minorities. Defeat in the Arab-Israeli war of 1948 led, with other factors, to a weakening of the Egyptian regime of Farouk, but it left the army with its reputation almost intact, as the military defeats could be blamed on governmental incompetence, the equivalent of the 'stab in the back' by German socialists and Jews in 1918.

These political attitudes of the military, and indeed the total role of the military in politics depend on two variables. Firstly, there is the nature of the military itself. Some armed forces are more professionalised than others, and this will affect the prestige of the military in society and will affect the degree of pride and feeling of separateness with which the military reflects its distinctive values and attitudes.[6] Conscript armies will differ from volunteer armies, though few match the military conscription of the Swiss, with their conception of a citizen army with intermittent military service for all males from twenty to fifty years. The social background of recruits will vary from the emphasis on élite recruitment in some armed forces to reliance on peasant and lower-middle-class recruits in others. Specialisation and technical and administrative competence will differ, having profound effects on the ability of the military to influence and control the decision-making process. It may be that the leanings to violence, the lack of political experience and the attempt to apply military values and procedures to the process of government are disabilities of all armed forces, whether they are trying to influence or actually seize control of the government.

The second variable is the nature of the political system. Direct military intervention is less likely in industrialised liberal democracies or in socialist systems controlled by one party. Conversely, in states in which civilian governments lack prestige and have not succeeded in winning the allegiance of the people, the ability of the military to intervene directly is enhanced. The military lacks the basis of legitimacy that civilian governments have, with their right to rule often based on traditions and conceptions of popular sovereignty, and therefore there must be serious weaknesses in the structure of the civilian government for military intervention to be successful. This political stability is not always based on the level of socio-economic development – a comparison of Germany between 1918 and 1933 and India since 1947 is sufficient to cast doubts on the certainty of that relationship – but the lower the level of economic development, the greater the likelihood of a weaker basis of legitimacy for the civilian governments.

The interaction of these two variables, the nature of the military and the strength of the civilian government, does not submit to any simple superimposed pattern. The cleavages between the values of civil and military authorities, the intensity with which these values are held, and the complexity of the government process itself, all complicate the nature of the relationship. To examine the role of the military in politics more closely and to emphasise these variables, we shall look at examples of (1) limited interference by the military; (2) direct interference; (3) interference leading to military rule.

Limited interference in the political process

Direct military intervention in the political process is the exception rather than the rule in liberal democracies and socialist states such as the Soviet Union.[7] While the armed forces attempt to influence governmental policy, especially in the fields of foreign policy and defence, and try to win concessions for themselves, the frequency of attempts to threaten the displacement of the civilian government or of refusals to carry out its commands is low. The histories of such liberal democracies as the United States, Canada, Britain, the Scandinavian countries, Holland, Belgium and Switzerland, to give a few examples, have been relatively untroubled by military challenges to the legitimacy of the civilian government, in spite of the martial past and imperial glories that some of these states have enjoyed. The United States, one of the first states to win independence from European domination by force of arms, provides an outstanding example of this subordination of the military. Only once, at the birth of the republic, was there a serious danger of active, direct military intervention against the civilian government, but Washington refused to lead the army on such a speculative venture. The paramountcy of civilian legitimacy survived the bloody civil war of 1861–5 and remains a cardinal feature of American government in the present period of American ascendancy in international politics.

Likewise, since the experience of army control under Cromwell in the seventeenth century, Britain has escaped the problem of overt military involvement in the processes of government. The Curragh mutiny of 1914 provides an inconclusive exception. Several officers in the British army in Ireland resigned because of the possibility of their being sent to fight the Ulster Volunteers. Three points should be noted in respect of this incident. Firstly, the period 1910–14 was an exceptional period in British politics, and the Irish Home Rule issue was but one aspect of an unusual breakdown of the consensus among the British ruling élites. Secondly, the resigning officers were from the northern part of Ireland and objected to forcing Protestant Ulster into self-governing union with the Catholic south. Thirdly, the officers did not disobey orders, but merely resigned when given this option by their commanding officer. Perhaps more relevant to the role of the military in British politics were the relations that 1914–18 war prime ministers had with their generals. Lord Kitchener was difficult to remove from the cabinet in spite of his incompetence, and Prime Minister Asquith's problem was not solved until the military leader was drowned on the way to Russia in

1915.[8] Lloyd George struggled to exercise full control of the military between 1916 and 1918, when with the backing of George V, Haig and the other British military leaders were at times able to resist civilian control of the direction of the war.[9] These problems did not recur in the Second World War, and it should be noted that war conditions are exceptional in affecting the civilian–military relationship in all political systems.

Liberal democracies of this type are characterised by a long history of independence, national unity, a relatively stable process of industrialisation and an orderly and accepted means of transferring political power. These, allied to the notion of popular sovereignty developed with the liberal theories of the state in the nineteenth century, provide a strong basis of legitimacy for civilian governments. Other groups in the political process, such as political parties, can effectively challenge the moral authority of the military to intervene directly in politics. Moreover, the military in these societies lacks the prestige it receives in other political systems, and there is less emphasis on separateness from civilian society. In Britain the higher ranks are drawn from the upper classes in society, thus, to a degree, sharing the values of civilian élites, reflecting a balance that exists in society as a whole.[10] The effect of the long British influence on the Indian army and to lesser extent on the Malaysian armed forces may be a factor in the avoidance in these states of direct military intervention since independence, although the history, economic development and social structure offer sharp contrasts with the more industrialised liberal democracies.

Yet within liberal democracies the military, while respecting the legitimate supremacy of the civilian government, does play an important role in the political process. President Eisenhower, in his farewell message in 1961, warned of a 'military–industrial complex' that could dominate the government of the United States. The size of the American military budget, the complexity of the military machine and the overlap between foreign policy and military strategy have given rise to fears that the armed forces are exercising too great an influence on political decision-making. Yet civilian supremacy is a fundamental principle of American government. As one writer has pointed out:

> Not only is meaningful civilian supremacy accepted in principle by military and civilians alike, but military officers are essentially willing to accept the actions and decisions that flow from it (however much they may deplore specific ones). The leadership of the Department of State in foreign policy is accepted in the same spirit. Similarly, the State Department accepts military participation in foreign policy.[11]

It follows from this that the military is one group among many attempting to influence relevant decision-making, and the controls are essentially similar to those exercised over other groups in the American system of government. The American military shares the fundamental values of American society as a whole, and the degree of control rests on the efficiency of the civilian organisations, such as the Department of Defence, in imposing their own more detailed directives.

In socialist states such as the Soviet Union, civilian supremacy over the armed forces is as marked as in most liberal democracies. For periods before 1942 the Soviet army had a dual system of control in which the orders of the military commander had to be countersigned by a political commissar appointed by and responsible to the Communist Party. Efficiency often demanded the abolition of this system, but in periods of political uncertainty it was restored. Trotsky had magnificently created the Red Army to defend the Bolshevik revolution of 1917, but it never achieved the independence of civilian control of other revolutionary armies in history. The most complete period of political subjugation of the armed forces occurred during the Stalinist period, and his great purges of 1937–8 ensured that there would be no political threat from the military. These purges even included the removal of Marshal Tukhachevsky, one of the architects of Bolshevik triumphs in the civil wars before 1921.

With Stalin's death in 1953, and the lengthy struggle over his succession, the Soviet military appeared to acquire more direct political influence. Army units ensured the fall of Beria, the feared and hated chief of police, and the support of the Soviet leaders was important in the triumph of Khrushchev in his defeat of Malenkov in 1955, and the routing of his remaining political opponents in 1957. The army was suspicious of Malenkov's emphasis on consumer goods and decreases in the military budgets. It was rewarded for its support by an increase in military spending and the appointment of Marshal Zhukov as minister of defence.

However, this increased independent role for the army was short-lived. Khrushchev, aware of the dangers, counter-attacked: Zhukov was demoted in 1957, and full civilian supremacy was restored. This restoration was summed up in the words of a Central Committee of the Communist Party resolution of October 1957:

> The chief source of the might of our army and navy lies in the fact that the Communist Party, the guiding and directing force of Soviet Society, is their organiser, leader, and instructor. We must always remember V. I. Lenin's instructions to the effect that the 'policy of the military department, as of all other departments and institutions, is pursued in strict accordance with the general directives given by the Party in the person of the Central Committee and under its direct control'.[13]

Thus the Soviet military is firmly controlled for the most part by civilian governments; the legitimacy of the Party's supremacy is recognised. The transfer of power from one leader or group of leaders to another, because the transfer is less institutionalised than in liberal democratic systems, does offer possibilities for increasing military influence, but chiefly the political concerns of the Soviet armed forces centre on issues of vested interest such as the size of the military budget, the size of the army and technical developments in methods of warfare.[13] These are issues which do not lead to a military challenge to the established tradition of civilian supremacy.

This supremacy was partly ensured in the past by systems of dual control and periodic purges. In recent years the military has been incorporated into the policy-making process through its representatives on the Central Committee and often through the presence of the minister of defence in the Politburo. Other mechanisms of control are, firstly, the activities of the secret police, whose organisation runs throughout the armed forces, and which is responsible to the Party. Secondly, members of the armed forces are subject to more overt political indoctrination than their equivalents in liberal democracies, and they are encouraged to identify with the regime by joining the Communist Party; over 90 per cent of the officers, and a large number of the rank and file, are Party members. Thirdly, the military officers form a privileged class in regard to conditions and pay. After the revolutionary period titles were fully restored, discipline over the rank and file increased, and after the army purges in the late 1930s officer privileges were either introduced or existing ones increased. The gulf between officers and men has generally been re-emphasised. Officers are encouraged to accept the status quo and the underlying ideology of the state.

The Soviet Union, then, is similar in many respects to liberal democracies with extensive accommodation between military and civilian authorities. The term 'military-industrial complex' has been applied to the USSR as well as to the United States.[14] A similar pattern would appear to exist in the other East European socialist states with the obvious exception of Poland.[15]

Direct interference

Direct interference by the military in politics, but falling short of the assumption of power by the military, may occur in any type of political system. The military may merely exert direct pressure to attempt to achieve a particular political goal, may create the conditions for a change of government or even dictate what type of civilian government achieves power. The army mutinies in Kenya, Tanzania and Uganda in 1964, which led to the respective governments calling for British military assistance to put them down, had their roots in dissatisfaction with army pay and conditions, and the rate of Africanisation of senior ranks; they were not consciously aimed at overthrowing the existing governments, and were certainly not a step towards establishing military governments.[16] It is difficult to find general reasons underlying the military interventions in other African states with similar problems of development, and with British influences in the military and political structures. The Ghanaian coups of 1966 and 1972, the Nigerian coups of 1966 and 1975, and the Sudanese coup of 1985, partly represented clashes between different élites, protests against corruption and the protection of military vested interests.

Nevertheless, in spite of these difficulties in finding common denominators for different levels of military intervention, there are some factors which tend to inhibit full military control. The triumph of liberal democracy in France after 1870 was sufficient to survive several military crises in the early years of the Third Republic. The McMahon scare of 1877, the Boulanger crisis of 1886 and the Dreyfus scandal at the turn of the century were overcome and it appeared that France had finally secured the subordination of the military to the civilian government.[17] Yet the intervention of the military was crucial in the collapse of the Fourth Republic in 1958. An explanation lies in the reverses of French foreign policy and the contraction of her overseas empire since 1945. The disastrous reverses in Indo-China, the military success followed by the political defeat in the Suez crisis of 1956, and the clash of European settlers and north African nationalists, especially in Algeria, had weakened the army's faith in the governments' directives. French civilian institutions were highly developed, but the instability of the successive governments and the 'immobilisme' of the politics of the Fourth Republic allowed the army, and especially the army in Algeria, to challenge the legitimacy, the right to rule, of the French government. Before 1958 the army had controlled Algeria and directed the war there with increasingly little reference to the government in Paris, and flagrant acts of insubordination were only lightly punished by the civilian authorities. A significant factor in the 1958 crisis was that no important sector of French society was willing to defend the regime. Also, once the army had reached the position of open defiance of the government, de Gaulle provided an alternative source of authority to which civilians as well as the army could appeal.[18] If the events of 1958 are compared with the army revolt of 1961, it can be seen that in the second crisis the army did not confront a weakened civilian government. Moreover the attempted coup was confined to the army in Algeria, and was not supported by army units in France or those stationed in Germany. President de Gaulle was able to rally all important sections of French society in opposition to the rebellious generals, and the revolt which had achieved success in Algeria soon crumbled in the face of this united civilian hostility.[19]

Two examples expose the limitations of the military's role in the political process. The German army enjoyed unparalleled prestige in the German Empire after 1871; responsible only to the Emperor, bound by rigid professional loyalties which were reinforced by the upper-class background of its officers, it supported the political system but was not the government. After 1918, the size of the army was limited and the country threatened by internal political upheavals with the army drawn more firmly into the political arena to restore its previous independence and prestige. Von Seekt, chief of the army command in the early years of the Weimar Republic, summed up the attitude of the army with the observation: 'The army serves the state, and only the state, for it is the state'.[20] The army leaders intrigued against the governments of the Weimar Republic, not to achieve absolute power, but to insure the independence of the army. Thus the army welcomed the authoritarian Nazi government of 1933 in the belief that Hitler's aims coincided with those of the army and that Hitler's mass movement would legitimise the stronger foreign policy which the army desired. However, by 1938 Hitler had succeeded in crushing the last vestiges of military independence and had established complete civilian control.

The Spanish army had been one of the main props of the Franco regime since the civil war in the 1930s. This conservative loyalty had been reinforced by the overwhelming upper-class background of the officer corps and the willingness of Franco to expand military strength. It was not surprising that the armed forces viewed developments after the dictator's death in 1975 with some suspicion. It opposed, with some success, military reforms to limit the size of the army and was completely opposed to the legalisation of left-wing parties such as the Communist Party. The reduced political importance of the military was instrumental in leading to the unsuccessful military coup of February 1981. The failure of the abortive coup forced the army reluctantly to recognise the legitimacy of the Socialist accession to power in 1982 while the Spanish membership of NATO and the EEC has lessened, although not removed, the likelihood of direct military intervention.[21]

The French, German and Spanish examples illustrate the relationship between the strength and legitimacy of the civilian government and the political power of the military. When the civilian government is attempting to establish its legitimacy as with France during the Fourth Republic, Germany under Weimar, and Spain in the post-Franco period of 1975 and 1982, the military will act with a degree of independence and either oppose the government or not seek to actively defend it. However with the installation of civilian legitimacy with the election of a de Gaulle, the accession to power of a Hitler or the popular election of a Socialist government, the independence of the military is reduced.

Military control

There are difficulties in measuring the exact degree of military interference short of direct military control, and arriving at a broad classification of the reasons why this particular level is reached in particular regimes. The same problems are present in an examination of regimes that suffer direct military control. Some states may be described as being controlled by military–civilian coalitions: Finer gives the examples of Jordan, Morocco, Bahrain and the Sultanate of Oman.[22] Military governments may become more civilianised after the passage of time without any dramatic political changes taking place. This has happened in Egypt since the military coup of 1952; Spain offers an illustration of the army seizing power after a prolonged civil war, but gradually becoming an important, not dominant, prop of the existing regime. Some military dictatorships are camouflaged by presidential elections and representative assemblies, with the military leaders assuming civilian status in order to perpetuate army control, as in Brazil. Army control may be distinquishable from the continual replacement of one civilian government by another, a persistent factor in

Syrian politics since 1945.[23] There are examples of the military relinquishing control, direct political control that is, for short periods in some cases. The Burmese army, seizing control in 1958, surrendered it partly after eighteen months, but returned to assume full control again in 1962. In Ghana, the army seized control in 1966, with civilian rule again in 1969 for a short period. Further moves towards civilian rule were again interrupted by the military coup of 1981. The Greek army surrendered control in 1974 after a period of military dictatorship lasting from 1967.

Thus the degrees of control make any system of rigid classification difficult. Nevertheless. the frequency of military takeovers in Latin America, the Middle East, the new nations of north and sub-Sahara Africa and South-East Asia does indicate the links between military dictatorship and the level of socio-economic development, the strength of civilian institutions and the nature of the military response to the problems that face these states.[24]

In the states that experience direct military control the legitimacy of the existing political institutions and of the ruling élites is disputed. The regime has not acquired the respect that puts it beyond the challenge of the armed forces. Thus, far from meeting widespread opposition to its intervention, the army may be welcomed as a means of ridding the state of the old corrupt and inefficient politicians. The colonels' seizure of power in Egypt in 1952 took place against a backcloth of a discredited political system that concentrated power in the hands of a narrow oligarchy which appeared to be manipulated by British imperial interests and was symbolised by an ineffectual, pleasure-loving hereditary ruler; it was this government that had taken the country to the humiliating defeat at the hands of the Israelis in the 1948 war. The cautious colonels were pushed on from their original intention of replacing one civilian government by another to seizing complete political control by the hollowness of the existing political system and the lack of support it received.[25] A similar selfish ruling group provided easy opposition for the Iraqi army's seizure of power in 1958. The prime minister, Nuri-es-Said, who was murdered with the king during the coup, had long resorted to emergency laws to ensure his political survival, but the government's failure to implement social reforms, its seeming rejection of the Arab cause against Israel, and the claims that it was assisting the aims of British foreign policy in the area, left it without serious support.

The failure of the existing political institutions to establish a legitimate base and to win the respect and support of powerful groups within the state is a particular problem for new nations that have recently emerged from colonial domination. These difficulties are increased if the level of socio-economic development has not allowed the emergence of strong political parties, trade unions and a business and professional class to rival the military's influence. The gap between rich and poor may preclude the development of a stable consensus within the country, and if the state is in a sensitive area of international politics, such as the Middle East, there is great emphasis on large military budgets assisted by the outside interference of the great powers.

The complexity of these variables is illustrated by Argentina's recent history. Long independent with a relatively high level of economic development and strong trade union and party organisation, the country's instability led to a military coup in 1976. The Falklands defeat in 1982 paved the way for the restoration of civilian government, but President Alfonsin was still being forced, in the face of military revolts, to compromise with the armed forces in 1987.[26]

However, the low level of economic development may lead the army to intervene on the part of radical forces in the country aiming at a more egalitarian social structure, as was the case with the Egyptian coup, but generally the military tends to support conservative groups, as the Brazilian army did when it overthrew the left-wing president Goulart in 1964 and established a right-wing dictatorship. There are often tensions between senior and junior officers in regard to right and left political orientations. An added complication is that of external military aid. The United States is a lavish provider of aid in the forms of technical assistance, training, money and weapons to armies in underdeveloped countries to counter any possible threats to pro-Western governments, and this assistance not only strengthens the military inside the state, but is also designed to encourage anti-radical tendencies. The American government encouraged the Chilean army to overthrow the radical Allende government in September 1973, and the ensuing military dictatorship brutally suppressed any form of left-wing political activity.[27]

Regional differences inside the state may be so acute as to precipitate crises leading to direct assumption of power by the military. This can occur in states with a long history of independence and unity such as Spain, but is particularly a problem facing new states and those states in which tribal loyalties take precedence over loyalty to the central government. Nigeria since independence is a clear example of regional divisions leading to military dictatorship. The state was a federal structure based on regions loosely adhering to the main tribal divisions, with political power being mainly controlled by the conservative, Muslim, feudal north in alliance with either of the two more advanced, sophisticated, mainly Christian coastal regions, the Yoruba west and the Ibo east. The army failed to overcome the tribal tensions within its own ranks, but the predominance of the Ibo officers, who had joined the army to advance the interests of their own region, led to a military coup in 1966 in which the northern and western military officers were the chief victims. General Ironsi, while trying to promote the 'one Nigeria' concept, was identified with eastern Ibo interests, which led to a tribal counter-coup in the same year. This time the Ibo tribe suffered the most and a series of massacres of Ibo in the northern region led to a split in the military dictatorship of General Gowan and General Ojukwu; a civil war saw the end of Ibo secessionist aims with the victory for the federal military government in 1969.[28]

The nature of the armed forces is a factor of great significance in the establishment of a military government. In some states the army is identified with nationalism, the protection of the general interest, and embodies the values of order and efficiency. Thus, when the heady wine of independence has evaporated and the unity of the groups that have fought for independence is cracking, the army is resorted to in order to support national as opposed to sectional interest; that is, if the army has maintained its own unity. This is true even when the army did not win prestige in the struggle for national independence. Certainly in new and underdeveloped countries the military may monopolise certain administrative skills and possess most of the trained manpower of engineers, surveyors, etc. The military is often the most 'westernised' or 'modern' structure in a traditional, rural, tribal and hierarchical society. Even where tribal and other differences exist, the army provides a structure where they are most likely to be minimised. The impact of rival training schemes in America, the Soviet Union, Britain and China may produce tensions within the military of a particular state that could destroy its unity and professional image. It was fear of Nkrumah's mistrust of the army, his spies and his proposals to train more officers in Soviet Russia that finally induced the army to bring down his regime in 1966 and establish a period of military dictatorship.

The degree of professionalisation of the army is important, but a factor that may cut across it and have important consequences itself is the area of recruitment. Armies in the Middle East have tended to draw their officers from the lower-middle classes, and these groups have joined because there was no other organisation capable of effecting the reforms in the political system that they thought necessary, and they have implemented important social reforms after the military has achieved power. Political leaders in northern Nigeria looked upon military careers with disdain, as being below their feudal dignity, with the consequent domination by the coastal tribes. Armies, in fact, may lack a monolithic structure. The Portuguese army that seized control in April 1974 divided into several political groups ranging from the conservative General Spinola to the more radical General Goncalves. The political ferment in Portugal in the years after the coup tended to reflect the political conflicts within the armed forces more than the competition between the political parties.[29]

The existence of both institutional and economic crises has led to the relatively rare examples of military intervention in socialist states. In Poland the military came to play the dominant role after December 1981, not only through its administration of martial law and direct supervision of certain sectors of the economy, such as mining, but also through the increased participation of military personnel in the leading institutions of the Communist Party (PZPR). This may, of course, prove to be a relatively short-lived arrangement.

Certainly in China, when the military moved into a political vacuum during the Cultural Revolution and its aftermath, the military in the post-Mao period appears to have increasingly withdrawn from such an overtly political role.[30]

Conclusion

In all political systems the military possesses certain advantageous characteristics which allow it to intervene in the political process. But these advantages are marked by some corresponding defects which tend to inhibit certain types of intervention. The type of intervention, whether merely seeking influence or that of establishing a military dictatorship, will vary according to several criteria. These are the nature of the political system, the stability of the political institutions, and the level of socio-economic development. There are also the factors of the organisation, recruitment and degree of professionalisation of the armed forces, and the extent to which military values correspond to the values of civilian society. However, both these groups of variables will depend, to some extent, on the particular circumstances that occur at particular times; in other words, historical accidents. External pressures are now more important in the twentieth century, with the improvement of communications and the importance of international ideological alignments. Above all there is the need to base the various types of intervention on popular support, and the military is often reluctant to act unless it believes that it has some degree of popular support.

The problems facing the military do not end when the intervention is accomplished. The difficulties of retreating from a given level of interference are almost as great as effecting the intervention in the first place: we have already noted the example of the Argentinian military surrendering supreme political power in 1983, but continuing to threaten the civilian government. Moreover, the assumption of a high level of interference begins to change the military's relationship with the governmental processes. It becomes responsible for unpopular decisions, it risks losing the belief that it puts the wider national interest before narrower sectional interests, and the unity of the armed forces may be impaired. The military finds it difficult to restore its former relationship with civilian governments, and its leaders may risk penalisation. Often the very act of intervention may lose the army its most important asset, that of potential intervention. The factors that determine the level of military interference are seldom removed by the subsequent intervention and are usually a consistent feature of the political system.

References

1. *The Guardian* (9 July 1982). See also S. Declo, *Coups and Army Rule in Africa* (New Haven, Conn., 1976) pp. 5–6. The term 'military' in this chapter includes the navy and air force as well as the army.
2. H. Thomas, *The Spanish Civil War*, 3rd ed. (London, 1977) p. 91.
3. S. E. Finer, *The Man on Horseback*, 2nd ed. (London, 1976) p. 5.
4. An interesting example of this authoritarian attitude is the comment of a young Pakistan army officer in April 1970 helping to organise elections in West Pakistan: 'They are going to have democracy whether they like it or not. The army will see to it. Any trouble, anyone attempting to disrupt democracy, that's where we step in.' (Quoted in *The Times*, 28 April 1970).
5. Quoted in J. W. Wheeler-Bennett, *The Nemesis of Power. The German Army in Politics, 1918–45*, 2nd ed. (London, 1964) p. 31.
6. See S. P. Huntington, *The Soldier and the State* (Cambridge, Mass., 1957).
7. See A. R. Ball and F. Millard, *Pressure Politics in Industrial Societies* (London, 1986) pp. 243–80.
8. See P. Magnus, *Kitchener. Portrait of an Imperialist* (London, 1958) chs 14, 15, 16. See also P. Guinn, *British Strategy and Politics 1914–18* (Oxford, 1965).
9. See A. J. P. Taylor, *English History, 1914–1945* (Oxford, 1965) pp. 97–100. See also Lord Beaverbrook, *Men and Power 1917–21* (London, 1956) for a more detailed account of Lloyd George's struggle with his generals.
10. See C. Wright Mills, *The Power Elite* (Oxford, 1956) ch. 8 for a different emphasis on the role of the military in American politics.
11. B. M. Sapin, *The Making of United States Foreign Policy* (New York, 1966) p. 171.
12. Quoted in M. Fainsod, *How Russia is Ruled* 2nd ed. (Cambridge, Mass., 1967) p. 485.
13. See E. Warner, *The Military in Contemporary Soviet Politics* (New York, 1977). See also, R Kolkowicz, 'Military Intervention in the Soviet Union: Scenario for Post-Hegemonial Synthesis', in *Soldiers Peasants and Bureaucrats*, eds R. Kolkowicz and A. Korbonski (London, 1982) pp. 109–38.
14. M. Agursky and H. Adomeit, 'The Soviet Military–Industrial Complex', *Survey*, 24. (1979) pp. 106–124.
15. See Ball and Millard, *Pressure Politics in Industrial Societies*, pp. 245–6.
16. See W. F. Gutteridge, *Military Regimes in Africa* (London, 1975). However, while Uganda has suffered civil war and a series of military coups since the overthrow of Milton Obote by Idi Amin, Kenya and Tanzania have escaped direct military rule

although there was an abortive coup by air force officers in Kenya in August 1982. Mugabe in Zimbabwe, in spite of the guerrilla war background to independence and the military activities of his opponents, has kept civilian government intact since independence in 1980.

17. See D. Thompson, *Democracy in France*, 2nd ed. (Oxford, 1952) pp. 147–63 for an outline of these crises in the Third Republic.
18. For a brief account of the events leading up to the crisis of May 1958 see P. H. Williams, *Crisis and Compromise. Politics in the Fourth Republic*, 3rd ed. (London, 1964), pp. 44–57.
19. See Finer, *The Man on Horseback*, pp. 85–8.
20. Quoted in F. L. Carsten, *The Reichswehr and Politics 1918–1933* (Oxford, 1966) p. 400. See also D. Cameron Watt, *Too Serious a Business* (London, 1975) pp. 43–7.
21. See J. Hooper, *The Spaniards. A Portrait of New Spain* (London, 1987) pp. 61–79.

PART FOUR

Values and Politics

13

Ideologies and Political Change

The importance of values in politics

At several points in our discussion of the political process, we have noted the importance of political ideas. Indeed, the first steps in the development of the study of politics were motivated by the desire to find the 'best system of government'.[1] Constantly the problem of evaluation and the difficulty of scientific objectivity have been of supreme importance in the practice and the study of politics. The relationship between the political process and political ideas can be seen at various levels: it can be seen in the nature of the rules that regulate the political process; in the influence that these ideas have on the policies of governments; in the political motivation of individuals in the political system; in the methods of studying politics and the political values of the students of politics.

The rules and constitutions that are drawn up for each state strongly underline the influence of ideas in the political process. The English Bill of Rights of 1689 was designed to prevent the return of despotic kings and was based on the belief that good government was only possible when political power was dispersed among the landed aristocracy represented in Parliament.[2] The American constitution is based on both a belief in popular sovereignty and the fear of democracy; thus power was widely dispersed among representative institutions.[3] The constitution of the Soviet Union declares the intention of realising communist aims of economic and political equality.[4] The constitution of South Africa, a constitution that pays lip-service to the principles of liberal democracy, still defends apartheid on the grounds that the dominant South African whites are granting self-determination, i.e. separate development, to the South African blacks.[5]

Likewise the decision-making process in all political systems is affected by the value system in which the decisions are made. The Arab countries' hostility to the state of Israel often works against what could be thought to be the economic interests of these countries. Nehru of India conducted foreign policy in the 1950s partly on the basis of the need for a bloc of countries unaligned to the large power alliances of the Soviet Union and the United States, and he defended this policy as morally necessary. It was of course attacked, especially by the American-aligned states, as unnecessarily morally simplistic and unmindful of Indian economic and defence interests. President de Gaulle based French foreign policy between 1958 and 1968 on an ideal of French greatness which necessitated a greater degree of independence from the United States. French foreign policy of the period cannot be understood without reference to these values of the French President.

The political actions of every individual in the political system, at whatever level, are only comprehensible within some value framework. Individuals are prepared to fight for causes, often realistically hopeless causes, or to undergo savage ill-treatment and torture in the belief that some political values are superior to others. At some levels this claim for the influence of political ideals is simplistic and obvious, but in the study of political science, especially with the emphasis on scientific method, it is necessary to remind ourselves about the whole range of political motivations.

Political ideologies

It is not difficult to illustrate the relationship between political values and ideals with both the practice and study of politics. When these ideals form an articulate, coherent, systematic pattern, we speak of political ideologies. Political ideologies have been described as 'action-related "systems" of ideas',[6] in the sense that they are sets of ideas concerning change or defence of existing political structures and relationships. All ideologies are concerned with the nature of the distribution of political power; they are essentially normative arguments to espouse a programme of reform or reaction – thus they are not simply political philosophies. They demand action, not just observation and analysis. They may be particularly linked to one group in society, but it is always claimed by its supporters that a particular ideology has a wider and impartial relevance to all interests in the political system.

There are different types of ideologies, some being more coherent and better articulated than others. Indeed the dividing line between a loose collection of political ideas and an integrated ideology is often difficult to distinguish clearly. Fascism as a political ideology is interesting in this respect. We have seen that 'fascist' can be used as a term of abuse with little reference to the political values and ideas of the abused; it is commonly used to denote the extreme right-wing of the political spectrum. However, if fascism is analysed within an historical context, as it must be in order to correctly understand this particular set of political ideas, the easy description of right-wing extremism disappears. The problem with examining fascism as an ideology is, firstly, that it belongs to a distinct period of European history, especially Central European history between 1918 and 1945.[7] Secondly, there is no collection of sacred texts for fascism as there is for liberalism, communism, etc. Hitler's *Mein Kampf* stands up poorly in comparison with the writings of John Stuart Mill and especially in comparison with the work of Karl Marx. Thirdly, fascism, born of a particular historical set of circumstances, expressed itself in negative terms; fascism was opposed to Marxism, liberal democracy, the Jews, the Slavs, and so on, but the positive aspects were never as clearly articulated. The concept of the corporate state remained unclear, for example, and although European fascists did consistently unite under their different nationalist banners, it was, perhaps, their acceptance of the need for a distinctive type of political leadership that distinguished them clearly from other sets of political idealists.[8]

Ernst Nolte has offered an approach to the analysis of fascism:

> Neither anti-parliamentarianism nor anti-semitism is a suitable criterion for the concept of fascism. It would be

> equally inprecise to define fascism as anti-communism ... Fascism is anti-Marxism which seeks to destroy the enemy by the evolvement of a radically opposed yet related ideology and by the use of almost identical and yet typically modified methods, always, however, within the unyielding framework of national selfassertion and autonomy.[9]

Thus it can be seen that the difficulties in providing a clear statement of fascism as an ideology, while immense, do not prevent discussing fascism as an ideology. If we were to examine populism, another much abused term, the difficulties of conceptualisation would probably be even greater.[10] Yet, nevertheless, we can still talk of a populist ideology.

Compared with fascism and populism, however, Marxism is a comprehensive ideology with a highly sophisticated basis of philosophical, sociological, historical and economic analysis. The philosophical concepts of Marxism are, in part, derived from Hegel, particularly the concept of the dialectic, i.e. that the clash of conflicting elements within society accounts for change and progress. The Marxist view of human progress rests on what is often called 'the materialist view of history'. Marx saw human beings as essentially social beings moulded by particular stages of economic and social development; the values and attitudes of individuals are, in particular, a product of the economic class to which the individual belongs, while the class itself is defined by the different relationship within a society to the means of production. Initially, in the Marxist view, there were no classes because the economic division of labour did not exist. This was the first stage of human history, known as the era of 'primitive communism'. As the division of labour emerged, so did classes develop. In Marxist sociology those classes with economic power also wielded political power. Thus the feudal lords controlled the peasantry throughout Western Europe because of their control of the land which the peasants worked. However, as the balance of economic power shifted from the feudal lords to the rising commercial manufacturing classes, so did the political relationships shift: the struggles of the bourgeoisie with the landed aristocracy (the 'clash of opposites' of the Marxist dialectic) resulted in the transfer of political power to the bourgeoisie.

Similarly, contemporary capitalism is characterised by the struggle of two opposing classes, those who own the means of production – the capitalist class or bourgeois class – and those who possess nothing but their own labour – the proletariat. Marxist economics emphasises the contradictions within capitalism which give rise to ever-deepening economic crises. At the same time the exploitation of the proletariat makes it an agent of revolutionary change and the means of transition to a new socio-economic structure based on the nationalisation of the means of production.

It is at this point that the prescriptive and descriptive elements of Marxism merge. Marxists tend to argue that the emergence of socialism, and ultimately the establishment of a communist society, are possible of realisation. At the same time the prescriptive element emerges when Marxists argue that this socialist society would be a progressive society in that there would no longer be class exploitation but mutual co-operation. Advanced communism would not rest upon the division of labour and so would be classless society free of economic and therefore political inequalities. Indeed politics would disappear, the state would cease to exist, and society would not be ruled by a dominant political class; rather, it would be administered on the basis of social structures emerging from the people themselves in the form of volunteer forces co-operating to serve the needs of the collective.[11]

This brief survey of a highly developed, coherent and well-articulated ideology illustrates the essential nature of political ideologies: that there is analysis, explanation and prescription in all political ideologies even though the levels of complexity differ enormously. It is with this basic outline of the nature of ideology that we can now turn to look at the functions performed by ideologies in the political system.

Functions of ideologies

Although, as we have seen, ideologies have varying degrees of internal self-consistency and coherence, we can still make certain generalisations in regard to their functions within the political system. One of the problems, however, in discussing these functions is that ideologies differ in terms of their positions on the left-right spectrum.[12] There is also the difficulty that in some political systems the existence of ideology is strenuously denied, and so the word 'ideological' becomes a term of abuse. It has been fashionable in liberal democracies to speak of 'the end of ideology'.[13] The argument claims that ideologies have become irrelevant to the understanding of the politics of industrially developed, liberal democratic states, for there is less ideological commitment in these political systems, and that there is little conflict . Thus the divisions in American, West German, British, and French societies are not over the nature of the political system, nor the distribution of power within those systems, but over the methods to increase the general rate of economic growth.

The supporters of this type of approach point not only to the minimal political differences between the main contenders for power in these political systems – i.e. the American Republican and Democratic parties or the conservative and social democratic parties in western Europe – but also the changes that have been wrought in the western European communist parties.[14] There are two objections to these arguments regarding the relevance of ideology in modern political systems. Firstly, a movement from one ideological stance to another does not necessarily mean a decline in ideological commitment. Here the supporters of the 'end of ideology' argument have possibly confused ideology with revolutionary utopianism. The two are not always interchangeable. Secondly, there will be an ideological base to the political system even though there is widespread agreement and acceptance of the political values that constitute the ideological base. The absence of ideological conflict within liberal democracies does not constitute the absence of ideology.[15] Liberal democracy, as we saw in Chapter 3, is clearly based on a set of unambiguous political values that are interrelated and coherent. All political systems are ideological.

Some systems appear more ideologically based than others because either their ideology is constantly paraded or there is a deep ideological conflict within the system. No matter how weakly articulated, there is, none the less, an ideological base to all systems.

Perhaps the most important function of an ideology in a political system is to legitimise the political structures and the distribution of political power within that system. Thus liberal democratic government is said to rest on the will of the people as expressed by their elected representatives; so a government constituted after a general election or a presidential election is said to have authority from the people which is less challengeable than immediately before an election. The government's right to act is legitimised by reference to the liberal democratic tenet of popular sovereignty. We have seen that the pluralists have defended liberal democracy by attempting to modify democratic theory. Thus, in this view, the political élites compete for the consent of the governed; there may be no equality in the distribution of power, but there is a plurality of competing groups. J. A. Schumpter has underlined this accommodation of minority rule with liberal democracy: 'The principle of democracy then merely means that the reins of government should be handed to those who command more support than do any of the competing individuals or teams.'[16] He further observes that 'democracy does not mean and cannot mean that the people actually rule in any obvious sense of the terms "people" and "rule". Democracy means only that the people have the opportunity of accepting or refusing the men who are to rule them ... [by] free competition among would-be leaders for the vote of the electorate.'[17] So the actual process in liberal democracies is constantly defended by reference to a set of principles which, while not totally static, seek to legitimise the process at all times.

This process of ideological legitimisation can also be clearly seen in socialist systems. Marxism became the official political doctrine of the Soviet Union after the triumph of Lenin and the Bolsheviks in 1917. The legitimacy of the Soviet government is defended by reference to Marxism-Leninism.[18] The conflict between Stalin and Trotsky in the 1920s may have been a personal struggle for power, but it was conducted in the framework of ideological arguments about 'socialism in one country'. The policies of Stalin, especially his purges of party comrades in the 1930s, were necessary, it was argued, because in dialectical fashion the class struggle intensifies as socialism draws nearer, and so constant vigilance was essential to maintain the purity of the regime against enemies who were seeking to undermine its ideological basis. The political purges were certainly excused by these ideological references. Whether they should be viewed as a sincere adaption of Marxism-Leninism or a cynical justification of Stalin's personal power is another question.[19] The Soviet invasion of Czechoslovakia in 1968 was justified on the grounds that it was necessary to defend socialism from internal and external enemies and that the Warsaw Pact countries had a socialist duty to aid their comrades in Czechoslovakia.

Ideologies allow the framing of demands in the political system in recognisable forms. The American Democratic party was quite fearful that its criticism of the misdeeds of President Reagan might be interpreted as seeking partisan advantage, and was careful to wrap its criticisms of the Irangate scandals in terms of the aims of the Founding Fathers of the Constitution.[20] The debate about British membership of the European Economic Community was partly couched in the language of parliamentary independence, the ability to exert democratic influence on a powerful executive, and the bureaucratic threat to representative government. American doctors long argued their case against state assistance for the costs of medical treatment with reference to 'socialised medicine'. In all these cases it is very difficult to separate the ideological emphasis from the individual and group advantage. Demands are often made in ideological terms; therefore without reference to the ideological framework of the political system, these demands either cannot be understood or may be misinterpreted as sectional. The language of politics is also the language of ideology.

It is difficult to explain the involvement of individuals in the political process without reference to some ideological framework. Certainly, financial gain, social status, a sense of belonging to a larger group and, of course, the seeking after political power will explain a great deal of political participation, but sometimes these explanations will be insufficient. The explanation can often be found by reference to some ideological goal; the party activist may believe that in the near or distant future his party will gain power and change the political system to produce a fairer, more just, more equal society. It is these goals that may explain the participation in what could be viewed as a dreary round of party committee meetings or the canvassing of votes in constituencies that are a lost cause. The Campaign for Nuclear Disarmament in Britain or the campaign in the United States in the 1960s against the war in Vietnam provide examples of political involvement based on some form of ideological commitment.

Ideologies provide an excellent tool for the political élites in every political system to achieve varying degrees of mass involvement in the political process. This is clearly seen when a state wages war, particularly the large-scale wars of the twentieth century, characterised by exhortations to save democracy, socialism, the motherland, against external dangers.[21] Nationalistic exhortations are understandably the ones most stressed. We have defined ideology as 'an action-related system of ideas', a definition clearly apposite in this area of mass mobilisation. Hitler, with his successful orchestration of mass rallies in Germany, is the most outstanding example of the use of this élite weapon. It is sometimes argued that such mobilisation is more obviously used in political systems where the degree of legitimacy is thin. But the dividing line between political systems is exceedingly narrow; certainly mass mobilisation by means of ideological exhortation is common in all political systems, and political parties are an excellent example of one agent of such manipulation. There is scarcely a political system in which reference to a party congress or party convention does not underline this important function of ideology.

Ideologies are as much a factor in the stability and political unity as a source of challenge to the existing political structures. They can be used to support the dominant political élites and so disarm their rivals, and they may be used to divert attention away from difficult internal problems. Above all they are a means of legitimising the government and the policies of the government. Ideologies are not the same as the values and attitudes of the political culture. They provide the language in which to conduct an examination of the political processes. They are programmes for action and instruments of evaluation. They are a response to and a means of changing the existing political system, and it is to this relationship to political change that we must now turn our attention.

Ideologies and change

A major function of ideologies in modern political systems is that of legitimisation of existing political structures, but ideologies also help to accommodate change. They are a means of explaining political changes, and assist in their acceptance. Political change is a universal phenomenon, yet the speed and the extent varies from political system to political system. It is a consequence of a whole host of interrelated factors, individuals, social structure, level of economic development, as well as political institutions and political ideas. There is not one single variable but many; ideologies may help to legitimise the process of change, but they are only one aspect: political parties may be the most important ideological carrier and interpreter.

Political changes need not be dramatic, but naturally a great deal of interest centres on the nature of revolutionary as opposed to gradual change. Yet the problem of identifying the 'causes' is equally difficult even within the shorter time span. If, for example, we were to ask the question 'What were the causes of the downfall of the Austro-Hungarian Empire during the First World War?', our analysis, isolating some of the more important factors, would include the following generalisations:

1. The multi-national nature of a dynastic empire in a period of nationalism.
2. The conservative, unrepresentative nature of the Hapsburg government leading to the opposition of both liberals and socialists.
3. The overcentralised system of government, located mainly in Vienna and vested in the Imperial Court.
4. The individual political failings of the Emperor Franz Joseph.
5. The lack of raw materials within the Empire, the inability to exploit those that did exist, and the low level of economic development compared with the Empire's European rivals.

Thus we already have various political, individual, economic and ideological reasons for the weakness of the Empire. But one more must be included:

6. The impact of war on this 'ramshackle' structure.

As Foreign Minister Aerenthal observed in regard to the Hapsburg welcome for the 1914 war: 'We were bound to die. We were at liberty to choose the manner of our death, and we chose the most terrible.'[22]

War can, in some ways, be regarded as the catalyst of political change; Marx once observed: 'The redeeming feature of war is that it puts a nation to the test. As exposure to the atmosphere reduces all mummies to instant dissolution, so war passes extreme judgement on social systems that have outlived their vitality.'[23] The role of war was at its most dramatic in the downfall of the Tsarist government in Russia in 1917, but here again we see the interrelation with other factors. Could we say that the Bolshevik revolution would have occurred later in 1917 but for the decision of the liberal Kerensky government to continue to wage against the Germans? A series of unprofitable (for our purposes) hypotheses follow, but the question is an indication of the importance of the interconnectedness of all factors.

The degree of change will depend on the degree of stress to which the political system is subjected and the ability of the system to adapt itself to certain changes. It is here that we meet the problems of terminology and conceptual complexity. Modern political scientists are particularly interested in the underdeveloped countries, states that have newly won their independence and/or fail to attain the levels of industrialisation of more economically advanced states. Thus there is enphasis on modernisation and on the links between social and economic structures and political structures, connected to the whole idea of political stability as opposed to instability.[24]

There is a difference between change and progress; the nineteenth-century and early-twentieth-century liberal optimism based on the healing powers of liberal political institutions and national self-determination has been replaced partly by the equally optimistic belief in progress based on improvements in economic performance. It may be that the so called underdeveloped countries have been singled out for theorising partly because so little is known of the detail of their political processes, compared to those of, say, Britain, France or the United States, that generalisations may more easily be made. The danger remains that of attributing change to one cause, in this case economic development levels. One need only reflect on the political convulsions of Germany between the wars and compare these to the survival of liberal democracy in the United States or France, to agree that there is a most complex interrelationship.

Without straying into the free will versus deterministic arguments, it could be said that there is often too much emphasis on mono-causal, preordained sequences of events. We have mentioned, for example, the role of the individual in the process of change; he cannot be seen as the helpless pawn of impersonal forces, but neither is he completely independent of patterns of change. Christopher Hill once gave an interesting insight into the individual's place in the process of change when he said that Oliver Cromwell 'was Napoleon to his own Robespierre, Stalin to his own Lenin and Trotsky'.[25] No one can deny that France was visibly affected by the period of de Gaulle's rule from 1958 to 1968, yet at the same time the reforms of the civil service in the 1940s and 1950s, the economic developments of the period, the effects of Common Market membership, and even such factors as the moderation of the ideological position of the Communist Party, were all factors of some importance preventing a return to the pre-1958 pattern of politics, even if the political and constitutional steps could be taken. The political institutions of the state permit or impede change, and political stability can be said to result from the harmony of individuals, political institutions and the dominant ideologies of the political system. Yet political stability does not imply absence of change; it means the ability of the system to absorb change without violent upheavals.

References

1. See Chapter 1.
2. See M. Ashley, *The Glorious Revolution* (London, 1966).
3. See R. A. Dahl, *Democracy in the United States*, 4th ed. (Boston, 1981) pp. 4-11.
4. See D. Lane, *State and Politics in the USSR*, (New York, 1985) pp. 287–9.
5. See L. Thompson and A. Prior, *South African Politics* (New Haven, Conn., 1982).
6. See C. J. Friedrich and Z. K. Brzezinski, *Totalitarian Dictatorship and Autocracy* 2nd ed. (New York, 1965) p. 88.
7. Of course, Japan may be described as a 'fascist' state in the same period. See Barrington Moore, *The Social Origins of Dictatorship and Democracy* (London, 1967) ch. 5.
8. See Chapter 3 for a discussion of the concept of totalitarianism and its relationship to fascism.
9. E. Nolte, *Three Faces of Fascism* (London, 1965) pp. 20–1. The original is italicised after my hiatus.
10. For a discussion of populism, see D. MacRae, 'Populism as an Ideology', in *Populism. Its Meanings and National Characteristics*, ed. G. Ionescu and E. Gellner (London, 1967).
11. On Marx, see D. McLellan, *Karl Marx: His Life and Thought* (London, 1967). Of course it should be remembered that contemporary Marxist approaches differ considerably from one another in their views of the work of Marx, including his discussion of ideology.
12. See Chapter 7, note 30.
13. 'For the radical intellectual who had articulated the revolutionary impulses of the past century and a half, all this has meant an end to the chiliastic hopes, to millenarianism, to apocalyptic thinking – and to ideology. For ideology, which was once a road to action, has come to a dead end.' D. Bell, *The End of Ideology* (New York, 1960) pp. 369–70. A different but still hostile approach to ideology is provided by a British Conservative: 'Ideology seems inseparable from class; hence the Tories can only remain a national party if they remain free from ideological infection', Ian Gilmour, *Inside Right. A Study of Conservatism* (London, 1977) p. 132.
14. For the mass Communist parties of France, Italy and Spain these changes include, *inter alia*, the abandonment of the principle that their assumption of power would constitute the inauguration of the 'dictatorship of the proletariat'. There has been considerable discussion as to whether the ideological changes associated with Eurocommunism represent genuine evolution of views or a fraudulent ploy designed to deceive. See R. Tannahill, *The Communist Parties of Western Europe* (Westport, Conn., 1978) and G. Schwab, ed. *Eurocommunism. The Ideological and Political–Theoretical Foundations* (London, 1981).
15. There is some argument about the distinction between political culture and ideology. See W. T. Bluhm, *Ideologies and Attitudes* (Englewood Cliffs, NJ, 1974).
16. J. A. Schumpeter, *Capitalism, Socialism and Democracy* 4th ed. (London, 1954) pp. 273.
17. Ibid, pp. 284–5.
18. See J. M. Gilison, *The Soviet Image of Utopia* (Baltimore, 1975). Also Lane, *State and Politics in the USSR*, pp. 141–6.

19. For a criticism of Stalin's manipulation of Soviet ideology for personal gain, see I. Deutscher, *The Unfinished Revolution* (London, 1967). An examination of the reasons for the political purges of the 1930s can be found in R. Conquest, *The Great Terror* (London, 1971) and J. Arch Getty, *The Origins of the Great Purges* (Cambridge, 1985).
20. This ability to defend many aspects of American life in ideological terms can be seen in a booklet on American National Parks: 'The National Park idea is a legacy of the American Revolution, a national outgrowth of the democratic ideals of opportunity and equality for all. To set aside outstanding places of beauty and history for all to enjoy was in direct opposition to English and Continental practice where kings removed entire villages to protect hunting preserves and great estates were maintained for the pleasure of the nobility', *The Bicentennial and the National Parks*, National Park Services (US Department of the Interior, 1976).
21. This rallying call was given a peculiar class slant in Britain during the Second World War:

    Your Courage
    Your Cheerfulness
    Your Resolution
    Will Bring
    Us Victory.

    Quoted in A. Calder, *The People's War* (London, 1969) p. 61.
22. Quoted in A. J. P. Taylor, *The Hapsburg Monarchy, 1809–1918* (London, 1951) p. 232.
23. Quoted in A. Marwick, *Britain in the Century of Total War* (London, 1970) p. 13.
24. D. Apter *The Politics of Modernisation* (Chicago, 1965), and D. Apter, *Some Conceptual Approaches to the Study of Modernisation* (Englewood Cliffs, NJ, 1968).
25. C. Hill, *Oliver Cromwell* (Historical Association Pamphlet, 1958) p. 22.

Bibliography

General and introductory works

Almond, G. A. (ed.), *Comparative Politics Today*, 2nd ed. (Boston, Mass., 1980).
Blondel, J., *The Discipline of Politics* (London, 1981).
Brown, A., *Soviet Politics and Political Science* (London, 1974).
Cowling, M., *The Nature and Limits of Political Science* (Cambridge, 1963).
Crick, B., *In Defence of Politics*, 2nd ed. (London, 1982).
Crick, B., *The American Science of Politics* (London, 1959).
Dahl, R., *Modern Political Analysis*, 4th ed. (Englewood Cliffs, NJ, 1984).
Downs, A., *An Economic Theory of Democracy* (New York, 1957).
Dragnich, A., and Rusmussen, J., *Major European Governments*, 7th ed. (Homewood, Illinois, 1986).
Easton, D., *A Systems Analysis of Political Life*, 2nd ed. (Chicago, 1979).
Garson, G. D., *Political Science Methods* (Boston, Mass., 1976).
Harris, P. B., *Foundations of Political Science* (London, 1975).
Holmes, L., *Politics in the Communist World* (Oxford, 1986).
Isaak, A. C., *Scope and Methods of Political Science*, rev. ed. (Homewood, Ill., 1975).
Leftwich, A. (ed.), *What is Politics?* (Oxford, 1984).
Lewis, P. G., Potter, D. C. and Castles, F. G., *The Practice of Comparative Politics*, 2nd ed. (London, 1978).
Mackenzie, W. J. M., *Politics and Social Science* (London, 1967).
Smith, G., *Politics in Western Europe*, 4th ed. (London, 1983).
White, S., Gardner, J. and Schöpflin, G., *Communist Political System. An Introduction*, 2nd ed. (London, 1987).

Individual countries

Britain

Dearlove, J. and Saunders, P., *Introduction to British Politics* (Cambridge, 1984).
Drucker, H., Dunleavy, P., Gamble, A. and Peele, G., *Developments in British Politics 2* (London, 1986).
Moran, M., *Politics and Society in Britain* (London, 1985).
Rose, R., *Politics in England*, 4th ed. (London, 1985).

France

Ehrmann, H. W., *Politics in France* (Boston, 1983).
Pickles, D., *Problems of Contemporary French Politics* (London, 1982).
Wright, V., *The Government and Politics of France*, 2nd ed. (London, 1983).

United States

Dahl, R. A., *Democracy in the United States*, 4th ed. (Boston, 1981).
King, A. (ed.), *The New American Political System* (Washington, 1978).
McKay, D., *American Politics and Society*, 2nd ed. (Oxford, 1983).
Robins, L. (ed.), *The American Way. Government and Politics in the United States* (London, 1985).

USSR

Hammer, D., *USSR: The Politics of Oligarchy*, 2nd ed. (Boulder, Col., 1986).
Hill, R. J., *Soviet Union* (London, 1985).
Hough, J. and Fainsod, M., *How the Soviet Union is Governed* (Cambridge, Mass., 1979).
Lane, D., *State and Politics in the USSR* (London, 1985).

West Germany

Childs, D., *West German Politics and Society* (London, 1980).
Edinger, L. J., *West German Politics* (New York, 1986).
Smith, G., *Democracy in West Germany*, 3rd ed. (Aldershot, 1986).

Political Power

Bachrach, P., *The Theory of Democratic Elitism* (London, 1969).
Bell, D. V. J., *Power, Influence and Authority* (New York, 1975).
Bottomore, T. B., *Elites and Society* (London, 1964).
Connolly, W. E. (ed.), *The Bias of Pluralism* (New York, 1969).
Cox, A., Furlong, P. and Page, E., *Power in Capitalist Society* (Brighton, 1985).
Dahl, R. A., *Who Governs?* (New Haven, Conn., 1961).
Dahl, R. A., *Dilemmas of Pluralist Democracy* (London, 1982).
Dunleavy, P. and O'Leary, B., *Theories of the State. The Politics of Liberal Democracy* (London, 1987).
Harrison, R. J., *Pluralism and Corporatism* (London, 1980).
Jessop, B., *The Capitalist State* (London, 1982).
Lindblom, C., *Politics and Markets* (New York, 1977).
Machiavelli, N., *The Prince and the Discourses*, ed. M. Lerner (New York, 1950).
Miliband, R., *The State in Capitalist Society* (London, 1969).

Mills, C. W., *The Power Elite* (Oxford, 1956).
Newman, O., *The Challenge of Corporatism* (London, 1981).
Nordlinger, E., *The Autonomy of the Democratic State* (London, 1981).
Parry, G., *Political Elites* (London, 1969).
Poulantzas, N., *Political Power and Social Classes* (London, 1973).
Prewitt, K. and Stone, A., *The Ruling Elites. Elite Theory, Power and American Democracy* (New York, 1973).
Schmitter, P. and Lehmbruch, G., *Patterns of Corporatist Policy Making* (London, 1979).
Schmitter, P. and Lehmbruch, G., *Trends Towards Corporatist Intermediation* (London, 1979).
Solomon, S. (ed.), *Pluralism in the Soviet Union* (London, 1983).
Therborn, G., *What Does the Ruling Class Do When It Rules?* (London, 1978).
Westergard, J. and Resler, H., *Class in Capitalist Society. A Study of Contemporary Britain* (London, 1975).
Wrong, D., *Power. Its Forms, Bases and Uses* (Oxford, 1979).

Representation, elections and electoral systems

Bogdanor, V. and Butler, D. (eds), *Democracy and Elections* (Cambridge, 1983).
Bogdanor, V., *The People and the Party System. The Referendum and Electoral Reform in British Politics* (Cambridge,1981).
Butler, D. and Ranney, A., *Referendums. A Comparative Study of Theory and Practice* (Washington, 1978).
Butler, D. and Kavanagh, D., *The British General Election of 1983* (London, 1984).
Finer, S. E. (ed.), *Adversary Politics and Electoral Reform* (London, 1975).
Harrop, M. and Miller, W. L., *Elections and Voters. A Comparative Introduction* (London, 1987).
Mackenzie, W. J. M., *Free Elections* (London, 1958).
McLean, I., *Elections*, 2nd ed. (London, 1980).
Palmer, N., *Elections and Political Development* (Durham, NC, 1975).
Pitkin, H. F., *The Concept of Representation* (Cambridge, 1967).
Pomper, G. and Lederman, S., *Elections in America*, 2nd ed. (New York, 1980).
Rae, D., *The Political Consequences of Electoral Laws* (New Haven, Conn., 1967).

Political culture and voting behaviour

Adams, J. S., *Political Participation in Communist Systems* (New York, 1981).
Almond, G. A. and Verba, S. (eds), *The Civic Culture Revisited* (Boston, Mass., 1980).
Barbrook, A., *Patterns of Political Behaviour* (London, 1975).
Brown, A. (ed.), *Political Culture and Communist Studies* (London, 1984).

Brown, A. and Gray, J., *Political Culture and Political Change in Communist States*, 2nd ed. (London, 1979).
Butler, D. and Stokes, D., *Political Change in Britain*, 2nd ed. (London, 1974).
Crewe, I. and Denver, D. (eds), *Electoral Change in Western Democracies* (London, 1985).
Dunleavy, P. and Husbands, C. T., *British Democracy at the Crossroads* (London, 1985).
Friedgut, T., *Political Participation in the U.S.S.R.* (Princeton, NJ, 1979).
Harrop, M. and Miller, W. L., *Elections and Voters. A Comparative Introduction* (London, 1987).
Heath, A, Jewell, R. and Curtis, J., *How Britain Votes* (Oxford, 1985).
Himmelweit, H. *et al.*, *How Voters Decide* (London, 1981).
Lipset, S. M., *Political Man*, 2nd ed. (London, 1983).
Mason, D. S., *Public Opinion and Political Change in Poland 1980–1982*, (Cambridge, 1985).
Robertson, D., *Class and the British Electorate* (Oxford, 1984).
Rose, R., *Electoral Participation* (London, 1980).
Rose, R. and McAllister, I., *Voters Begin to Choose* (London, 1986).
Stacey, B., *Political Socialisation in Western Society* (London, 1978).
White, S., *Political Culture and Soviet Politics* (London, 1979).

Political Parties

Ball, A. R., *British Political Parties*, 2nd ed. (London, 1987).
Bell, D., *Contemporary French Political Parties* (London, 1982).
Beyme, K. von, *Political Parties in Western Democracies* (Aldershot, 1985).
Castles, F. (ed.), *The Impact of Parties* (London, 1982).
Chambers, W. N. and Burnham, W. D. (eds), *The American Party System: Stages of Political Development* (New York, 1975).
Daalder, H. and Mair, P., *Western European Party Systems* (London, 1983).
Duverger, M., *Political Parties*, 2nd ed. (London, 1962).
Finer, S. E., *The Changing British Party System, 1945–1979* (Washington, 1980).
Fischer-Galati, S., *The Communist Parties of Eastern Europe* (New York, 1979).
Frank, P. and Hill R., *The Soviet Communist Party*, 3rd ed. (London, 1987).
Frears, J. R., *Parties and Elections in the French Fifth Republic* (London, 1977).
Irving, R., *The Christian Democratic Parties of Western Europe* (London, 1979).
Lange, P. and Maurizio, V. (eds), *The Communist Parties of Italy, France and Spain* (London, 1981).
Layton-Henry, Z. (ed.), *Conservative Politics in Western Europe* (London, 1982).
Nugent, N., *The Left in France* (London, 1982).
Paterson, W. and Thomas, A. (eds), *The Future of Social Democracy* (Oxford, 1986).
Polsby, N. W., *The Consequences of Party Reform* (Oxford, 1983).
Pridham, G., *The Nature of the Italian Party System* (London, 1981).
Rose, R., *Do Parties Make a Difference?*, 2nd ed. (London, 1984).

Schwab, G. (ed.), *Eurocommunism. The Ideological and Political Theoretical Foundations* (London, 1981).
Sartori, G., *Parties and Party Systems*, vol. 1. (Cambridge, 1976).
Sorauf, F. J., *Party Politics in America*, 5th ed. (Boston, Mass., 1984).
Tannahill, R., *The Communist Parties of Western Europe* (Westport, Conn., 1978).
Wattenberg, M. P., *The Decline of American Political Parties, 1958–80* (Harvard, 1984).

Pressure groups

Alderman, G., *Pressure Groups and Government in Great Britain (London, 1984)*.
Ball, A. R. and Millard, F., *Pressure Politics in Industrial Societies* (London, 1986).
Berger, S. (ed.), *Organising Interests in Western Europe* (London, 1981).
Castles, F. *et al.*, *Decisions, Organisations and Society*, 2nd ed. (London, 1976).
Cerny, P. (ed.), *Social Movements and Protest in France* (London, 1982).
Eckstein, H., *Pressure Group Politics* (London, 1960).
Finer, S. E., *Anonymous Empire*, 2nd ed. (London, 1966).
Lowenhardt, J., *Decision Making in Soviet Politics* (London, 1981).
Marsh, D. (ed.), *Pressure Politics. Interest Groups in Britain* (London, 1983).
Paterson, W. and Kolinsky, M., *Social and Political Movements in Western Europe* (London, 1976).
Presthus, R., *Elites in the Policy Process* (London, 1974).
Skilling, H. G. and Griffiths, F. (eds), *Interest Groups in Soviet Politics* (Princeton, NJ, 1971).
Wilson, G. K., *Interest Groups in the United States* (Oxford, 1981).
Willetts, P. (ed.), *Pressure Groups in the Global System* (London, 1982).
Wootton, G., *Interest Groups* (Englewood Cliffs, NJ, 1970).
Wootton, G., *Pressure Groups in Contemporary Britain* (Farnborough, 1979).

Assemblies

Blondel, J., *Comparative Legislatures* (Englewood Cliffs, NJ, 1973).
Boynton, G., *Legislative Systems in Developing Countries* (Duke, NC, 1975).
Green, M., *Who Runs Congress?*, 4th ed. (New York, 1984).
Hale, D. (ed.), *The United States Congress* (London, 1983).
Judge, D. (ed.), *The Politics of Parliamentary Reform* (London, 1983).
Loewenburg, G. and Patterson, S. C. *Comparing Legislatures* (Boston, Mass., 1979).
Mezey, M. L., *Comparative Legislatures* (Durham, NC, 1979).
Norton, P., *The Commons in Perspective* (London, 1981).
Nelson, D. and White, S., *Communist Legislatures in Comparative Perspective* (London, 1982).

Patterson, S. C. and Wahlke, J. (eds), *Comparative Legislative Behaviour* (New York, 1972).
Vanneman, P., *The Supreme Soviet* (Durham, NC., 1977).

Executives

Albrow, M., *Bureaucracy* (London, 1970).
Barber, J. D., *The Presidential Character. Predicting Performance in the White House* (Englewood Cliffs, NJ, 1972).
Beck, C. *et al.*, *Comparative Communist Political Leadership* (New York, 1973).
Bialer, S., *Stalin's Successors* (Cambridge, 1980).
Blondel, J., *World Leaders* (London, 1980).
Brown, R. G. S. and Steel, D. R., *The Administrative Process in Britain*, 2nd ed. (London, 1979).
Cerney, P., *Elites in France* (London, 1981).
Fry, G., *The Changing Civil Service* (London, 1985).
Greenwood, J. and Wilson, D., *Public Administration in Britain* (London, 1984).
Kellner, P. and Crowther-Hunt, Lord, *The Civil Servants* (London, 1980).
King, A. (ed.), *The British Prime Minister*, 2nd ed. (London, 1985).
Mackintosh, J. P., *The British Cabinet*, 3rd ed. (London, 1977).
Neustadt, R. E., *Presidential Power*, 2nd ed. (New York, 1964).
Page, E. C., *Political Authority and Bureaucratic Power* (Brighton, 1985).
Rose, R. and Suleiman, E. N., *Presidents and Prime Ministers* (Washington, 1980).
Seidman, H., *Politics, Position and Power*, 3rd ed. (Oxford, 1980).
Smith, G. B., *The Soviet Procuracy and the Supervision of Administration* (Leiden, 1978).
Smith, G. B., *Public Policy and Administration in the Soviet Union* (New York, 1980).
Suleimann, E. N. (ed.), *Bureaucrats and Policy Making* (New York, 1984).

Judiciaries

Abraham, H. J., *Freedom and the Court. Civil Rights and Liberties in the United States*, 3rd ed. (New York, 1977).
Barry, D. D. *et al.* (eds), *Soviet Law After Stalin* (Leiden, 1977).
Cobler, S., *Law, Order and Politics in West Germany* (London, 1978).
Dworkin, R., *Law's Empire* (London, 1986).
Griffith, J. A. G., *The Politics of the Judiciary*, 2nd ed. (London, 1981).
Hazard, J. N., *The Soviet Legal System* (New York, 1984).
Hodder-Williams, R., *The Politics of the Supreme Court* (London, 1980).
Juviler, P., *Revolutionary Law and Order: Politics and Social Change in U.S.S.R.* (New York, 1976).
Patterson, A., *The Law Lords* (London, 1982).

The military

Adelman, J. (ed.), *Communist Armies in Politics* (Boulder, Col., 1981).
Bebler, A. (ed.), *Military Rule in Africa: Dahomey, Ghana, Sierra Leone and Mali* (London, 1981).
Carsten, F. L., *The Reichwehr and Politics 1918–33* (Oxford, 1966).
Finer, S. E., *The Man on Horseback*, 2nd ed. (London, 1976).
Gutteridge, W. F., *Military Regimes in Africa* (London, 1975).
Herspring, D. and Volyges, I., *Civil–Military Relations in Communist Systems* (Boulder, Col., 1978).
Howard, M. (ed.), *Soldiers and Governments: Nine Studies in Civil–Military Relations* (London, 1976).
Kolkowicz, R. and Korbonski, A. (eds), *Soldiers, Peasants and Bureaucrats* (London, 1982).
Perlmutter, A., *Political Roles and Military Rulers* (London, 1981).
Philip, G., *The Military in South American Politics* (London, 1985).
Sanford, G., *Military Rule in Poland* (London, 1986).
Schiffrin, H. (ed.), *Military and State in Modern Asia* (Jerusalem. 1976).
Warner, E., *The Miltary in Contemporary Soviet Politics* (New York, 1978).

Ideology

Arblaster, A., *The Rise and Decline of Western Liberalism* (Oxford, 1984).
Bell, D., *The End of Ideology* (New York, 1960).
Benewick, R. *et al.*, *Knowledge and Belief in Politics* (London, 1973).
Bracer, K., *The Age of Ideologies* (London, 1985).
Dahl, R. A., *A Preface to Democratic Theory* (Chicago, 1956).
Dolbeare, K. M. *et al.*, *Readings in American Ideologies* (Chicago, 1973).
Drucker, H. M., *The Political Uses of Ideology* (London, 1974).
Hibbin, S. *et al.*, *Politics, Ideology and the State* (London, 1978).
Holmes, L. (ed.), *The Withering Away of the State?* (London, 1981).
Larrain, J., *The Concept of Ideology* (London, 1979).
Lipset, S. M., *Political Man* (London, 1983).
Lively, J., *Democracy* (Oxford, 1975).
McLellan, D., *Ideologies* (London, 1986).
Macpherson, C. B., *Democratic Theory* (Oxford, 1973).
Manning, D. J., *The Form of Ideology* (London, 1980).
Nisbet, R., *Conservatism* (London, 1986).
Peele, G., *Revival and Reaction: The Right in Contemporary America*, (Oxford, 1984).
Plamenatz, J., *Ideology* (London, 1971).
Poulantzas, N., *Political Power and Social Classes* (London, 1973).
Seliger, M., *Ideology and Politics* (London, 1976).
Schubert, G., *Political Attitudes and Ideologies* (London, 1977).
Taras, R., *Ideology in a Socialist State: Poland* (Cambridge, 1984).
Therborn, G., *The Ideology of Power and the Power of Ideology* (London, 1980).

Index